KU-532-138

THE FOUR-WHEELED MORGAN
Volume 2

By the same author:

THE FOUR-WHEELED MORGAN
Volume 1: The Flat-Radiator Models

THE FOUR-WHEELED MORGAN

Volume 2: The Cowled-Radiator Models

by KEN HILL

MOTOR RACING PUBLICATIONS LTD
28 Devonshire Road, London W4 2HD

ISBN 0 900549 54 8
First published 1980

HERTFORDSHIRE
COUNTY LIBRARY

629.222

8953829

8 OCT 1980

Copyright © 1980 — Ken Hill and Motor Racing Publications Ltd

All rights reserved. No part of this publication may be reproduced,
stored in a retrieval system, or transmitted, in any form or by any
means, electronic, mechanical, photocopying, recording or otherwise,
without the prior permission of Motor Racing Publications Ltd

Photosetting by Zee Creative Ltd, London SW16
Printed in Great Britain by Page Bros. (Norwich) Ltd, Norwich

Contents

Introduction

The year 1954 heralded the beginning of a new chapter in the history of the Morgan Motor Company, for this was the year in which the company felt obliged to introduce a new body style, the first fundamental change since the introduction of the four-wheeled Morgan.

For some five or so years, Britain's major car manufacturers had been gradually changing their designs to a more streamlined appearance, and in offering more sweeping and curving lines it had become necessary for them to move away from the traditional upright integral radiator and free-standing headlamps. Instead, the headlamps were being inserted into the wings, while a separate radiator core was being mounted a little further back in the chassis, so enabling a curved grille to be placed in front of it. These two comparatively simple modifications opened up all kinds of alternatives to body designers and stylists, and a glance at photographs of cars from the early-1950s period will reveal what a wide variety of solutions were adopted at that time.

As more manufacturers altered the design of their cars in this way — and the major car producers were in the vanguard of this trend — so, inevitably, the radiator and headlamp manufacturers changed their own products and production schedules to meet the changing needs. Although this did not mean that the supply of the traditional components would be discontinued completely (the components industry was prepared to keep them in limited production) it did mean that factories would have to remain tooled-up for what would be very limited production runs. The annual requirements of the Morgan Motor Company, for example, could probably be produced in a matter of 10 to 14 days. Understandably, a result of these short-run production cycles would have to be an increase in price, and if the small-volume car manufacturers could not absorb this, it would have to be passed on to the customer.

In a typically shrewd move, H. F. S. Morgan decided that his sports cars would be subtly changed to make use of the new components, but without altering their traditional character. Although the price increases being asked on existing radiators and headlamps was not excessive at the time, he realised that further price changes could only be upwards until perhaps, before too long, Morgan would be paying twice or triple the former price. To delay now, would merely be to delay the inevitable. A number of other small manufacturers were unwilling to make the change, and in due course they were to go out of business or become absorbed into one of the major groups. This was the era of takeover bids, from which the Morgan Motor Company itself was not immune (there was an overture from Triumph, and later there would be another one from Rover, with which Triumph by that time had its own links, but both were successfully resisted).

The first cowled-radiator Morgan to be produced was not the true design as we know it today, but rather an interim model, a sort of half-way house. Some present-day owners of these cars say that they are really the last of the flat-radiator Morgans, but I cannot subscribe to this, and to me they will always be the first of the cowled-radiator cars.

Morgan owners are traditionally diehards, and just as their predecessors in 1936, whose world had long revolved around three wheels, thoroughly disliked the introduction of the four-wheeled Morgan, so in 1954 many Morgan enthusiasts deeply regretted the styling change. Indeed, dissent was so deep that the Morgan 4-4 Club had to hold several committee meetings before it was agreed that the new car would be acceptable by the membership. It is difficult to understand, today, how a body design which is held in such high regard and is the hallmark of all that is best in Morgans could have been the subject of so much controversy at the time of its introduction. But once again 'H. F. S.' was proved right, in time the critics were silenced, and the cowled-radiator cars were to serve the Morgan Motor Company well in guiding it through the difficult years which were to come.

In Britain, the Fifties was the decade of the road rallies, with scarcely a weekend going by without at least one being organized by a motor club. It was a form of motor sport to which the Morgan proved itself to be well suited, as a glance at the competitions chapter of this book will confirm. But unfortunately these events became increasingly unpopular with other people, farmers, villagers and even townspeople objecting violently to rally routes passing through or close to their properties, especially at night.

Legislation to control the proliferation of this type of event became inevitable, the emphasis in rallying moved to the more sophisticated stage events, and simultaneously the sport entered the 'win at any cost' period, with major manufacturers and their sponsors spending vast sums to secure publicity-earning victories. It meant that the smaller manufacturers and the private owners were being squeezed out, and the Morgan Motor Company was one of the victims, no longer being able to enter teams in events such as the RAC Rally, in which they had done so well in the past. It was particularly sad that the highly financed teams were effectively excluding from the sport the very people — the motor sports enthusiasts — to whom they were aiming to sell their own products.

Yet Morgans have continued to do well in other branches of the sport, and in recent years their racing activities have undergone a renaissance at club level, while the Morgan sports car has now become not only a status symbol but also a source of investment, a state of affairs which some true Morgan enthusiasts consider to be lamentable. However, they should remember that the widening of the Morgan market has helped the Morgan Motor Company considerably and enabled it to continue to manufacture cars for the dedicated enthusiast.

During the years covered by this volume several different models have been produced, some having only a very limited production spread over a number of years, which has given rise to doubts regarding the numbers actually produced. I hope that my extensive researches in this area will have clarified the picture for many people. I also hope that those enthusiasts who have read my earlier book, which concentrates on the flat-radiator models and includes information on maintenance, will find this book to be a useful and interesting companion. If they serve to stimulate even further the worldwide interest in Morgans, in my opinion the very best of production sports cars, I shall be more than pleased.

April 1980

Ken Hill

Acknowledgements

I am indebted to many people for their unstinted co-operation during the preparation of this book for without their help it would never have reached the publisher.

Firstly, I must record my thanks to Peter Morgan and the staff of the Morgan Motor Company, whose enthusiasm and unfailing assistance with the provision of works records and personal recollections have once again proved so valuable.

I am also indebted to Michael Ware and Peter Brooks of the National Motor Museum, Beaulieu, for placing their expertise, library and records at my disposal; to John N. Edwards for his invaluable assistance in connection with the construction of the bodies for the Plus-4-Plus coupe and the E. B. Morgan; to all the Presidents and Secretaries of Morgan clubs around the world, who so readily supplied so much information and photographs; to the President and Secretary of the Morgan Sports Car Club for the supply of information and their permission to reproduce extracts from the club magazine *Miscellany;* to Peter Askew, Chris Lawrence, Cyril Charlesworth and a large number of other Morgan enthusiasts, who so readily gave me information, recollections and photographs; and to Jenny Lee, for her help in the production of the completed manuscript.

I have obtained information from material and notes left by the late Dick Pritchard. The material had been collected by him over 40 years and the exact origin of much of it is unknown. I know that he assembled material from most motoring magazines, including *Autosport* and *Motor Sport,* both of which he read regularly. It has been impossible to establish the exact source of certain material and reports which I have received from club members from all round the world, and therefore I express my sincere thanks to all such writers and magazines as may have helped me with some of the detail of this book. Finally, my thanks to my wife, Janet, who has helped me so much in the research and compiling of this book. K.H.

A pair of four-seaters depicting the two stages in the evolution of the cowled-radiator Morgan. On the left is a 1969 4-4 and alongside it a 1954 Plus-4 with the transitional front-end.

Chapter 1

Maintaining the tradition

Throughout its 70 years of production the Morgan motor car has relied on outside suppliers for its engine, and consequently the timing of the introduction of new models, and their specification, has been to a large extent dependent upon engine supplies from these outside sources.

Sometimes a model has been changed simply because its engine has ceased to be available, either because production has stopped or because the manufacturer concerned has no longer been interested in supplying Morgan with the small numbers required. Perhaps the most significant example of Morgan production car policy being dictated by an engine supplier was when Triumph terminated production of the four-cylinder TR4A engine; it was this decision which brought about the end of the Morgan Plus-4 series.

It was a worrying situation for the Morgan Motor Company, but its solution came about in a most unusual way. Peter Morgan was asked by a high-ranking Rover executive whether he would consider a take-over bid by the Rover Company. Peter immediately answered 'No', then added, 'but I would like to use your V-8 engines'. To his amazement the Rover man agreed, and so was to be born the fastest production Morgan ever, the Plus-8.

So, we find that in the period covered by this book, since the advent of the first cowled-radiator models, we have three major engine suppliers — Ford, Triumph and Rover, all powering variations on a classic theme which has stood the test of time and seemingly has an inexhaustible life ahead of it. During this period, as we shall see, there have been many minor changes in detail design, so many, in fact, that it has not been possible to list them all and link them to specific chassis numbers, and for a very good reason — no such information exists, even at the factory.

Over the years there have been numerous subtle changes in body details and to items of equipment as outside suppliers have altered the specification of their components. These changes, sometimes to a larger part, at other times to something a little smaller, have been accepted by the factory as a normal part of the problem of building cars in a relatively low volume but over many years. Wherever possible I have collated data on the more significant of these changes, and in particular I hope I have been able, through my researches, to provide Morgan enthusiasts with more information than they may have had before on the rarer models, such as the Plus-4-Plus and the Plus-4 four-seater Drop Head Coupé.

Meanwhile, Morgan's research and development department continues to be fully occupied, a lot of their work being to ensure that cars meet the ever more stringent regulations imposed in all of their markets. Along with every other car manufacturer they are longing for the day when some measure of uniformity of requirements is adopted by countries throughout the world, so that products can be improved for the customer rather than to meet the demands of the faceless legislators.

For those to whom 'all Morgans look the same', the variety of different models must be very confusing, and I hope that the remainder of this chapter will go some way towards helping them to identify one model from the other, and to understand the logical progression in specification which has taken place over the years without altering the basic character of these unique sports cars.

Morgan 4-4 Series 2

This model was introduced at the London Motor Show in 1955 and remained in production until October 1960. Production covered the Chassis Number sequence A200-A586, the prototype car having Chassis Number A200. Apart from one special Drop Head Coupé (Chassis Number A553) all cars had open two-seater bodywork.

Designed to sell alongside the Plus-4, the 4-4 was reintroduced to the Morgan range to fill the large gap which existed for a low-priced sports car (the 4-4 cost approximately £714 in 1956, compared with £894 for the Plus-4, £939 for the Triumph TR2 and £961 for the MGA). Listed as a 'Tourer' by the factory, the 4-4 was powered by the 1,172cc side-valve Ford Anglia engine and three-speed gearbox, and although the car's performance was modest by sports car standards there existed a wide range of moderately priced tuning kits for this engine for those who wanted more power, while another bonus for 4-4 buyers was the wide availability of Ford service and spare parts. At the time of announcement, the 4-4's specification was as follows:

Engine: Ford Anglia 100E, four cylinders in line, side valves, bore 63.5mm, stroke 92.5mm, displacement 1,172cc, maximum power 36 bhp at 4,400 rpm, compression ratio 7 to 1.
Transmission: Single dry plate clutch. Ford three-speed gearbox. Ratios 17.29, 8.91 and 4.44 to 1. Synchromesh on second and top. Open Hardy Spicer propeller shaft to Salisbury hypoid-bevel axle unit.
Suspension: Front, independent with sliding pillars, coil springs and Armstrong telescopic shock absorbers. Rear, live axle with semi-elliptic springs and Armstrong piston-type shock absorbers.
Steering: Cam gear, 2½ turns from lock to lock.
Brakes: Girling hydraulic, two-leading shoes at front. 9in diamter drums, 1¾in wide shoes.
Wheels: Pressed steel with hub caps. Tyres 5.00 × 16in, pressures 18 psi front and rear.
Fuel: 8-gallon tank, rear-mounted.
Dimensions: Wheelbase 8ft; length 12ft; width 4ft 8in; height 4ft 2in with hood up; track 3ft 11in.
Weight: 14 cwt (with five gallons of fuel).

4-4 Series 2 Competition Model

This model was produced alongside the normal Series 2 from 1957 until 1960, the earliest Chassis Number being A272. The main mechanical changes were an Aquaplane aluminium cylinder-head, increasing the compression ratio to 8 to 1, and the replacement of the single Solex carburettor with twin SU carburettors. Power output was increased to 40 bhp at 5,100 rpm and a special exhaust system was fitted. The Competition Model was similar in all other respects to the normal Series 2.

4-4 Series 2 Drop Head Coupé

This car was built specially for a Miss Skinner, a relative of H.F.S. Morgan, on Chassis Number A553, and was equipped with Ford 100E engine B427103C. The car was finished in yellow and was delivered on February 1, 1960 with the Registration Number 380 AAB.

4-4 Series 3

This model was introduced at the London Motor Show in October 1960 and remained in production until December 1961. Production covered the Chassis Number sequence A590-A648, and the prototype car was built on Chassis Number A589. This model was produced as an open two-seater only, and is sometimes referred to as the 50th Anniversary car because it coincided with this milestone in the company's history. However, there was no such official designation.

The main change from the Series 2 was the substitution of the Ford 105E overhead-valve engine and four-speed gearbox for the earlier engine-transmission package. External identification points were the different rear lights and the removal of the fasteners for the side-screens to the outside of the doors. At the time of announcement the specification was as follows:

Engine: Ford 105E, four cylinders in line, overhead valves, bore 80.86mm, stroke 48.41mm, displacement 997cc, maximum power 39 bhp at 5,000 rpm, compression ratio 8.9 to 1.
Transmission: Single dry plate clutch. Ford four-speed gearbox. Ratios 18.1, 10.54, 6.21 and 4.4 to 1, reverse 23.7 to 1. Synchromesh on second, third and top. Open Hardy Spicer propeller shaft to Salisbury hypoid-bevel axle unit.
Suspension: Front, independent with sliding pillars, coil springs

Prototype of the 4-4 Series 3, a model which marked the substitution of the Series 2's 1,172cc Ford side-valve engine with the new 997cc overhead-valve engine as fitted to the Anglia, together with a four-speed instead of the previous three-speed gearbox.

Below left: Dixon Smith competing in a Curborough sprint with the prototype 4-4 Series 2. The damaged left front wing and bumper suggests that one of the marker barrels may have got in his way! Below: The low body lines of this 4-4 in the United States are exaggerated by the tall roll-over bar protruding through the tonneau.

11

Morgan hoods have been improved progressively over the years. This 4-4 four-seater not only reveals the snug fit of the top and side screens, but also shows the greatly improved rear and three-quarters vision as a result of generously sized window cut-outs.

A dramatic shot of Chris Jenkins driving his one-month-old 1965 4-4 Series 5 to a class win in the Pirbright production car trial that year. The car had barely 800 miles on the clock at the time.

and Armstrong telescopic shock absorbers. Rear, live axle with semi-elliptic springs and Armstrong piston-type shock absorbers.
Steering: Cam gear, 2.7 turns lock to lock.
Brakes: Girling hydraulic with 9in drums. Disc front brakes optional extra.
Wheels: Pressed steel with hub caps. Tyres 5.20 × 15in.
Fuel: 8-gallon tank, rear-mounted.
Dimensions and weight: As Series 2.

4-4 Series 4

Produced between December 1961 and December 1962 as an open two-seater within the Chassis Number sequence B650-B849. The introduction of this model was brought about by the availability of the Ford Classic engine, which enabled Morgan to offer a relatively low-cost sports car capable of being used in competitions without having to resort to costly modifications. In standard form its improvement in performance over the Series 3 was substantial, the 0-60 mph acceleration time being reduced from 26 seconds to 16.5 seconds, while the top speed went up from 80 mph to 92 mph. The car was very well received, and it was only discontinued after a year because of the availability of a new 1½-litre engine from Ford. The specification of the Series 4 was as follows:

Engine: Ford 109E, four cylinders in line, overhead valves, bore 80.96mm, stroke 65.07mm, displacement 1,340cc, maximum power 62 bhp at 5,000 rpm, compression ratio 8.5 to 1, single SU H450 carburettor.
Transmission: Borg and Beck single dry plate clutch. Ford four-speed gearbox. Ratios 18.8, 11.0, 6.0 and 4.56 to 1. Synchromesh on second, third and top. Open Hardy Spicer propeller shaft to Salisbury hypoid-bevel axle unit.
Suspension: Front, independent with sliding pillars, coil springs and Armstrong telescopic shock absorbers. Rear, live axle with semi-elliptic springs and Armstrong piston-type shock absorbers.
Steering: Cam and sector, 2¼ turns lock to lock.
Brakes: Girling hydraulic with 11in front discs and 9in rear drums.
Wheels: Pressed steel with hub caps. Tyres 5.60 × 15in.
Fuel: 8½-gallon tank, rear-mounted.
Dimensions: As Series 2.
Weight: 13 cwt (dry).

4-4 Series 5

Produced as open two-seater between December 1962 and January 1968 within Chassis Number sequence B850-B1495. The addition of a 1½-litre version to Ford's 'Kent' series of engines gave Morgan a welcome shot in the arm in that it enabled the Malvern company to offer a sports car which, even in standard form, could outpace the rival Austin-Healey Sprites, MG Midgets and Triumph Spitfires. Whereas the 109E Classic engine, welcome though it had been to Morgan, was tending to be left behind in the performance stakes, the 116E replacement was so successful as a Morgan engine that it would be adopted for more than five years. The Series 5 specification was as follows:

Engine: Ford 116E, four cylinders in line, overhead valves, bore 80.97mm, stroke 72.74mm, displacement 1,498cc, maximum power 65 bhp at 4,800 rpm, compression ratio 8.3 to 1, single Zenith 33N carburettor.
Transmission: Ford single dry plate clutch. Ford four-speed all-synchromesh gearbox. Ratios 16.2, 10.92, 6.44 and 4.56 to 1, reverse 18.1 to 1. Alternative gearbox ratios available (see Competition Model). Open Hardy Spicer propeller shaft to Salisbury hypoid-bevel axle unit.
Suspension: Front, independent with sliding pillars, coil springs and Armstrong telescopic shock absorbers. Rear, live axle with semi-elliptic springs and Armstrong lever-arm shock absorbers.
Steering: Cam and lever.
Brakes: Girling hydraulic with 11in front discs and 9in rear drums.
Wheels: Spoked, fitted with Dunlop 5.20 × 15in or 155 × 15 tyres.
Fuel: 8½-gallon tank, rear-mounted.
Dimensions: Wheelbase 8ft; length 12ft; width 4ft 8in; track 3ft 11in front, 4ft 1in rear.
Weight: 16½ cwt.

4-4 Series 5 Competition Model

An increase in compression ratio and a change in carburettor, together with a closer-ratio gearbox, all from the Ford Cortina GT, helped to give this model a significantly better performance than the standard Series 5, with a 0-60 mph acceleration time of 11.9 seconds and a top speed of 95 mph. The changes in specification, which brought with it a purchase price of £1,437 compared with £1,304 for the standard model, were as follows:

Two views of a unique Morgan. Although the 4-4 Series 2 was only offered to the public as an open two-seater, a special drop-head coupe was produced for a Miss Skinner, a relation of the Morgan family. Its Chassis Number was A.553, its Engine Number Ford 100E B.427103C, and finished in yellow, it left the factory on February 1, 1960 with the registration number 380 AAB.

Engine: Ford 116E GT, maximum power 83.5 bhp at 5,200 rpm, compression ratio 9 to 1, Weber DCD 22 carburettor.
Transmission: Ford four-speed all-synchromesh gearbox, ratios 14.54, 9.82, 5.8 and 4.1 to 1, reverse 16.22 to 1.

4-4 1600

This model has been in production since January 1968, when once again Morgan took advantage of the availability of another Ford engine to enhance the performance of the 4-4 models. Offered with open two-seater or four-seater bodywork. The Chassis Number sequence under which this model is produced began at B1600, and the specification on the car's introduction at a price of £1,495 was as follows:
Engine: Ford 2737E, four cylinders in line, overhead valves, bore 81mm, stroke 77.7mm, displacement 1,597cc, maximum power 74 bhp at 4,750 rpm, compression ratio 9 to 1, single Zenith or Ford carburettor.
Transmission: Ford 7½in diaphragm-spring clutch. Ford four-speed all-synchromesh gearbox. Ratios 12.19, 8.24, 5.73 and 4.1 to 1, reverse 13.63 to 1. Open Hardy Spicer propeller shaft to Salisbury hypoid-bevel axle unit.
Suspension: Front, independent with sliding pillars, coil springs and Armstrong telescopic shock absorbers. Rear, live axle with semi-elliptic springs and Armstrong lever-arm shock absorbers.
Steering: Cam and lever.
Brakes: Girling hydraulic with 11in front discs and 9in rear drums.
Wheels: Pressed steel or spoked, fitted with 5.60 × 15in tyres on 4J rims or 4½J (spoked) rims.
Fuel: 8½-gallon tank, rear-mounted.
Dimensions: As Series 5 except track 4ft front and rear.
Weight: 16½ cwt (two-seater).

4-4 1600 Competition Model

Basically similar to the standard 1600 models, but equipped with the Ford 2737 GT engine of the Cortina GT, with a compression ratio of 9.2 to 1, a twin-choke Weber carburettor and a power output of 95.5 bhp at 5,500 rpm. Priced at £1,551, the Competition Model was introduced in January 1969, the first Chassis Number being B1799. The model was discontinued in November 1970 when the Ford 2737 GT engine was adopted for all 4-4 1600 models.

4-4 1600 specification changes

The following are the more significant changes during the production run of the 4-4 1600, identified by date and Chassis Number:

January 1969, from B1740, four-seater model introduced.

October 1969, from B2014, new dashboard, based on Plus-8 design, with tachometer to right of steering column on right-hand-drive cars and all other instruments and rocker-type switches in oval panel in centre of dashboard.

November 1970, from B2276, Ford 2737 GT engine standard for all models, collapsible steering column introduced.

February 1971, from A2381, Chassis Number prefix 'A' adopted with change to Ford 2265E engine brought about by Ford's replacement of 2737 GT engine with single-overhead-camshaft engine for Series 3 Cortina GT. Ford 2265 engine basically similar to 2737 GT, with pushrod-operated overhead valves. Mechanically operated clutch fitted.

October 1971, from A2559, dual braking system introduced. Extra padding provided around dashboard. Protruding instead of flush-mounted rear light assemblies.

May 1972, from A3060, improved fresh-air heater fitted.

November 1974, from A3367, windscreen demisting vents introduced.

January 1977, from A3905, aluminium body offered as optional extra.

Morgan Plus-4 (TR2 engine)

The first Plus-4s, announced in October 1950, fell within the flat-radiator era of Morgan history, and consequently have been covered in detail in Volume 1 of **The Four-wheeled Morgan.** They were powered by the 2,088cc Standard Vanguard engine, and even after the change to cowled radiator bodywork this power unit continued to be offered, until 1958, as an alternative to the 1,991cc Triumph TR2 engine, which was first made available in the Plus-4 in October 1953. Understandably, the TR2-engined cars, being of superior performance as well as falling conveniently within the 2-litre class limit, were the more popular.

The first TR2 engine was originally fitted into the first of the cowled-radiator cars, Chassis Number T3000, although subsequently it was removed and transferred into the works car, which carried the registered number KUY 387. Production of Plus-4s continued until

An early cowled-radiator Plus-4 with the reverse-curvature rear-end incorporating stowage space for the twin spare wheels behind the fuel tank. The outline of the tank is no longer visible externally.

The conversion of the Plus-4 to a cowled-radiator design was most tastefully carried out and in many people's opinion actually enhanced the car's classic appearance.

The Plus-4 four-seater, with its extended passenger compartment necessitating an almost straight rear panel with a vertically mounted single spare wheel behind it.

Below: This is the simpler rear-end treatment which was possible when the second spare wheel was dropped from the Plus-4 two-seater's specification. Below right: This picture by P. Boisvieux reveals a Morgan with a history; it is the 1967 Plus-4 four-seater which was originally owned by Brigitte Bardot.

The most snug of all the Plus-4s, the cowled-radiator drop-head coupe in its original guise with twin spare wheels behind a reverse-curvature rear panel.

The later drop-head body style displayed by the immaculate 1961 Plus-4 owned by Jerry Boston of Cleveland, Ohio, which carries the Chassis Number 4854 and has been a regular concours prizewinner.

January 1969, the last Chassis Number being 6853 (the prefix letter, P for the Vanguard and T for the TR engine, was dropped after the former engine ceased to be available in 1958). The TR2 engine progressively gave way to the TR3 and TR4 engines as these were introduced by Triumph.

In addition to the choice of open two-seater and open four-seater Tourer bodies, the Plus-4 was also produced at various times in other body styles, which are covered later in this chapter.

The earliest cowled-radiator Plus-4s appeared with bodywork changes confined to the front of the car, the traditional pair of upright-mounted spare wheels still being featured at the rear. However, by October 1955 the twin spares had been replaced by a single wheel set into the rear panel. At the same time overriders were fitted to the front bumper. The first Chassis Number featuring these modifications was 3400. The introduction of the TR2 engine meant that, at approximately £830, the Plus-4 was the cheapest car on the British market able to reach 100 mph, although testers found that the last two or three miles per hour took quite a long run to achieve. The specification of the TR2-engined Plus-4 on its announcement was as follows:

Engine: Triumph TR2, four cylinders in line, overhead valves, bore 83mm, stroke 92mm, displacement 1,991cc, maximum power 90 bhp at 4,800 rpm, compression ratio 8.5 to 1, twin SU carburettors.
Transmission: Borg and Beck 9in single dry plate clutch. Moss four-speed gearbox, synchromesh on second, third and top. Ratios 12.51, 7.43, 4.9 and 3.73 to 1, reverse 16.09 to 1. Open Hardy Spicer propeller shaft to Salisbury hypoid-bevel axle unit.
Suspension: Front, independent with sliding pillars, coil springs and Girling telescopic shock absorbers. Rear, live axle with semi-elliptic springs, Silentbloc bushes and Girling hydraulic shock absorbers.
Steering: Cam and sector, 2¼ turns lock to lock.
Brakes: Girling hydraulic, 9in drums with two leading shoes front and rear.
Wheels: Pressed steel with hub caps fitted with 5.25 × 16in tyres.
Fuel: 11-gallon tank, rear-mounted.
Dimensions: Wheelbase 8ft; length 11ft 8in; width 4ft 8in; track 3ft 11in.
Weight: 16½ cwt.

Plus-4 (TR3 engine)

Outwardly identical to the TR2-engined model which it replaced, this model, which was introduced in 1954, was visibly different beneath the bonnet in the size of its carburettors and its different inlet manifold. The more powerful engine helped the car's top speed to 105 mph, and there were improvements in acceleration times, although fuel consumption, which had been such a strong point of the earlier TR2 engines, had suffered. The TR3-engined Plus-4 went on to the market at just under £894 with a specification as follows:

Engine: Triumph TR3, four cylinders in line, overhead valves, bore 83mm, stroke 92mm, displacement 1,991cc, maximum power 100 bhp at 5,000 rpm, compression ratio 8.5 to 1, twin SU H6 carburettors.
Transmission: As TR2-engined cars.
Suspension: As TR2-engined cars.
Steering: As TR2-engined cars.
Brakes: As TR2-engined cars.
Wheels: As TR2-engined cars.
Fuel: As TR2-engined cars.
Dimensions and weight: As TR2-engined cars.

Plus-4 four-seater Drop Head Coupé

In the heyday of the Morgan three-wheelers there was a Family model which proved deservedly popular, and perhaps the closest we have seen to a family-type four-wheeled Morgan is this variant of the Plus-4, which was announced publicly in 1954 and at £879 was the most expensive car in the current range. Weighing 84 pounds more than a four-seater Tourer, performance inevitably suffered slightly, but this did not prevent examples from appearing in competitions, and one, owned by T. Dixon-Smith, was sufficiently impressive to be described by the motoring Press as 'indecently quick'.

Two prototype cars had been built in 1951 and 1953 with the then current flat radiator, although both were subsequently altered to the later bodywork. The 1953 car became the personal car of H.F.S. Morgan, who used it until his death in 1959. A total of 51 cars were produced with this bodywork, including the two prototypes, 29 being destined for the home market, 18 for the USA, two for Spain and one each for Belgium and Australia. All cars sold in the UK were fitted with the Vanguard engine, while export cars had the TR power unit.

Above left: Another variation on the Plus-4 theme, this time a drop-head coupe with two occasional seats in the rear. Above: This example, which was photographed by Roger Moran and reveals the large rear screen panel and the lid for the recessed spare wheel, was originally exported to the U.S.A. but has since been purchased by an English Morgan enthusiast.

This concours prizewinner is the last Plus-4 drop-head coupe to have been built. Carrying Chassis Number 3428, it is owned by Barbara and Gerry Willburn of the Plus-4 Club of Southern California and used as everyday transport.

MORGAN PLUS-4 FOUR-SEATER DROP HEAD COUPÉ

Production Record

Date left factory	Chassis number	Engine type	Engine number	Gearbox number	Axle ratio	Coachwork colour	Upholstery colour	Destination
September 1951	P. 2227	V1	V 122 ME	113	4.1	Blue	Black	Works
March 1953	P. 2612	V1	V 420 ME	435	4.1	—	—	Works
July 1954	P. 3144	V2	V 730	822	4.1	Blue	Black	U.K.
October 1954*	3179	V2	V 686	799	4.1	Ivory	Black	U.K.
November 1954	3207	TR2	TS 5810	898	4.1	Ming Blue	Beige	U.S.A.
November 1954	3211	V2	V 762	871	4.1	Blue	Black	U.K.
December 1954	3214	V2	V 749	840	3.73	Ivory	Black	U.K.
December 1954	3222	V2	V 765	809	4.1	Black	Red	U.K.
January 1955	3230	V2	V 732	825	4.1	Green	Black	U.K.
January 1955	3234	V2	V 767	842	4.1	Red	Black	U.K.
January 1955	3235	V2	V 713	930	3.73	Green	Black	U.K.
January 1955	3237	V2	V 740	962	4.1	Green	Black	U.K.
January 1955	3238	V2	V 719	958	3.73	Blue	Black	U.K.
February 1955	3243	TR2	TS 5138	837	N/A	Ivory	Red	U.S.A.
February 1955	3250	V2	V 761	950	3.73	Blue	Black	U.K.
March 1955	3254	V2	V 760	929	4.1	Blue	Black	U.K.
March 1955	3256	TR2	TS 5028	921	3.73	Red	Black Leather	U.S.A.
March 1955	3259	V2	V 698	956	4.1	Green	N/A	U.K.
March 1955	3261	TR2	TS 4195	935	3.73	Ivory	Black Leather	U.S.A.
March 1955	3264	V2	V 664	957	4.1	Green	Black	U.K.
March 1955	3266	V2	V 769	992	3.73	Ming Blue	Grey Leather	U.K.
March 1955	3267	V2	V 783	968	3.73	Green	Beige	U.K.
April 1955	3274	TR2	TS 4925	940	3.73	Black	Red	U.S.A.
April 1955	3283	V2	V 741	976	4.1	Blue	Black	U.K.
May 1955	3289	TR2	TS 5598	967	3.73	Red	Black Leather	U.S.A.
May 1955	3290	V2	V 721	961	N/A	Blue	Black	U.K.
May 1955	3298	TR2	TS 4602	N/A	3.73	Black	Red Leather	U.S.A.
June 1955	3300	V2	V 734	849	4.1	Green	Black	U.K.
June 1955	3302	TR2	TS 4927	941	3.73	Blue	Black Leather	U.S.A.
June 1955	3307	V2	V 781	1018	3.73	Ming Blue	Beige	U.K.
July 1955	3319	TR2	TS 5694	944	3.73	Black	Red	Belgium
July 1955	3322	V2	V 706	1037	4.1	Green	Black	U.K.
July 1955	3323	TR2	TS 4824	982	3.73	Off White	Red Leather	U.S.A.
August 1955	3332	TR2	TS 6018	996	3.73	Maroon	Black	Australia
August 1955	3335	TR2	TS 5251	1006	3.73	Red	Beige Leather	U.S.A.
August 1955	3339	TR2	TS 5466	1003	3.73	Black	Red Leather	U.S.A.
September 1955	3342	V2	V 693	1023	4.1	Leaf Green	Black	U.K.
September 1955	3346	TR2	TS 5968	1014	3.73	Ming Blue	Red Leather	U.S.A.
September 1955	3348	V2	V 759	1045	4.1	Primer	Beige Leather	U.K.
September 1955	3354	TR2	TS 5866	1050	3.73	Black	Beige Leather	U.K.
September 1955	3356	V2	V 775	1053	4.1	Blue	Black	U.K.
October 1955	3368	TR2	TS 7775	1046	3.73	Ivory	Red Leather	U.S.A.
November 1955	3372	TR2	TS 6060	1054	3.73	Red	Black Leather	U.S.A.
November 1955	3374	TR2	TS 6230	1048	3.73	Black	Red Leather	U.S.A.
November 1955	3375	V2	V 18 ME	1055	4.1	Blue	Black	U.K.
November 1955	3393	V2	V 707	1154	4.1	Green	Black	U.K.
December 1955	3394	TR2	TS 8199	1092	4.1	Blue	Light Grey	Spain
December 1955	3398	TR2	TS 7901	1063	4.1	Ivory	Red Leather	Spain
December 1955	3400	V2	V 778	1065	3.73	Ivory	Black	U.K.
February 1956	3419	TR2	TS 8293 ME	1107	3.73	Blue	Black Leather	U.S.A.
February 1956	3428	TR2	TS 8287 ME	922	4.1	Red	Black Leather	U.S.A.

*1954 London Motor Show car.

The Plus-4 underwent many changes during its 18-year life. The 1,991cc TR2 engine was made available in 1954, the TR3 engine in 1957, when the radiator cowl was lowered, the 105 bhp TR4 2,138cc engine took over in 1963 and the same year a Plus-4 Super Sports was added to the range, powered by a modified 120 bhp version of the TR3 engine to keep it within the 2-litre class. This model can be identified by the air intake on the right side of the engine cover. Wire wheels had become an option with disc brakes in 1959, and the sloping tail (similar to the 4-4's) had been standardized in 1958.

Apart from the different seating arrangements, the main change from the two-seater Drop Head Coupé Plus-4 came at the rear, where even a small luggage compartment had been provided. The door windows were also larger on the four-seater, and there were modifications to the hood and its frame. The accompanying table offers full details of each of the cars produced and its destination.

Plus-4 (TR4 and TR4A engine)

With the introduction of the TR4 the Triumph, and therefore the Morgan, sports cars were moved into the over-2-litre class, but performance was considerably enhanced, especially when the increase in capacity was followed, for the TR4A, by a further increase in power. This was to be the last of the series of four-cylinder TR engines, and therefore the last of the Morgan Plus-4s, a car which had enjoyed, and indeed would continue to enjoy for many years to come, a fine competitions record.

The first of the 2,138cc TR4 engines was produced in 1961, and the first to the uprated TR4A specification in 1965 enabling Morgan to uprate the specification of the Plus-4 priced from £816 as follows:

Engine: Triumph TR4 or TR4A, four cylinders in line, overhead valves, bore 86mm, stroke 92mm, displacement 2,138cc, maximum power (TR4) 100 bhp at 4,600 rpm, (TR4A) 104 bhp at 4,700 rpm, compression ratio 9 to 1, twin Stromberg or SU carburettors.
Transmission: Borg and Beck 9in single dry plate clutch. Moss four-speed gearbox, synchromesh on second, third and top. Ratios 11.05, 6.5, 4.5 and 3.73 to 1, reverse 11.05 to 1. Otherwise as TR2-engined cars.
Suspension: As TR2-engined cars.
Steering: As TR2-engined cars.
Brakes: Girling hydraulic, 11in front discs and 9in rear drums.
Wheels: Spoked, fitted with Dunlop 5.60 × 15in or 165 × 15 tyres.
Fuel: As TR2-engined cars.
Dimensions: Wheelbase 8ft; length 12ft; width 4ft 8in; track 3ft 11in front, 4ft 1in rear.
Weight: 16½ cwt.

Plus-4 Super Sports

When this car was announced in 1961 it offered arguably the best value in terms of performance for money available at that time anywhere. With acceleration figures of 0-60 mph in 7.8 seconds and 0-100 mph in 22.8 seconds, it was tailor-made for competitions, and was to earn countless successes.

Engines for the Super Sports were sent from the works to Chris Lawrence's workshop at Westerham Motors, Acton, where they received the now famous Lawrencetune treatment. Basically this consisted of completely stripping the engine and sending the clutch, flywheel, connecting rods and crankshaft to Jack Brabham (Motors) Ltd for balancing. While this was happening, Lawrence's workshop team polished and gas-flowed the cylinder-head, the compression ratio was raised to 9 to 1, and a high-lift camshaft was fitted. At the same time the engine was given a cast-alloy inlet manifold and an unusual square-section four-branch exhaust manifold, while a pair of either 42 or 45 DCOE Weber carburrators were added. The engine was then returned to the factory, where it was fitted into a standard Plus-4 chassis, which in turn was covered by a light-alloy body and wings. Finally, an oil-cooler was mounted in front of the radiator, but behind the grille. The changes in specification of the Super Sport from the normal Plus-4 were as follows:

Engine: Triumph TR series, fully balanced, displacement 2,196cc, maximum power 125 bhp at 5,500 rpm, two twin choke 42 or 45 DCOE Weber carburettors, tubular exhaust manifold, oil-cooler and remote header tank cooling system.
Wheels: 72-spoke, wide-rim.
Weight: 15½ cwt (dry). Many examples were fitted with individual bucket seats in place of the conventional bench-backed seats.

Plus-4 four-seater Super Sports

This car was built specially for Eric White of Allon White & Son (Cranfield) Ltd., the Morgan Main Agent, and was collected from the factory in November 1966. Eric White's recollections of this car, which had a Westminster Green coach finish and was trimmed in black leather, are recorded in the final section of this book.

Plus-4 specification changes

The following are the more significant changes and milestones during the production run of the Plus-4, identified by date and Chassis Number:

February 1956, at 3428, final four-seater Drop Head Coupé.

October 1957, from 3790, lower front cowl introduced to special order.

October 1958, at 3923, lower front cowl withdrawn.

October 1958, from 4003, wider seats on four-seater tourer.

October 1958, from 4023, altered rear end on all models with single spare wheel recessed into sloping panel. 12-gallon in place of 11-gallon fuel tank, narrower running boards.

May 1959, from 4203, front-wheel disc brakes available as optional extra, but only with wire wheels.

October 1959, from 4368, front-wheel disc brakes available as option with pressed-steel wheels.

September 1960, from 4644, front-wheel disc brakes fitted as standard.

September 1960, from 4647, improved steering introduced.

September 1960, from 4650, revised instrument panel with toggle switches.

March 1961, from 4806, Super Sports model introduced.

October 1961, from 4974, deeper windscreen and lower door sills introduced on two-seater Drop Head Coupé.

June 1962, from 5155, 2,138cc engine adopted as standard, but 1,991cc engine still available to order. Instruments changed to white figures on black dials.

October 1962, from 5237, Super Sports fitted with 2,138cc engine as standard, but 1,991cc engine still available to order. Body line lowered to reduce frontal area.

October 1965, from 6079, Competition Model introduced with four-branch exhaust manifold, wire-spoked wheels with wider tyres, adjustable rear shock absorbers and body height reduced to that of 4-4 model.

November 1966, at 6387, Competition Model discontinued.

December 1966, from 6393, body line of two-seater tourer lowered.

January 1968, at 6656, Super Sports model discontinued.

November 1968, at 6833, four-seater tourer discontinued.

December 1968, at 6850, two-seater tourer discontinued.

January 1969, at 6853, two-seater Drop Head Coupé discontinued.

Plus-4 production

Records reveal that a total of 3,853 TR-engined Plus-4s were produced, the breakdown according to engine being as follows:

TR2-engined cars	366
TR3/TR3A-engined cars	1,871
TR4/TR4A-engined cars	1,523
Super Sports	93

Morgan Plus-4-Plus Coupé

Perhaps the most controversial of all Morgan models, the Plus-4-Plus first appeared at the 1963 Motor Show in London, where it received a very mixed reception. Some described the closed glass-fibre-bodied car as having a Jaguar XK150 front and a Lotus Elite rear, while many die-hard Morgan purists were almost lost for words.

For several years prior to this model's introduction Peter Morgan had been considering the possibility of producing a 'fully enclosed Morgan'. In 1962, after making a very detailed study of a Debonair GT body (similar to one which was fitted to Roy Clarkson's well-tried and very successful rally car of the mid-fifties), he contacted the manufacturers, E.B. Plastics Ltd., of Tunstall, Stoke-on-Trent. This company had been producing two-seater open sports car bodies for several years and the Debonair GT saloon since about 1960. (They also produced cabs for Foden and ERF trucks and Austin-Parkinson electric vehicles, quite apart from varied applications of glass-fibre moulding for the motor industry in general.)

Peter Morgan asked them if they could produce a similar body for the Morgan chassis, though retaining some of the classic Morgan lines, which was interpreted as retaining a Morgan-style frontal appearance incorporating a somewhat similar radiator grille. There was to be no overhang at the front, and no mechanical changes were to be needed to the chassis. In fact, the only chassis change necessary were to be a pair of sheet-steel extensions which were to be bolted on each side of the engine, and which linked the front suspension mountings to the bulkhead, thereby making the structure much sturdier.

John N. Edwards, the founder and managing director of E.B. Plastics, designed and produced drawings of variations on the Debonair GT theme, and Peter Morgan selected the one which was to be put into production, but before the final go-ahead was given a scale model of the proposed car was made and submitted for approval.

Charley Lloyd, of Leola, Pennsylvania, used these pictures of his 1967 Plus-4 Super Sport to help sell the car, which he described as being one of 14 built and fitted with a TR4 engine with Lawrencetune manifolds, Weber carbs, tuned exhaust and an oil cooler. The black-painted and trimmed aluminium-bodied car had only covered 5,700 miles at the time. The excellent fit of the soft top is typical of modern-day Morgans.

This is the only Plus-4 four-seater Super Sports to have been built by the factory. Registered EMJ 266E, it was owned originally by Eric White of Allon White & Son (Cranfield) Ltd., the well-known Morgan agents.

Bob Burrows, president of the Ohio Morgan Owners, in the cockpit of his 1967 Plus-4 two-seater, Chassis Number 6553, which is seen in its original unrestored condition and is used daily.

Three photographs by John H. Sheally II of his immaculate 1967 Plus-4 two-seater roadster, which must be one of the most frequently photographed of all Morgans. The high-angle view on the left gives an indication of the extravagent care with which Morgan enthusiasts throughout the world maintain their cars.

Next, a full-scale pattern was made, using wood formers, and this was then panelled in light alloy on which many long hours were spent producing a very high quality cellulose finish. The first mould was made from epoxy resin, and while the first body was being prepared in this mould Peter Morgan sent a Plus-4 chassis (A5379) to the Tunstall works. The body was mounted, cellulosed, fitted with lights and other equipment and trimmed. It was given a pair of individual seats with a common bench-type back, but all subsequent cars of this model were to be supplied with bucket seats. The prototype car was then registered 869 KAB and Peter Morgan collected it from the Tunstall works. This was the only Plus-4-Plus to be produced in this way, all future cars being finished, cellulosed and trimmed back at the Morgan factory after the body had been fitted at the Tunstall works.

Extensive road testing included a tour of Spain, and this revealed a problem associated with the very stiff front end of the car, which meant that the front suspension was having to work harder than would have been the case had the usual flexing of the chassis been able to absorb some of the worst shocks. Nevertheless, the car retained the Morgan's famed roadholding capabilities and it still handled like a car from Malvern should. When the production car was unveiled its specification was as follows:

Engine: Triumph TR4, four cylinders in line, overhead valves, bore 86mm, stroke 92mm, displacement 2,138cc, maximum power 105 bhp at 4,750 rpm, compression ratio 9 to 1, twin Stromberg CD carburettors.
Transmission: Borg and Beck 9in clutch. Moss four-speed gearbox, synchromesh on second, third and top. Ratios 11.08, 6.51, 4.49 and 3.73 to 1; reverse 11.08 to 1. Open Hardy Spicer propeller shaft to Salisbury hypoid-bevel axle unit.
Suspension: Front, independent with sliding pillars, coil springs and Armstrong telescopic shock absorbers. Rear, live axle with semi-elliptic springs and Armstrong lever-arm shock absorbers.
Steering: Cam gear, 2¼ turns lock to lock.
Brakes: Girling hydraulic with 11in front discs and 9in rear drums with 1¾ in wide shoes.
Wheels: 72 spoke with 5.60 × 15in tyres.
Fuel: 10-gallon tank, rear-mounted.
Dimensions: Wheelbase 8ft; length 12ft 8in; width 5ft 1in; height 4ft 3in; track 3ft 11½ in front, 4ft 1in rear.
Weight: 16¼ cwt (dry).

Although the car had been received quite well by the motoring Press when it was announced at just over £1,275, public reaction was less satisfactory, and the car was only produced spasmodically over the next four years, even though the works prototype car had done well in competitions in the hands of Peter Morgan. It has been widely quoted that 50 cars were produced in the Plus-4-Plus series, but the correct figure is in fact 26, as Mr. Edwards has been able to confirm. In addition, two spare body shells were made. Of the 26, only eight remained in Britain apart from the prototype, which is still retained at the works in dismantled form following an accident. Of the remainder, 10 went to the USA, three to Canada, and one each to Switzerland, Belgium, Holland and Japan. The full list of Chassis Numbers and delivery details is as follows:

Chassis Number	Date left factory	Sold to	
A5379	April 1963	U.K.	Index Number 869 KAB (Prototype)
A5504	September 1963	U.K.	Index Number DUY 997B (1963 London Motor Show)
A5530	November 1963	U.K.	Index Number 3095 JN
A5544	November 1963	U.S.A.	
A5558	December 1963	Canada	
A5575	January 1964	U.K.	Index Number ANP 351B
A5592	January 1964	Canada	
A5606	February 1964	U.S.A.	Now owned by John Sheally, President Washington D.C. Club
A5612	February 1964	Switzerland	
A5619	March 1964	U.S.A.	
A5625	March 1964	U.K.	Index Number CLB 801B
A5650	April 1964	U.K.	Index Number BUY 280B
A5657	April 1964	U.S.A.	
A5678	May 1964	U.S.A.	
A5686	June 1964	U.S.A.	
A5702	June 1964	U.S.A.	
A5722	July 1964	U.K.	Index Number CUY 708B
A5723	July 1964	U.S.A.	
A5737	August 1964	Belgium	
A5758	August 1964	U.S.A.	

This Lawrencetune hardtop, which was designed and developed by Chris Lawrence, was made initially to fit the low-line Plus-4 models, although it could also be used for the 4-4 when supplied with different fittings. Moulded in resin-bonded glass-fibre, it was normally supplied white with a flock-sprayed inner finish and it weighed 22 lbs.

The biggest surprise at the Earls Court Motor Show in 1963 was the appearance of a contemporarily styled glass-fibre-bodied two-seater closed coupe on the Morgan stand, an event which staggered the traditionalists and amazed the avant garde alike. Virtually the same as the traditional Plus-4 beneath the skin, the Plus-4-Plus was a brisk performer, but not quite right for the particular niche in the enthusiast market which the Malvern company had nurtured so effectively. The slightly exaggerated roof line was intentional in order to provide acceptable headroom as well as impressive roof strength.

Smoothly styled it may have been, but the Plus-4-Plus soon found its way on to the traditional Morgan competition terrain of greasy, unmetalled hills. Here is Peter Morgan tackling two of the sections on the 1964 Land's End Trial.

A5794	October 1964	U.S.A.	1964 London Motor Show Car
A5908	March 1965	U.K.	Original Index Number
			CNN 289C now RAR 444
A5989	May 1965	Japan	(American Serviceman)
A6124	December 1965	U.K.	Index Number KBF 267D
A6373	November 1966	Canada	
A6436	January 1967	Holland	

E.B. Morgan

During 1963, John N. Edwards and his brother of E.B. Plastics Ltd., who had begun the production of Plus-4-Plus bodies, discussed with Peter Morgan the possibility of purchasing a supply of 4-4 chassis with a view to clothing them with a modern-style open two-seater body and retailing the cars as E.B. Morgans.

Initially one chassis was obtained, and a prototype was produced towards the end of 1963. The glass-fibre body was built by a short-cut economy method without using a proper pattern and mould, which would be produced at a later stage if the prototype performed satisfactorily and seemed acceptable as a commercial proposition.

The car certainly did perform well, and John Edwards well remembers a journey to the Duple Coachworks at Blackpool, for whom his company were producing Massey-Ferguson tractor cabs under sub-contract. While travelling at over 100 mph along the M6 motorway he suddenly heard and felt a machine-gun-like staccato rattle. He managed to slow and eventually stop the car, when he found that the cross-ply tyres, which were standard equipment on the 4-4 but only recommended for up to 85 mph sustained speed, had thrown their treads. Fortunately, no car damage had resulted, and in due course five new Dunlop radials were fitted in their place.

Shortly after this episode E.B. Plastics was sold to E.R.F. Engineering Ltd., of Sandbach, Cheshire, John Edwards joining the board, and it was decided not to continue with the E.B. Morgan project. In 1965 the prototype car was sold, and it was not until 1978 that it was heard of again, when it was discovered in a poor condition in a yard in Surrey. It transpired that the car was still owned by the person to whom John Edwards had sold it all those years earlier, and a sale was agreed. During the intervening period the body had survived remarkably well apart from some starring behind the rear wheel arches caused by stones thrown up by the wheels. The bonnet had been modified in an apparent attempt to get more air to the non-standard Weber carburettor which had been fitted, and certain other modifications had taken place which suggested that at one time there had been an attempt to prepare the car for racing. However, it is the intention of the new owner to restore the car to its original condition and specification.

Morgan S.L.R. (Sprinzel Lawrencetune Racing)

This car was designed and developed as a direct result of Chris Lawrence's successes at Le Mans, Spa, Monza and elsewhere in the early-sixties. In order to remain competitive in the mid-sixties he needed a faster car than his basically standard-bodied Morgans, and late in 1963 he was offered a new Porsche 904. However, he wanted to remain loyal to Morgan and so he decided to use the TR4-engined Plus-4 as the basis of a new car.

Lawrence had tuned a couple of rally cars for John Sprinzel, which had proved quite successful, and after some discussion the two drivers teamed up to form Sprinzel Lawrencetune Racing. Sprinzel managed to obtain some financial support from B.P., and this, together with money put in by each party, plus definite orders for two cars provided sufficient finance to begin development.

The regulations governing Group 4 GT racing at that time allowed for body modifications provided that the weight of the original car was not cut by more than 15 per cent. The aerodynamic body of the S.L.R. was designed jointly by Sprinzel and Lawrence, and was made in aluminium by Williams and Pritchard and attached to the bare chassis with very light sub-frames. No drastic chassis modifications were required, but a small amount of strengthening was done to the transverse bulkhead, and sub-frames were provided for mounting the shock absorbers.

Three cars were to be built on Morgan chassis and one on Neil Dangerfield's ex-Sid Hurrell Triumph TR4 (SAH 137), which had run so well at Monza in 1963. One of the Morgans was the works prototype of the Plus-4 Super Sports (170 GLP), this car being an exact replica of Lawrence's Le Mans car, for which it had acted as back-up for that event.

The modified TR4 engine had a new cross-flow cylinder-head with staggered 90 degrees-angled valves, a development which had been financed jointly by Lawrencetune and the Morgan Motor Company, but which was never actually completed. Several problems were encountered, especially concerning the lubrication of the rockers, and another irritation was the oiling up of the 10mm spark plugs,

J. N. Edwards' camera captures an historic moment as the wooden former on which the glass-fibre bodies of the Plus-4-Plus were to be constructed arrives at the Tunstall works of E.B. Plastics Ltd.

Controversial though they may have been at the time of announcement, Plus-4-Plus coupes have since become highly prized collector's items. This example, owned by C. Sampson, is pictured at the MOG '79 gathering at Knebworth House.

The S.L.R. Morgan (the initials stood for Sprinzel Lawrence Racing) was a successful effort to give the racing Morgan a more slippery shape, although its appearance in marque races caused a certain amount of controversy at the time. The example photographed above by Charles J. Smith on a rainy day at Silverstone in 1976 was still enjoying an active life at a Bentley Drivers Club meeting.

Three views of an experimental open two-seater body by E.B. Plastics Ltd., mounted on a 4-4 chassis. The photograph upper left, by E. Winfield, shows the state in which this car was found, in 1978, in need of restoration, while the two lower photographs were taken when the E.B. Morgan had been restored to its original state.

which had a narrow heat band. As Chris explained, 'If you could get on to the front row of the grid and could get away at the start you were alright. Otherwise, the plugs nearly always oiled up.' Another complication of this cylinder-head on the 2-litre engine was that the valves were so large that it was impossible to obtain a compression ratio of 10 to 1, which it is felt would have been ideal. Instead, the c.r. was a modest 6.8 to 1, but even so the engine developed more torque than the standard engine.

The cars also had larger stub axles and steel hubs, which had been developed as a result of numerous breakages which had occurred in the 1961 and 1962 seasons. During this period the Lawrencetune-prepared race cars developed such a high 'g' factor that the standard hubs could not take the strain, something which the manufacturers concerned were at first reluctant to accept, although in due course they were persuaded to change the material and increase the size. The stronger hubs were to be fully race-proved and have since been adopted as standard equipment for the Plus-8.

The S.L.R. Morgans achieved some notable competition successes, and Chris Lawrence used one to lower the class lap record at Goodwood from 1 minute 42 seconds to 1 minute 39 seconds, then went on to take a brilliant third place overall at Spa, splitting six Porsche 904s, which could never have been described as road cars. From time to time the cars are still seen in action, giving a good account of themselves, and one wonders how much they might have achieved had not Chris Lawrence suffered a serious road accident in 1964, which prevented any further development of the S.L.R.s.

Morgan Plus-8

The discontinuation of the four-cylinder Triumph TR engine may have been a blow to some Morgan enthusiasts, but to others it was a blessing in disguise in that it opened the door to the most exciting and powerful Morgan production car to date, the Plus-8, thanks to Peter Morgan's successful negotiation for the supply of Rover V-8 engines.

Although he has often voiced his regret that Rover have not fully exploited the potential of this fine engine, even in its standard form (and to some extent it has suffered a detuning over the years) it has given Morgan a truly exhilarating sports car. Announced in October 1968, it earned some exciting headlines from the motoring Press, but the one I liked best was the one word chosen by Michael Bowler, now Editor of *Thoroughbred and Classic Cars,* but at that time writing for *Motor* — 'TRANSMOGRIFICATION', by which, of course, is meant 'to transform in magical or surprising manner'. How true! Of all the models introduced by the Morgan works none has been so startlingly different in performance terms as the Plus-8, the Chassis Number sequence for which began at R7000 (the prototype car).

Aside from its phenomenal acceleration and all-round performance, it incorporated certain other changes in Morgan design which perhaps have tended to be overlooked, even though they represented quite a departure from traditional construction methods. Notable of these was the replacement of the wooden floor by steel from the pedal board to the seat-mounting points. Another change was to Restall bucket seats instead of the traditional bench-type seats, and these were adjustable, albeit only over a very limited distance. The new model also brought about the introduction of a triple windscreen wiper system, while in conformity with changing safety regulations the cockpit switches were of the rocker type. As with all previous models, the Plus-8 has been refined in specification over the years (some of the major landmarks are listed below) but when announced the car's specification was as follows:

Engine: Rover aluminium V-8-cylinder, overhead valves, bore 88.9mm, stroke 71.12mm, displacement 3,528cc, maximum power 184 bhp at 5,200 rpm, compression ratio 10.5 to 1, twin SU HS6 carburettors.

Transmission: Borg and Beck 9½in single dry plate clutch. Moss four-speed gearbox with synchromesh on second, third and top. Ratios 10.63, 6.24, 4.4 and 3.58 to 1. Hypoid-bevel final drive with Power-Lok limited-slip differential.

Suspension: Front, independent with sliding pillars, coil springs and Girling telescopic shock absorbers. Rear, live axle with semi-elliptic springs and Girling lever-arm shock absorbers.

Steering: Cam gear worm and nut.

Brakes: Girling servo-assisted with 11in front discs and 9in rear drums.

Wheels: Cast magnesium alloy with five-stud fitting. Dunlop SP Sport 185 VR-15 high-speed tyres.

Fuel: 13½-gallon tank, rear-mounted.

Dimensions: Wheelbase 8ft 2in; length 12ft 3in; width 4ft 10in; track 4ft 1in (front), 4ft 3in (rear).

Weight: 16¼ cwt (dry).

Morgan entered a new league with the
introduction of the Rover V8-powered Plus-8. In
anticipation of a tight engine fit the prototype car
(left) was equipped with twin bulges on the
bonnet top, although these subsequently proved
unnecessary. The lower left picture shows the
works car with hood erected and alloy wheels
replacing the wire-spoke-type of the prototype,
while immediately below the famous MMC 11
number graces one of the more recent
aluminium-bodied cars with wider wheels and
tyres.

Introduction of the Plus-8 brought about a change from the traditional bench-backed seats to individual bucket seats, while progressive improvements have been made to the specification ever since. This is a 1976 model with triple screen wipers and a full-width bumper visible here.

Eric White replaced his four-seater Plus-4 Super Sports with another unique Morgan, in this case a four-seater Plus-8, which originally was registered XMJ 84L, but now carries the number 23 HEW. The wide-section spare tyre and tow bar contribute to an unfamiliar appearance.

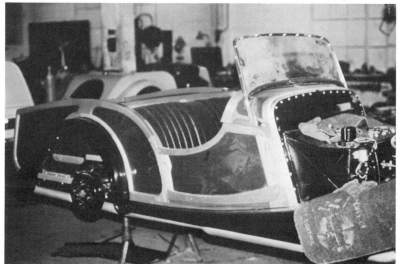

Above: Another unique Morgan. This car, which was photographed by Peter Askew in the factory undergoing repairs after being involved in an accident, was built to test both automatic transmission and a coupe body on a Plus-8 chassis. It was decided not to put the car into production because of potential limited demand and because the additional weight adversely affected performance and the car has since been used by Mrs. Jane Morgan. It was registered on January 1, 1971 and carries the Chassis Number 7317. Right: Two views of a novel pick-up conversion of a Morgan carried out by Steve Miller of San Francisco and photographed by Roger Moran.

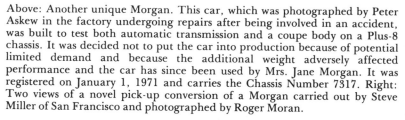

Plus-8 specification changes

The following are the more significant changes which have taken place during the production run of the Plus-8 open two-seater, identified by date and Chassis Number:

October 1971, from R7482, dual braking system introduced, increased dashboard padding and protruding instead of flush-fitted rear lights.

May 1972, from R0000, Moss gearbox replaced by Rover 3500S all-synchromesh gearbox. Internal ratios: 3.62, 2.12, 1.39 and 1.0 to 1, reverse 3.42 to 1.

May 1973, from R7602, improved fresh-air heating installed.

October 1973, from R7660, rear-axle ratio changed from 3.58 to 3.31 to 1, front track to 4ft 4in, rear track to 4ft 5in.

November 1974, from R7838, windscreen demisting vents fitted.

October 1975, from R7983, aluminium-bodied version introduced as Sports Lightweight.

January 1977, at R8186, Sports Lightweight discontinued at this Chassis Number.

January 1977, from R8200, Rover five-speed gearbox fitted. Internal ratios: 3.321, 2.087, 1.396, 1.0 and 0.833 to 1, reverse 3.428 to 1. Full-width front and rear bumpers. Instrument panel revised. Aluminium body now supplied as optional extra.

Plus-8 four-seater

Although at least four of these cars exist, only one of them was made at the factory. This was built specially for Eric White of Allon White & Son (Cranfield) Ltd., the Morgan Main Agents, as an experimental exercise. The other cars were built by their owners, and at least one of them was the result of a rear-end shunt.

The Plus-8 four-seater is more than simply a graft of a 4-4 four-seater body on to a Plus-8 chassis. The changes in specification include a larger fuel tank, larger seats (which are fixed), and changes to the rear timbers, the bulkhead and the steering shaft measurements. The Plus-8 is also fitted with twin-servo, twin-circuit brakes.

There were three reasons for not putting this model into series production, and they are the same as apply in respect of the automatic-transmission Plus-8, a prototype of which was also built. Firstly, it would have meant another model in the range at a time when the factory's main interest was in maximizing production of the existing models in order to help reduce the long waiting lists for them. Secondly, the four-seater models have to offer a compromize in handling qualities because of the considerable change in weight distribution whenever a third or fourth passenger is carried, nearly all of the additional weight being carried over the back wheels. This is not so critical in the case of the 4-4, but the greatly increased power and torque of the Plus-8 makes it less desirable to offer a car with this performance potential in a form which allows the balance to be so markedly changed with the passenger load. Thirdly, because of the inevitably limited demand for such a car, sales could not justify the cost involved in putting the car into production. Eric White's recollections of his car are recalled in the final section of this book.

Location of Chassis Numbers

Chassis Numbers are always stamped on the top of one of the chassis cross-members on the offside. In the case of the two-seaters, the Drop Head Coupés and the Plus-4-Plus Coupés it will be found on the member immediately behind the gearbox. On the four-seaters it can be found on the member immediately behind the front seats.

It is a sound policy to make a note of as many numbers as possible in respect of the major components of your car — chassis, engine, gearbox, rear axle, and so on — which will be most useful if ever you require to order or identify replacement parts. This is particularly important if you are not the first owner of the car, the components of which may have been changed as a result of wear and tear or even an accident. The more numbers you can quote the better.

Chapter 2

Morgans on trial and track

For as long as Morgans have been built they have enjoyed an active and successful competitions career, and the Morgan family have always encouraged this aspect of Morgan ownership, being firm believers that sports cars should be enjoyed in their natural environment, namely in sport.

Although during many seasons the competitions achievements of Morgans have been spearheaded by works entries, by far the greatest percentage of appearances have been by private owners, and in events as widely spaced as the countries in which Morgans have been sold.

Races, rallies, hill-climbs, reliability trials, off-road events and driving tests, all these and other motor sporting activities have proved within the scope of Morgans, and the events concerned have ranged from major internationals to the smallest club affairs staged for perhaps only a handful of competitors. To have mentioned them all, of course, would have been impossible, for in many cases records simply do not exist. Also, even those which have been recorded by clubs or individual competitors, not to mention the motoring Press, are so numerous that they would have filled this entire book on their own.

I have had to be selective, therefore, and this has not been easy, because what may be dismissed as of minor interest and of no real significance to some Morgan enthusiasts may well have been judged of special importance to others, notably those who were concerned with the event in question in one way or another. So, on the pages which follow, the reader will find, in roughly chronological order, mention of a very wide cross-section of events in which Morgans

participated over a period of 26 years, in many cases successfully, but in some instances less so.

I cannot expect that all of this material will be of particular interest to every single reader, but I hope that in making my selection I shall have ensured that all who read it will find a great deal of it of genuine interest, and that those items which are skipped over briefly by some, will be especially welcomed by others. Above all, I hope that this look back at Morgan competitions history over more than a quarter of a century will emphasize once again the versatility of Morgans as true sports cars, to be enjoyed at every opportunity, however important or modest the occasion. (Certain events which were organized by the Morgan 4-4 Club or the Morgan Sports Car Club are recorded under the history of these clubs, later in the book.)

1954

The traditional start to the motor-sporting year in Britain is the M.C.C.'s Exeter Trial, but although over the years Morgans have usually done well in this event, on this occasion they did not particularly excel and gained only four second-class and two third-class awards, one of the latter going to the well-known motoring journalist Peter Garnier.

More encouraging was the Thames Estuary A.C.'s Cat's Eyes Rally on the night of February 6, when B. Clarke, navigated by Ian MacKenzie, beat 211 other entries to emerge the overall winner, with a clean sheet, at the end of the 320-miles event, parts of which were covered by thick ice. Another Morgan driven by Hugh Denton finished second in its class behind Clarke's car.

Howard Sturrock was in good form that month, taking third place overall in the Scottish S.C.C.'s Moonbeam Rally and following it up a week later with a class win in the Falkirk and District C.C.'s rally. In March he missed the R.A.C. Rally to take part in the Clydesdale Rally, where he scored another class win, while also in Scotland Charles Robinson won his class a week later in the Rommanno Bridge autocross.

Britain's major rally, which started on the evening of March 9 with a 229-car entry split between the Hastings and Blackpool starting points, was to cover a road distance of 1,317 miles, but was to be decided by a series of special tests.

The entry included 11 Morgans, and at first things went well, with Alec Newsham's time of 21.7 secs in the first Morgan away only being beaten by 0.3 sec by a Triumph TR2. However, fog in the Welsh mountains was to play havoc with many of the Blackpool starters and some missed the final control. Anne and Chris Neil crashed their car but escaped with a few bruises, but W. O. Steel's passenger suffered a fractured collar-bone when one of the works team Morgans crashed into a wall. A garage test at Oulton Park was made more interesting by the use of genuine bricks and mortar, and Peter Morgan and Jim Goodall were second and third fastest in 53.4 and 54.6 secs, Peter being only 0.4 sec behind the leading car.

Morgans continued to do well in the tests, Jim Goodall being fastest of all in a scissors test and Peter Morgan climbing Prescott in 54.8 secs., 0.1 sec faster than Jack Sears' Jaguar coupé. Peter and Jim were also first and second in the Yorkshire tests, followed by John (Farmer) Moore. Hugh Denton in another Morgan just beat Peter to take the best time in a night test at Charterhall, and Jim Goodall and Barry Phipps both finished in the first six, while in the Lake District and Blackpool tests Peter was fastest both times. But all his hard work in the tests had been in vain and only two of the Morgans were to figure in the general classification at the finish, Jimmy and Mrs Ray taking seventh place and Alec Newsham eighth.

Over in East Anglia M. J. Warner took his Morgan to the Best Time of the Day in the first autocross meeting organized by the Eastern Counties M.C., and two weeks later he won a handicap event at their race meeting at Snetterton. Then, at the end of the month, A. L. Yarranton and his Plus-4 took second place overall in the very strenuous 400-miles Welsh Rally, organized on the night of March 27 by the Herefordshire M.C.

On Easter Saturday, April 17, two of five class records broken at the Lydstep hill-climb went to John Moore, in 35.5 and 35.1 secs, while Morgans also did well that weekend in the Scottish S.C.C.'s three-days Highland Rally, from which only 18 competitors emerged with clean sheets. The rally comprised a series of driving tests, on one of which Roy Clarkson established the best time in his special-bodied Morgan saloon (he was to finish third in class), interspersed with day and night navigation sections. Morgan drivers Anne Neil and Charles Robertson both slipped up on a deceptively simple garaging test, although Anne went on to win the ladies' award and fourth in her class, but the best result — a class win — went to Howard Sturrock.

Hugh Denton's time of 57.8 secs was sufficient to beat the field in the Northampton and District C.C.'s autocross meeting, although an HRG finished only 0.4 sec behind, while on the crowded roads of the West Country in May Dr. J. T. Spare won his class in the Torbay Rally one day and was a close second in class in the West Counties C.C.'s rally the next.

The next weekend he joined Hugh Denton and Barry Phipps to form a three-car team in the Ilfracombe Rally, from which Denton emerged the overall winner, Dr. Spare was second and Phipps won his class; needless to say they also scooped up the team prize from the other 69 competitors.

The Lancashire A.C.'s Morecambe Rally, however, proved less successful for Morgan drivers, Anne Neil dropping out with broken front suspension and John Moore having to drive the final test with a broken throttle pedal. However, Les Yarranton emerged a class winner, while L. Griffiths won the Bristol starting control prize.

Jimmy Ray received rare praise from the motoring Press when they recorded his class win on the R.S.A.C.'s Scottish Rally on June 7-11. *Autosport's* reporter remarked, 'Jimmy Ray was a delight to watch in all of the eight driving tests and his crisp handling of his familiar white Morgan wasted no movements in manoeuvrings and was always allied to speed.' Referring to one of the later tests, he went on, 'He never appeared to be motoring the Morgan really hard, but he skimmed around pylons and whipped the car in and out of garages so very tidily that he was a full two seconds better than his nearest opponent'. The other Morgan in this rally was driven by G. Hoyle, who finished second in the same class.

Jimmy Ray won two of the tests in the Plymouth M.C.'s Presidential Trophy Rally later that month, and a third went to Les Yarranton, but it was Dr. Spare who won the Morgan Cup award, and he was also a member of the winning team.

Clerk Hill, with an average gradient of one-in-eight over 250 yards, with two acute hairpins and several other bends, was used by the Lancashire A.C. for a hill-climb on July 4, where Peter Reece was easily best in class and third fastest overall with his climb in 30.5 secs.

Next weekend, down south, Dr. Spare was in action again, winning the Brighton Rally, the final tests for which were held on the famous Madeira Drive by the Brighton and Hove M.C. He won the Clayton Trophy, while the 1,301-2,000cc open class went to P.W.S. White in another Morgan. Dr. Spare then rushed down the coast to take part in the Taunton Rally the following day, and again he was the overall winner, with only 84 penalty marks against the 246 of the runner-up.

Having won the event in 1952 and 1953, Jimmy Ray hoped to complete the hat-trick on the London Rally on September 3-4, but he lost a lot of marks when he became stuck in the mud near one of the controls and he never really recovered. Jim Goodall was also out of luck, despite being fastest in the first and fourth tests, and the only Morgan to feature in the prize list was that shared by Nancy Mitchell and Doreen Reece, who took the ladies' award.

Morgans did considerably better, though, on the *Birmingham Post* Rally two weeks later. The first stage of the 400-miles route through the Welsh mountains left no margin for error, and half the entry were missing at the roll-call during the breakfast halt, when Jim Goodall and Peter Reece were amongst those still with a clean sheet. However, by the end of the rally Les Yarranton had moved to the top of his class, followed by Dr. Spare and Jim Goodall, while Miss A. Jervis was second in the ladies' contest. The previous weekend Yarranton had won an autocross event organized by the Worcestershire M.C. over two laps of a half-mile course at Shelsley Walsh, his time of 2 mins 8 secs being 3 secs ahead of Barry Phipps, whose Morgan was second in class and third overall.

The busy month of October brought outright wins for F. F. Rankin in the Durham A.C.'s navigation trial and for Howard Sturrock in the Lanarkshire M.C.'s Tamshies Turnout event, while class victories went to Jim Moore in the Pembrokeshire M.C.'s Lydstep hill-climb, F. D. Dundas in the Ayrshire Rally and E. Robertson in the MG C.C.'s Biggar Autocross event.

On the other side of the world the first Macau Grand Prix was held on October 31 and it attracted the entry of a Plus-4 four-seater owned by 'Dinger' Bell, currently the director of the Hong-Kong Royal Observatory. He had shipped the car out from England, and it now sported a TR2 cylinder-head, twin SU carburettors and a specially made aluminium bonnet. Dinger was first away from the Le Mans-type start, soon set the fastest race lap and led the field for five laps, when disaster struck as he was beginning to lap some tailenders; the front nearside brake drum sheared, and the whole unit, complete with wheel, came adrift, so ending the racing career of 'Betsy', as the car has always been known.

Back home, Anne and Chris Neil were fighting hard for first place in the Scottish Sporting C.C.'s Anniversary Run (celebrating 22 years of club competitions) until Anne misjudged the finish of a test, which meant that she had to be content with the ladies' award. The Neil sisters were also out of luck in the M.C.C.'s RedeX Rally the next weekend, after making a mess of the Elan Valley section, although Morgans did well amongst the 71 finishers out of the 334 who had started the 1,200-miles event. Les Yarranton, navigated by D. Thompson were second overall and won their starting control award, Jim Goodall and Peter Morgan each won their class, these three sharing the team award, while P. W. S. White was second in his class.

Very consistent driving by K. N. Lee on both the road and test sections put him in an unbeatable position before the final test of the M.G.C.C. North Eastern Centre's Goathland Rally, but once again he made the fastest time to underline his convincing victory, while in Scotland, the final rally of the year, the Falkirk and District M.C.'s Festive Rally, on December 12, was another success for Howard Sturrock, who finished second overall. The last event south of the border was the MG C.C.'s Trophy Trial on December 27, when T. D. Warren and I. D. L. Lewis scored first-class awards and H. J. C. Liddon a second-class award.

At the British Trials Drivers' Association annual dinner, a new prize, the *Autosport* Rally Navigators' Trophy, was presented to J. C. Dixon, navigator for Jimmy Ray, who won the Association's Gold Star rally competition (which excluded works drivers). Les Yarranton finished in third place, Dr. J. T. Spare was joint 12th and Howard Denton 23rd. In the Silver Star competition Dr. Spare was first,

Jimmy Ray fifth, Peter Reece seventh and K. N. Lee eighth, while Anne Neil was joint fourth in the Ladies' Silver Garter competition. So ended a really fine year for Morgan drivers.

1955

There were 13 Morgans amongst the 133 entries for the Exeter Trial this year, and after 325 miles and 10 observed sections they scored four first-class, five second-class and four third-class awards, while D. L. Lewis, H. H. Gould and Dr. J. T. Spare shared the team award, and Jim Goodall's first-class award secured for him one of only two Triple Awards won this time for successes in consecutive years.

Snow played havoc the next weekend with the Liverpool M.C.'s New Year Rally, in which two of the three Morgans entered were ex-Jimmy Ray cars. One of these, driven by Ken James and navigated by Peter Dingley, struggled through the drifts to emerge way out in front to secure the Stott Trophy.

The Maggi Carlo 450-miles night rally organized by the Bristol M.C. & L.C.C. on February 19-20 was the club's first rally and its name signified sponsorship from Maggi Soups. Snow, ice and a half washed away bridge were amongst the hazards of this well-organized event, which was won outright by Dr. Spare and his Plus-4.

The bad weather caused many events to be cancelled that month, but the North London Enthusiasts' C.C.'s Jacobean Trophy trial was staged on February 20, when A. J. Blair's Plus-4 finished runner-up to a winning Ford Prefect, while the same day D. Butterwick's Morgan was outright winner of the MG C.C. North East Centre's Bronte Rally.

The organizers of the fifth R.A.C. International Rally came in for a lot of criticism from *Autosport* editor Gregor Grant in March for underestimating the hazards caused by bad weather and narrow roads; competitors were repeatedly held up behind stuck cars, sometimes losing up to two hours as cars were manhandled up frozen lanes, while the marking system also left a lot to be desired. Peter Morgan was amongst those who crashed and had to abandon, and although Jim Goodall, Francis Dundas and Les Yarranton were amongst the Morgan finishers they had lost too many marks to be in the running for even a class award, while the outright winner, Jimmy Ray, had changed his Morgan for a Standard 10 on this occasion.

The Bolton-Le-Moors driving tests attracted 162 entries this year,

and Morgans did well, Peter Reece winning his class and Ken James and Harry Denton taking special awards, Reece and James also being members of the winning team. Dr. Spare was also back in the winners list on February 27 when he won the Plymouth M.C.'s 200 Trophy reliability trial.

In marked contrast, the Sebring 12-Hours race in scorching Florida sunshine on March 13 saw two Morgans amongst the 80 entries, and both were amongst the 49 finishers, that of Rothschild and Kunz finishing third in class behind a pair of Arnolt-Bristols, with the Morgan of Weitz and MacKenzie narrowly failing to take fourth place.

Harry Denton was back in action again the same weekend, winning the Chiltern C.C.'s Amersham autocross event, while in April the Herefordshire M.C.'s Welsh Rally, over a 350-miles course, saw some excellent Morgan performances in an event in which severe flooding brought the retirement of 17 cars. Barry Phipps and Angela Palfrey finished second overall to win the Peter Wray Challenge Trophy, while J. T. de Blaby and R. Dillow were fifth and Aileen Jervis and Miss M. Freeman were seventh.

The Morecambe National Rally in May brought a class win for Les Yarranton, while Francis Dundas and A. J. Blair in the other two Morgans entered shared the fastest time in the final test.

John Moore came to the starting grid for a seven-lap race in the B.A.R.C.'s first Members' meeting at Aintree to find his Morgan matched against 10 other cars, all of them Triumph TR2s, but he faced the daunting task with skill to cross the line the winner of the 2-litre race by four-fifths of a second. Morgans were also in the thick of the action at the Eight Clubs meeting at Silverstone, on June 4, beginning with a fine drive by D. Hiam, starting a handicap race from the five-seconds mark and snatching second place on the very last bend. Then John Moore pulled off a marvellous win from the 25-seconds mark in another handicap event and was concentrating so hard that he failed to see the chequered flag. He carried on for another lap until his nearside rear wheel came adrift as he sped through Woodcote Corner. The car spun to a standstill in the centre of the track, but he was surprised and relieved to find everyone else rolling past slowly on their way back to the paddock.

At the Aston Martin O.C. meeting on the same circuit on July 23 J. F. Looker, Ray Meredith and Barry Phipps finished third, fourth and fifth in a half-hour regularity trial to earn first-class awards in a type of event designed to acclimatize drivers with circuit racing.

Back in America, meanwhile, Gaston Andre took his Morgan to a class win before 30,000 spectators at a race meeting at Beverley Airport, New England, on July 4, and Mike Rothschild ran him a close second in the car which had gone so well at Sebring. Two months later, at Watkins Glen, the weather was so hot that the track had started to melt by the time the production sports car race, supporting the Grand Prix, got under way. However, Morgan stability was well demonstrated in the tricky conditions, and Gunnard Rubini and Gaston Andre finished first and third in their class, separated by an AC Ace.

The London M.C.'s excellent London Rally attracted no less than 454 starters for an event covering 650 miles in 26 hours, 200 miles of which involved night navigation in the Welsh mountains. There were also four driving tests in which Les Yarranton won the special award for the best aggregate performance of 66 seconds. Jimmy Ray proved to be the outright winner of the rally, for the third time, but although his previous victories, in 1952 and 1953, had been in Morgans, this time he was in a works-entered Triumph TR2. Other Morgan drivers, however, did well, the *Coupe des Dames* going to Yvonne Jackson and Lorna Kinns, while Dr. Spare and Jim Goodall were members of the runner-up team.

Patience and a cool head rewarded Peter Reece in a 30-lap production sports car race at the *Daily Despatch* Gold Cup meeting at Oulton Park on September 24. He had shot into the lead at the start with his Morgan, but was passed by an Austin-Healey on the second lap, and by a similar car on the third lap. He sat back, holding off the remainder of the field, for five laps while a hectic battle developed ahead of him. Then the two cars touched, crashed, and turned over, fortunately without serious injury to either driver, and Reece went through to a comfortable win by 38 seconds over the remainder of the field. On the same day E. S. Sneath finished second overall in the Lancs and Cheshire C.C.'s Lakeland Rally.

Back in America, Gunnard Rubini and Mike Rothschild continued to do well with their Plus-4s, finishing first and second overall in an inaugural race at Firchild Airport, Maryland, while Gaston Andre was third in their class, but in Britain Morgans' main efforts towards the end of this year came in rallies, with several successes and two significant near-misses. The Morgan team looked all set for the team prize in the M.C.C.'s National Rally, but Jim Goodall's car broke a half-shaft on the Eppynt test. However, Angela Palfrey took the ladies' award, Dr. J. T. Spare the prize for the lowest penalty score as well as his starting control award and he also won his class, followed by Les Yarranton and Peter Morgan in second and third places. Yarranton and Angela Palfrey also took their respective control awards. Finally, on the same weekend, Dick Pritchard took time off from his 4-4 Club duties to compete in the Nottingham Sports C.C.'s Autumn Rally, and navigated by Ernest Winfield was only just pipped for the premier award, but took a first-class award instead.

1956

The new season started off well for Les Yarranton, who was outright winner of the V.S.C.C.'s Measham Rally, while E. Cleghorn scored another Morgan success by winning the East Anglian M.C.'s Winter Rally on February 11. A third major success came during the same month when C. W. Whiteley and L. Hopps were outright winners of the Yorkshire S.C.C.'s Yorkshire Rally from a field of 140 starters. The event encompassed 40 controls along a 580-miles route, and as well as the overall victory Morgans were driven to the ladies' prize by Yvonne Jackson and to two first-class awards by A. R. Crowther and Dr. F. Townsend.

After the criticisms of the previous year, the 1956 R.A.C. Rally proved to be a first-class event, producing 213 starters and 48 retirements. The best Morgan performance went to Doc Spare, who was third overall and first in his class, while Les Yarranton took third place in the same class. Ladies' prizewinners Angela Palfrey and Aileen Jervis were driving an Austin on this occasion, although they were back in a 4-4 again the following day for a club event.

During a busy Easter weekend for motor sport R. Grant took a special prize for his test performances in the Highland Three Days Rally with his 4-4, while in the Herefordshire M.C.'s Welsh Marches Rally Les Yarranton scored a class win and Barry Phipps and Angela Palfrey took the prize for the best mixed crew; Yarranton and Phipps also took the team award.

Team prizes came thick and fast during this period, Peter Morgan, Jim Goodall and Les Yarranton scoring in the Midland A.C.'s *Birmingham Post* Rally on April 28-29, and Yarranton along with Doc Spare and Barry Phipps taking the prize on the Morecambe National Rally held on May 11-13. The latter event was held in three parts, the first day comprising a 300-miles road section followed by driving tests, the second being devoted entirely to more tests and the third day to a further set of tests for the W. W. Turner Trophy. Yarranton, who did well on the road section, then won his class in the first day of tests and was runner-up the following day, emerged overall winner of the contest.

There were two Morgans amongst the 101 entries for the R.S.A.C.'s Scottish Rally, covering 1,220 miles on the road and 14 driving tests, and both cars emerged with distinction, that of Doc Spare taking the Firth of Scotland award for performances in the tests, and Anne Neil's taking her to the ladies' prize for sports car drivers.

The versatility of Morgans was demonstrated well in the results lists of events staged in June, when A. J. Blair was a comfortable class winner in an autocross held at Dunstable by the Sporting Owner D.C., D. A. Walker and his Plus-4 were best overall amongst 70 competitors in the Yorkshire Centre of the B.A.R.C.'s Scarborough Rally, with Yvonne Jackson third in her class, and Pauline Mayman and Peter Morgan had great fun in scooping up first-class awards in the one-hour high-speed trial at the M.C.C.'s Silverstone meeting at the end of the month.

Silverstone was also the venue of the Aston Martin O.C.'s 21st birthday race meeting on July 21, when the most exciting event proved to be the 21-lap handicap relay race for the David Brown Trophy, entered by 24 teams of three cars each. With every driver scheduled to complete seven laps before handing over a sash to the team's next competitor the pits at times became a place for none but the brave-hearted, but from all the confusion the team of Ray Meredith, Barry Phipps and John McKechnie, all in Plus-4s, emerged the overall winners after completing the 21 laps at an average speed of 67.69 mph.

The following weekend Meredith was competing in the Bugatti O.C.'s hill-climb at Prescott, where he was second in his class, less than half a second behind the class winner, while across the Atlantic Gaston Andre had been busy again, finishing second in class and third overall in a national meeting of the S.C.C.A. at Beverly, north of Boston.

Alec Newsham did well to earn a first-class award with his well rallied Morgan in a very tough Lancashire Cup Rally staged by the Lancashire A.C. on August 25, and on September 1 Ray Meredith

was back at Silverstone again for the Sunbac meeting in which he won a six-lap race ahead of an Austin, with J. L. Parker-Heaton's Morgan in third place.

The final round of the *Autosport* Production Sports Car Club Championship took place at the Mid-Cheshire M.C.'s race meeting at Oulton Park, on September 22, over a duration of three hours, and Morgan hopes were pinned on the Plus-4 of John McKechnie, who still had a remote chance of winning his class. He had a trouble-free run and eventually crossed the line in third place which, after the handicaps had been applied, meant that he had finished second in his class and fifth overall. A sturdy effort.

The previous weekend Jim Goodall had a good outing, setting best time of the day in the Worcestershire A.C.'s autocross meeting as well as sharing the team prize with J. Looker and Barry Phipps, who also won their respective classes. Then, a few days later, the London Rally lived up to its reputation for being a tough event, and only 171 of the 308 starters completed the 750-mile course linking 40 control points. Once again Les Yarranton did well, taking the prize for the best aggregate time in the tests and offering praise to his navigator, D. Thompson, for some excellent work, while Mrs. Kinns received similar acknowledgement from Yvonne Jackson for navigating her to the ladies' award.

Alec Newsham won his class and collected a first-class award in the hotly contested Lakeland Rally on September 28-29, while Peter Morgan was back amongst the silverware a week later, taking a first-class award in the M.C.C.'s Derbyshire Trial, while Jim Goodall and A. T. Hall each earned a second-class award. The Blackpool and Fylde M.C.'s annual driving test meeting at Blackpool on October 27-28 brought a second place behind a TR2 for Les Yarranton, and in November he was a member of a winning team along with Peter Morgan and Jim Goodall in the M.C.C.'s National Rally. This event, over a 1,250-miles route, led from seven starting points to Harrogate, then through Yorkshire to the Lake District, on into Wales, then back into England for the finish at Hastings. Once again Morgans did well, Peter Morgan, navigated by Ray Meredith, winning his class, as did Barry Phipps.

This was the year of the big Suez Crisis and on November 20 the R.A.C. announced that no more motor sport permits would be issued until fuel supplies were re-established satisfactorily, then, on December 17, petrol rationing was introduced, and motor sport was resumed on a limited scale, one of the few events to take place being the Sheffield and Hallamshire M.C.'s standard car trial, in which E. S. Sneath used his Morgan's fuel ration to good effect to make the best overall performance.

The B.T.R.D.A.'s annual awards brought to an end another good season for Morgan drivers, with Les Yarranton finishing in joint fifth place in the Gold Star competition, while in the Silver Star rally competition Alec Newsham's 127 marks put him nine clear of his closest rival, and in the ladies' Silver Garter competition Angela Palfrey was first, Yvonne Jackson third and Anne Neil fifth.

1957

One of the first events to be held in the north of England since the fuel restrictions was the Lancashire and Cheshire C.C.'s driving test meeting at Barton Airport on February 10, when the entry was restricted to 65 cars and many would-be entrants had to be turned away. Alec Newsham was one of the lucky ones, and he ended up the winner of the over-1,900cc class in his well-known Morgan.

Doc Spare's Plus-4 had now passed into M. B. Jarrett's hands, and his driving in the Shenstone and District C.C.'s V.T. Fellowes Memorial Trial was 'an education to watch' according to one reporter. He won the Shenstone Trophy after being the only driver to reach the top of several of the hills, while D. G. Phillips took a second-class award in another Plus-4.

There seemed to be plenty of fuel in the U.S.A., and the Sebring 12-Hours race on March 23 was attended by 30,000 spectators, who saw the lone Morgan entry of Bob Grier and Bob Kennedy run like clockwork for 149 laps to be classified 28th. The 1½-miles circuit at Lime Rock, Connecticut, was opened on April 28, when Bill Shade and his Plus-4 just failed to split the two AC-Bristols which dominated the sports car race.

A much shortened version of the M.C.C.'s Lands End Trial was held on Easter Sunday, but the 60-miles course proved a really tough one, from which Peter Morgan in a 4-4 Series 2 and Jim Goodall in his Plus-4 emerged with first-class awards.

Two brothers fought a wonderful battle for sports car honours in the Hagley and District C.C.'s Spring Trial on April 28, H. L. Livingstone and his TR2 eventually beating J.F. and his Morgan by 186.4 to 186.6 secs, and the same weekend Alec Newsham took the premier award with his Plus-4 in a night navigation rally run by the North East Centre of the MG C.C. He and Mrs. Anne Hall (in a Standard 10) were the only drivers to complete the course with a clean sheet, and understandably Newsham was faster in the tie-deciding driving test.

Morgans were prominent in two race meetings at Goodwood during June, and J. Looker ended up with second place at each of them. In the first he fought a race-long battle with an AC Ace in a race in which John McKechnie could only manage to finish a distant fourth, while in the second, held in a slight drizzle, he spent most of his race avoiding spinning cars and inherited second place seconds from the finish. The highlight of this race was the wheel-to-wheel battle between McKechnie's Morgan and an MGA, the latter benefitting from disc brakes and closing right up on the last lap so that the two cars went into the final chicane side-by-side. Unfortunately, only the MG emerged on the right line, and McKechnie's Morgan exploded into view through the middle of the chicane wall in a shower of planks, coming to an abrupt halt.

On the same day Peter Morgan and Jim Goodall were at Silverstone for the M.C.C. race meeting and they competed in several events. One of the best was a 10-lap handicap in which they battled with an Austin-Healey and eventually led it across the line, Goodall fractionally ahead of Peter, who in a later race chased a Jaguar C-type and a Jowett Jupiter R4 across the line in the best-handicapped race of the day.

The Morgan of Pauline Mayman and Valerie Domleo finished eighth overall out of 110 entries in the well-organized Plymouth M.C. National Rally on July 28-29, which involved a 500-miles route from five starting points. A week later Pauline crossed the Irish Sea with her husband, Lionel Mayman, for the Kirkistown race meeting, but although he had no trouble in winning his race with his Cooper-Climax, Pauline's famous rallying Morgan could only manage third place on the race track, after a spirited drive through the field. Sometimes the two Maymans exchanged cars, and this was to happen at Silverstone later in the year at the Sunbac meeting, when Lionel had a hectic 20-lap sports car race with four other cars for second place behind the winning Austin-Healey. One by one the opposition spun away their chances, first a TR2, then another one, then came a collision between one of the TRs and a Jaguar XK120, which also delayed an AC Ace, so that Mayman was finally secure in second place.

This year's A.M.O.C. relay race for the David Brown Challenge Cup was spoilt by heavy rain and the Morgan team of two Plus-4s and a 4-4 did well to finish third behind the winning limit team of Morris Minors. This time 23 teams took part, and each of the three entries had to cover six laps. Earlier, J. R. Beasley and J. F. Brown in 4-4s and J. Looker and B. Phipps in Plus-4s all earned first-class awards in the preliminary 'half-hour blinds'.

A really tough London Rally early in September in which competitors had to battle with heavy rain, thick fog in the Welsh mountains and a bewildering assortment of sheep tracks which soon took a toll of cars and crews, brought 92 retirements out of an entry list of 240, and only 20 crews finished with less than 50 penalty marks. One of these was Pauline Mayman with Valerie Domleo, who lost just 34 points, which earned them eighth place overall and the *Coupe des Dames,* their Morgan being one of the few cars to reach the finish without dented bodywork or bent suspension. Later in the year they took another ladies' prize in the Oxford M.C.'s Boanerges Rally, then they reversed roles for the Hertfordshire Night Navigation Rally and were placed first overall.

As a supplement to the Guy Fawkes 200 Trial in late-October the Falcon M.C. ran a competition over the same course for production cars, omitting only the toughest of the trials-car sections, and once again Morgans did well over the remaining 12 Cotswold hills. F. A. Freeman picked up the Guido (Mr. Fawkes' correct christian name) Vase for the best performance in this section, while E. H. Dennis won the sports car class and Peter Morgan picked up yet another first-class award to bring his season to a close.

1958

Once again the R.A.C. Rally was the subject of criticism, this time because of misleading statements in pre-rally publicity which suggested that it could be covered on quarter-inch maps, being essentially 'non-navigational', also because of a marking system which penalized a competitor who tackled a difficult section and was late at the final control, more than another competitor who bypassed the section altogether. Nevertheless, it was a very tough event, and Les Yarranton, with J. P. Taylor, and Jim Goodall, with J. Thomas, could be well pleased that they took first and second places in their class.

Also in March, the Wolverhampton and South Staffs C.C.'s

Express and Star Rally brought A. E. Cleghorn and his Morgan a first-class award, while in the Colmore Trial for production cars four of the six major prizes went to Morgan drivers. The Langley Trophy for the best performance was won by J. S. Parry, with Frank Livingstone the runner-up, and H. B. Geddes was a class-winner in his Plus-4. E. M. Rogers, meanwhile, made good use of a course dried by gale-force winds to emerge the overall winner of the West Hants and Dorset M.C.'s Hartwell Cup Trial, his Morgan beating all the Specials.

The Midland A.C.'s National Rally on April 25-26 attracted 94 starters to the Civic Centre, Birmingham, but only 62 of them reached the breakfast halt at Llandrindod Wells. Afterwards came a route-card section and then the tests, with Les Yarranton's aggregate of 84 secs with his Plus-4 the fastest time. However, a puncture had lost him 50 marks at a control during the night, and so instead of winning the rally outright he finished third in his class, behind Pauline Mayman, who was the clear winner of the ladies' award.

On May 4 Peter Morgan returned to his Army days for a spot of 'square bashing' at Middleway Military Camp, Taunton, the location of the Taunton M.C.'s annual driving tests, and in an immaculate display he emerged the overall winner from a field of 80 entries, while Mrs. P. Livingstone took the ladies' award on this occasion.

Harleyford Manor, near Marlow, Buckinghamshire, was a popular hill-climb venue, and especially so for A. J. Blair on May 11, when his time of 25.32 secs in a Plus-4 earned him the sports car class win on a day when many single-seaters failed to break 26 seconds.

This year 21 teams contested the A.M.O.C. relay race at Silverstone for the David Brown Challenge Cup, Morgan being represented by three Plus-4s driven by J. Brown, R. Meredith and J. Looker. A spectacular spin by Ray Meredith at Becketts was the only untoward incident for the team, but they were just pipped for victory by a trio of MGs so that Morgan's impressive record over the three years of this event was now first, third and second.

Amongst the entries for the Tulip Rally in 1958 was the Plus-4 of Lyndon Sims, who was partnered by R. E. Stokes in place of the absent Alex Cleghorn, and they took second place in the 1,601-2,000 cc GT class, splitting two TR3As. The rally concluded with a race round the Zandvoort circuit, and the best duel of all was between Sims and Annie Soisbault in a TR3A, Lyndon managing to hold off her strong challenge to finish first.

Lew Spencer scored many victories in S.C.C.A. races at the wheel of the Plus-4 two-seater of Rene Pellandini, the Los Angeles-based West Coast Morgan distributor. This is 'Baby Doll No. 2' during a race in 1958.

The car's successor, 'Baby Doll No. 3', forming part of Pellandini's import car display in Los Angeles. The neat spare wheel mounting is shown to good advantage in this picture. Part of the backcloth shows this car leading a Triumph TR2 at Laguna Seca.

51

The Morecambe National Rally, organized by the Lancashire A.C., proved to be something of a navigator's nightmare with 31 control points to be plotted and a half-hour's lateness at any of them constituting a failure, something which only 28 crews managed to avoid. After six hours of driving through seemingly every farmyard in North Lancashire, Westmoreland and Yorkshire, then a series of driving tests on the sea front, Brian Harper took a well-deserved first-class award, while once again the Mayman/Domleo team took the ladies' prize.

Les Yarranton's time of 47.7 secs was good enough for best time of the day at the Midland A.C.'s production car hill-climb at Shelsley Walsh in July, with J. F. Livingstone backing him up in second place to underline the Morgan domination, while Tom Bryant took a class win at 1 min 47.2 secs in a West Hants and Dorset C.C. autocross event during August. Earlier he had given the marshals a bad fright when one of his rear wheels tore away from its studs and took an entirely different course during a preliminary run.

Yet more successes were on the way for Pauline Mayman and Valerie Domleo. First they took the ladies' award in the Liverpool M.C.'s Jeans Gold Cup Rally, in which R. M. Dobson finished second in the driving tests with his 4-4, and a fortnight later they repeated the success in the London Rally on September 19-20, which attracted an entry of more than 250 cars this time. Once again Les Yarranton proved himself the master of driving tests by taking the special award for the best aggregate time. Continuing their excellent form, the Mayman/Domleo then went on to win the *Coupe des Dames* in both the Worcester M.C. Autumn Rally and the Bournemouth Rally during October.

Meanwhile, the Hagley and District M.C.'s Chateau Impney hill-climb on September 28 had brought a class win with a new record time of 29.28 secs for Frank Livingstone and his Plus-4, with Ray Meredith taking third place in 30.06 secs with his 4-4. Brian Harper was also in great form around this time, and he followed a best performance in the driving tests on the MG C.C.'s Northern Rally with a good class win on the Buxton Rally, both in October.

When the final points tables were announced for the various B.T.R.D.A. competitions Brian Harper was placed equal ninth in the Silver Star and 10th in the Gold Star rally contests for 1958, while not surprisingly Pauline Mayman was outright winner of the ladies' Silver Garter as well as third overall in the Gold Star table, while J. F. Livingstone was runner-up in the Flather Star driving test competition.

1959

The Hagley and District L.C.C.'s production car trial on January 4 was contested over 11 hill sections, each with a distinct flavour of its own and calling for the most delicate throttle and steering control, and at the end of the day only one first-class award had been earned; it went to G. C. Filder and his Morgan. It was a good start to the Morgan year, and F. Freeman kept up the momentum by scoring an easy class win with his Plus-4 on the Jacobean Trophy Rally, which attracted 44 competitors to the London start.

Chris Lawrence also began his new racing season in great style, winning the marque scratch race at the first Goodwood meeting of the B.A.R.C.'s season by almost 10 secs at an average of 77.82 mph, then taking another easy win in a handicap race which concluded the programme.

Jeff Bradford looked all set to win the open-car class of the Falcon M.C.'s March Hare Trial on March 15 until his navigator got into a bit of a tangle and checked in at a control point too early, but P. G. Gough was there to uphold Morgan honour by taking the class win.

Lawrence looked as though he would repeat his Goodwood success at the Snetterton spring meeting on March 22, but on the last lap of his eight-lap scratch race his engine failed, and he trickled across the line, still finishing second in class before ending the day on the end of a tow rope.

The 1958 Mayman/Domleo domination of the ladies' classes in motor sport was clearly to continue the following year, and the next success came in the Scottish Sporting C.C.'s Highland Rally, when their performance in this 1,000-miles event also vanquished the majority of the male competitors. Next came a similar result, a week later, in the Midland A.C.'s *Birmingham Post* Rally, in which they were also joint second in the over-1,600 cc class. But shortly afterwards Pauline Mayman crashed while competing in a hill-climb at Prescott, and her injuries kept her out of the cockpit until the Bolton-Le-Moors Rally in August. The *Birmingham Post* event proved particularly successful for Morgan drivers, with Jim Goodall winning and Brian Harper being placed third in the over-1,600 cc class, and the team award going to Jim Goodall/D. E. J. Thompson,

Pauline Mayman, who, usually partnered by Valerie Domleo, became one of the most successful Morgan rally drivers of the period in her Plus-4, is stopped at a secret check during the 1959 R.A.C. Rally. (Photograph by *Autocar*.)

Lyndon Sims, with Barry Hercock, on the way to a class win in the 1960 Tulip Rally with what had started life as a Plus-4 drop-head coupe but had subsequently been fitted with a hardtop.

Peter Morgan/A. D. Moore and Les Yarranton/H. Rumsey. With 12 of the 71 starters completing the 400-miles route without loss of marks, driving test times were used to decide the overall winner, and Jim Goodall's aggregate time was just 0.8 sec slower than that of the winning Wolseley.

Meanwhile, Chris Lawrence's first full season of racing a Morgan was proving spectacularly successful. He took part in virtually every marque race and most of his wins were to be runaway successes, his final tally being nine marque races and one handicap race, and he finished second four times and third once, a record which made him a comfortable winner of the Freddie Dixon Trophy.

But other Morgan drivers also did well on the circuits, including P. Bradley, whose very fast run of 32 seconds at the B.A.R.C. sprint meeting at Aintree beat a Cooper-Bristol back into second place in the class for sports cars between 1,501 and 2,700 cc.

The Taunton M.C.'s autocross meeting in August was the first such event to earn a National permit, indicating the growth in stature of racing over a grass course, and nearly 100 competitors took part. Tom Bryant, whose Morgan had won the event in 1958, did well again, a first run in 1 min 32 secs being followed by a second in 1 min 29.8 secs, but this time his car was beaten by just one Special, which recorded 1 min 29 secs. Every competitor at this event went away with a special plaque commemorating their entry in this first National autocross.

Back in action again, and clearly having lost none of her earlier form as a result of her accident, Pauline Mayman, still with Valerie Domleo, resumed their winning run with *Coupes des Dames* victories in four events from August to October, the Bolton-Le-Moors, the Jeans Gold Cup, the London and the Bournemouth rallies, their partnership in Pauline's Plus-4 LES 898 having now surpassed the earlier record of the Neil sisters, Anne and Chris. The London Rally also brought a fine outright victory for Brian Harper with Ron Crellin; theirs was one of two 'clean sheets' on the road, the other going to P. P. Roberts in a Triumph Herald, and with the Morgan's aggregate test time of 53.6 secs against the 56.2 secs for the Triumph the victory was assured.

Valerie Domleo's navigational talents were too good for a works team to miss, and for the R.A.C. Rally in November she was teamed with Annie Soisbault in one of the works Triumph TR3As, while Doreen Freeman joined Pauline Mayman in the Plus-4. Peter

Morgan and D. E. J. Thompson shared another Plus-4 and Brian Harper and Ron Crellin were in a third for this important event.

Pauline started off well by being fastest of the ladies in the first test, and she also won a race at Crystal Palace which was the final test of the rally, but overall she did not have a happy time and was down in 45th place in the final classification. Peter Morgan, meanwhile, had earned the title 'King of the Tests', having won his race and lost only two marks from all the other tests, but like everyone else he had to wait for several months to know his final position. Potential winner Wolfgang Levy, driving a DKW, protested over the alleged inaccessibility of the Braemar and Blairgowrie controls due to snow-blocked roads, and wanted them scrubbed. Peter Morgan was amongst only 16 competitors to reach the Braemar control, taking the very difficult route over the Devil's Elbow to Blairgowrie, and some of the others who did so lost so much time that they had been forced to retire. If Levy's protest had been upheld he would have won the rally and gained second place in the European Championship, so a lot was at stake, but in the end it was turned down. This made Peter Morgan a class winner and sixth overall, and with Brian Harper 38th overall the Morgans were fourth in the team contest. Peter Morgan's effort was quite exceptional; he had lost just those two test marks, plus three more in the Welsh section. A magnificent end to his season.

1960

The Welsh Rally, the first important event of the new season, lived up to its reputation of being a rally which puts relentless pressure on vehicles and is tough on the crew, with never a let-up, the 400-miles route having its usual quota of mud, ice and fog. It proved to be particularly tough on navigators, so often the forgotten member of a successful crew when the time comes to applaud the winner. On this occasion Brian Harper and Ron Crellin were in supreme form, losing only 67 points throughout the entire rally and emerging the outright winners in the Plus-4, while Doc Spare was back in action again to take the Cardiff start award, while once again Pauline Mayman was amongst the prizewinners, this time with a class award.

Lyndon Sims and Roger Jones shared a Plus-4 for the Monte Carlo Rally this year, but they had a troubled drive from their Glasgow start, and in an event which saw only 152 of the original 311 starters reach Monte Carlo they struggled through to 125th place. On the brighter side, however, the Morgan was placed third overall in the manoeuvrability test.

The 1960 'Monte' will go on record as being the first in which the works teams really came to the fore, taking the first three places overall as well as the team prize and signalling an era during which highly financed works teams would dominate rallying at international level. The costs involved would be huge, and would squeeze out the smaller companies, the Morgan Motor Company amongst them, from active participation in major events.

Meanwhile, the smaller and independent teams still had a healthy calendar in Britain, and in the *Express and Star* Pauline Mayman and Valerie Domleo came very close to an outright victory, as well as their usual ladies' prize, beating all but an Austin-Healey Sprite, while leaving Brian Harper and Ron Crellin to uphold male Morgan honour with a win in the over-1,300 cc class. However, the tables were turned on the *Birmingham Post* Rally in April when the two Morgans were first and second in their class, Harper's this time being in front.

Chris Lawrence and Lionel Mayman were second and fourth, respectively, in an exciting marque race at the B.A.R.C.'s Oulton Park meeting that month, then Mayman went on to win his class in the *Autosport* Championship race at Mallory Park two weeks later, but was out of luck at the Maidstone and Mid-Kent Silverstone meeting at the end of the month. He was pressing the driver of an Austin-Healey hard on the third lap of his race when it spun right in front of the Plus-4 at Becketts, leaving him no room to avoid it. Fortunately neither driver was hurt.

Lyndon Sims, accompanied by Barry Hercock, easily won their class from an Alfa Romeo and a TR3A on the Tulip Rally, which started on May 1 at Noordwijk, finishing 14th overall, but not without an alarming incident along the way. After leaving Eindhoven they were on a wide level crossing when suddenly the gates dropped down, trapping them. They looked around to see an express train approaching, so Lyndon edged the hardtop Plus-4 as far off the tracks as possible and waited anxiously. After what must have seemed an eternity the express rushed by and went on its way, having missed the back of the Morgan by about two feet!

Lionel Mayman had no trouble in winning his *Autosport* Championship race at the Nottingham S.C.C. Mallory Park meeting on Whit Monday, while Robert Duggen won a great battle in his Plus-4 with an Aston Martin to finish in second place. Chris Lawrence, meanwhile, was preparing his car for the 25th R.A.C. Tourist Trophy race at Goodwood, scheduled for August 20. His Plus-4 was entered in the 2-litre class of a race which had attracted all the big names in motor racing, including Stirling Moss, Roy Salvadori, Innes Ireland and Graham Hill, and his practice time of 1 min 45.4 secs put him into 16th place on the 34-car starting grid. It was a three-hour race and after the first hour Chris was running second to Graham Hill in his class and was 12th overall. The routine refuelling stop came after about 1¾ hours of racing, everything was completed quickly, then the car refused to restart. It took 17 agonizing minutes to get the car going again, and Lawrence went on to finish 24th overall and eighth in his class. Afterwards a Lucas man discovered that the armature shaft bush had split, the pieces had vibrated into the starter where half of the bush had jammed the armature immovably. The luck of motor racing! As a small consolation he had a comfortable win with his Plus-4 in a marque race at the B.A.R.C. Oulton Park meeting, driving in a terrific rainstorm to a 14-secs advantage before going on to a second victory in the Formula Junior race in a Deep Sanderson-Ford, a car he had designed and built himself.

The season ended on a rather mixed note, for while Lionel Mayman finished third in his class behind an Austin-Healey and a Frazer Nash in the *Autosport* Championship, the works Morgan team of Peter Morgan, Brian Harper and Jim Goodall met with little success on the R.A.C. Rally, Peter's car being an early retirement when it hit a wall in thick fog. But on the other side of the world the Warwick Farm race circuit was opened at Sydney, Australia, on December 18, and the very first race was won easily by David McKay driving a Plus-4 prepared by Ken Ward, who with his brother had just formed a Morgan distributorship and had also founded the Morgan Owners Club of Australia.

Back at home, the results of this year's B.T.R.D.A. competitions made good reading for Morgan enthusiasts with Brian Harper and Ron Crellin joint winners of the Gold Star contest, while Pauline Mayman was fourth as well as second in the Silver Garter competition, the winning co-driver in this contest being her partner, Valerie Domleo. B. B. Jones was placed sixth in the production car trial championship, while in the Silver Star driving tests contest Brian Harper finished third and Pauline Mayman was listed 38th.

1961

Once again the South Wales A.C.'s Welsh Rally marked the beginning of the new season, but with little reward for Morgan drivers other than the fact that the Plus-4 of Brian Harper and Ron Crellin was one of the cars of the prizewinning team. But they did a lot better on the *Express and Star* Rally in February being declared outright winners after Harper had protested the original finishing order. The trouble concerned a road which was partially blocked by a red and white pole with a 'Road Closed' notice on it. Many entrants immediately made a detour and as a result lost time, while those who stopped and investigated found the road to be passable.

A somewhat lean spring for Morgan drivers was interspersed with a class win for J. Brown's Plus-4 at the Sevenoaks and District M.C.'s driving tests and for Ray Meredith in the Bugatti O.C.'s Prescott hill-climb. Then came a new class record in 33.64 secs for Peter Bradley and his modified and lightened Plus-4 in the Westmoreland M.C.'s Barbon Manor hill-climb, and on July 9 the rally-orientated London M.C. staged their first ever race meeting at Snetterton. Here, Hugh Braithwaite caused quite a stir by putting his Lawrencetune-prepared Plus-4 on to pole position then selecting reverse instead of first gear. Fortunately a collision was avoided, Hugh quickly found the correct gear and rushed off into a lead which was not to be challenged.

One of the closest finishes seen at Mallory Park for a long time occurred on July 23 when a combined Grand Touring and production sports car race was held at the B.R.S.C.C. meeting, bringing Lotus Elites and Morgans into direct conflict. Clive Sanderson put his Plus-4 on to pole position, but an Elite went into the lead on the first lap, then Sanderson fought past into first place on lap 2 and although he was hard-pressed for the remainder of the race he held on for a fine win, the first five cars crossing the line within as many seconds.

Three Morgans, driven by Richard Shepherd-Barron, Chris Lawrence and Peter Marten were entered for the Peco Trophy race at the Guards Trophy race meeting of the B.R.S.C.C. at Brands Hatch on August Bank Holiday Monday, and although Marten's car ran its bearings on the second lap, the other two Morgans went extremely well, Shepherd-Barron's winning its class at 77.09 mph and setting a new class record at 78.45 mph, while Lawrence kept his ahead of an AC-Bristol to finish in second place.

The same three drivers were at Goodwood a fortnight later for the 26th R.A.C. Tourist Trophy, when L. J. Fagg was named as co-driver for both Shepherd-Barron and Marten, and L. S. Bridge was down to drive with Lawrence. The Morgans did well in practice, but the same cannot be said for the race. Shepherd-Barron's car broke a half-shaft and was out of the race after only 14 laps, Marten was going well when his big-end bearings went on the 81st lap, and only Lawrence's car survived to give him 11th place overall and third in his class.

A week later Hugh Braithwaite had a cracking race with an AC-Bristol to finish a close second in a marque race at the B.A.R.C.'s Aintree meeting, then in September, Chris Lawrence, who earlier in the year had had his application to race at Le Mans turned down because his car was 'too old fashioned', travelled to Monza with Pip Arnold for the Coppa Inter-Europa. The three-hours race was held prior to the Italian Grand Prix and the Morgan drivers finished a very impressive third in class with their 'old' car, and might have been even higher had they and the car not been so troubled by the extremely hot weather.

The year ended spectacularly for Hugh Braithwaite, for after the three-hours final round, at Snetterton, of the *Autosport* Championship, he ended at the top of the table in his class, a fine effort after his first full season in his blue Plus-4, then a few weeks later he was the victim of a nasty experience at Brands Hatch when acting as a steward at a spring meeting; he ate a wasp along with a piece of meat pie . . . and they say that motor racing is dangerous!

Morgans were prominent at the B.A.R.C. meeting at Mallory Park at the end of September, when Peter Marten won the marque race in his Lawrence-tuned Plus-4, having led all the way, while John McKechnie had a thrilling race in his green 4-4, working his way through the field to press the leader very hard in the closing laps, to finish just two seconds behind after setting the fastest lap in 1 min 6.4 secs.

The B.R.S.C.C.'s Boxing Day meeting at Brands Hatch was full of excitement, the best race of the day being for the Peco Trophy, with the Morgans of Shepherd-Barron, Braithwaite and Marten in the entry list. The race developed into a great dice between Shepherd-Barron in his Morgan and David Seigle-Morris in his big Austin-Healey, Richard repeatedly passing on the bends only to be overtaken again along the straights. He pressed the more powerful

Above: A fine action shot by Fred Scatley of Chris Lawrence at the wheel of TOK 258. Above right: A high point in Morgan competitions history was reached at Le Mans in 1962 when Lawrence, partnered by Richard Shepherd-Barron, finished 13th overall and won the 2-litre GT class with their Lawrencetune-prepared Plus-4, which ran in hardtop form. Here is the car at Mulsanne corner. Right: Pip Arnold competing in the Coppa Inter-Europa race at Monza in 1961, when XRX 1 was fitted with a bulbous experimental hardtop.

car the whole time until, just before the finish, the Austin-Healey disappeared off the track towards the advertising boards, letting Richard slip by into the lead and Hugh Braithwaite into second place. Seigle-Morris recovered well and rejoined the track just in time to hold off Peter Marten's Morgan and take second place in the big class and fourth place overall.

This year's B.T.R.D.A. competition results once again brought the season to a close, and once again Morgans were amongst the honours, Brian Harper being declared the outright winner of the Silver Star rally award, while Pauline Mayman finished in seventh place in the Gold Star list and took the mixed-crew award.

1962

The new international season got off to an encouraging start for Morgan when a Plus-4 shared by A. Rogers and J. Bailey covered 141 laps in the Sebring 12-Hours race to win the 2,000 cc GT class, while nearer home Bill Jones, driving the ex-Peter Marten Lawrence-tuned Plus-4, fought his way through the field at the B.A.R.C. meeting in March to finish second to Bob Burnard's AC-Bristol in the marque race. Later the same day Ray Meredith finished a close second to David Eva's MGA Twin-Cam with his Plus-4 in the marque scratch race, then went on to a comfortable win in a handicap race.

John Terry's Plus-4 only just made it to practice for the Hagley and District L.C.C.'s speed trials at Wellesbourne Airfield, near Stratford-upon-Avon, on March 17, having had its engine refitted only hours before the event, but despite steering problems it took the major award, while Ray Meredith took the Hagley Trophy for the best time of the day by an unmodified car, as well as the special GT award.

Past winner Peter Morgan suffered dynamo trouble during the Midland A.C.'s *Birmingham Post* national rally, although he was a class winner in the driving test section of the event.

Pip Arnold found himself near the back of the grid for the 10-lap GT race in the B.R.S.C.C. meeting at Brands Hatch on May 5, but a magnificent display of driving took him through into the lead on the fourth lap, with a best lap time of 69.32 mph. Then, with the race seemingly sewn up, his engine blew up on lap 8. However, he was rather more fortunate in the Spa Grand Prix, when he joined Richard Shepherd-Barron and Hugh Braithwaite in contesting the 1,301 to 2,000 cc class, and ran through into fifth place behind a

pair of Porsches. However, it was a far from troublefree weekend for the Morgan drivers. Shepherd-Barron broke a crank during one of the practice sessions, but fortunately was able to locate a replacement in an old TR2 engine lying in a village about 100 miles away from the circuit, and after a lot of hard work had it fitted in time for the following day's practice; apparently it worked excellently, the engine pulling an extra 500 rpm down the straight during the race, and he went on to finish an excellent second behind the winning Porsche. Braithwaite, however, had a disastrous race, crashing at high speed and ending up with his car a terrible mess in a field on the right side of the circuit; he was extremely lucky to walk away from it unscathed.

Having lost his own car, he teamed up with Pip Arnold for the Nurburgring 1,000-Kilometres race, while Shepherd-Barron and Lawrence shared their Le Mans car, and the Savoye brothers entered a third Morgan. This was to prove the race of starter motor troubles, both the Lawrence-tuned cars being afflicted and between them they exchanged motors 12 times during the race. The Le Mans car succumbed on the circuit with engine trouble on the 25th lap after being timed at 10 mins 34.9 secs for a lap, and at the end of the day the only thing to celebrate was the third place in class for the Savoye car.

The most important race of the year, of course, was the Le Mans 24-Hours, on June 23-24, which as usual had been preceded by a special practice weekend in April, on the one dry day of which the Chris Lawrence/Richard Shepherd-Barron Morgan had lapped in 4 mins 56 secs, making it the eighth fastest of the cars present.

During practice on race week the Morgan drivers were more concerned with track familiarization and minor adjustments than in setting any unofficial records, and when the time came to line up for the 4.00 pm start on the Saturday both drivers were quietly confident that their car would do well. Theirs was one of 16 British cars amongst the 55 starters, and throughout the race they were never to be forced into an unscheduled pit stop. Their regular stops were made every three hours to change drivers, refuel and top up with oil, etc, and their only drama came when an exhaust pipe broke close to the manifold. An attempt was made to secure the pipe during the 7.00 am pit stop, but rather than waste a lot of time the car was sent back into the race sounding more like a Grand Prix car than a production sports car as it continued to lap at close to 100 mph. For every Morgan enthusiast present that year the last hour of the race was a nail-biting time, but the Morgan was still running well and it crossed the line in 13th place (the same position as the Fawcett/White car had managed in 1938) amongst only 18 finishers, but most important of all, it had won the 2-litre class at an average speed of 93.97 mph, having covered over 2,255 miles in the 24 hours. This was the most important Le Mans result in the history of Morgan.

Meanwhile, Morgans had continued to do well in far more modest events nearer home. Earlier in the month Chris Lawrence had arrived at Goodwood for the B.A.R.C.'s Whit Monday meeting with his Morgan sporting an aero windscreen, which contravened the regulations for marque sports cars. With the race stewards' permission he was allowed to compete, but not for an award, and he simply ran away with the race. However, it was still to be a Morgan victory because the TVR which had finished a distant second on the road had had all four wheels off the track at one point, which meant disqualification, so first place was inherited by Bill Jones, whose Morgan had fought and won a race-long tussle with an AC-Bristol. The same weekend Brian Haslem was the victor of a handicap race at the Eight Clubs meeting at Silverstone, finishing just one second ahead of a Lotus.

While Lawrence and Shepherd-Barron were busy at Le Mans, Pip Arnold was having a successful day at Goodwood, winning the B.A.R.C.'s marque race comfortably at 80.91 mph, while Bill Jones had a wonderful scrap with a TVR, an AC-Bristol and an MGA in a later marque race and shared with the MG driver the fastest lap at 83.24 mph.

The B.R.S.C.C.'s Brands Hatch meeting on July 22 was reported as being a day of spills and records, and it was also the occasion when Pip Arnold and his Morgan caused the overall winner of the G.T. race considerable embarrassment by sitting on the tail of his E-type Jaguar for much of the race. Arnold finished a close second, won his class and set a new class record lap at 71.54 mph, which was only 0.46 mph slower than the new record set with the E-type. But the main drama in this event came after the chequered flag. The Morgan lost a wheel coming down the hill from Druids, and the Morgan slid to a halt at the bottom. The breakdown truck was soon on the scene, but suddenly an AC came rushing up, and the driver only just succeeded in avoiding everyone on the track and what could

have developed into a very serious incident.

Back at the same venue on August 6, but using the long circuit, Lawrence and Arnold finished first and second, respectively, in their class in the 25-lap G.T. race, during which Lawrence lowered the class lap record to 1 min 59.4 secs, a speed of 79.90 mph, before rain intervened.

The most important race that month was the R.A.C. Tourist Trophy, at Goodwood, on August 18, when the entry for the 100-lap race included the Morgans of Lawrence, Arnold and Shepherd-Barron. Things went well until quarter-distance, at which point Shepherd-Barron was third in class, Lawrence was close behind him in fifth place, and Arnold was seventh. But then the leading Morgan started to trail exhaust smoke, and soon it was in the pits, to retire with a broken piston.

Then, after Arnold's routine refuelling stop it took three minutes to restart the engine, and a few laps later he was back again with a leaking fuel line, which was quickly tightened. Meanwhile, Lawrence had worked his way into the class lead by half-distance, but the Morgan was overtaken by a Lotus Elite on lap 63, after which the positions stabilized, Lawrence finishing second in class and eighth overall. Arnold was 14th overall and eighth in class after his delays.

As usual, the three-hours race at Snetterton, held this year on September 29, marked the end of the *Autosport* Championship in which Lawrence did very well to finish third overall behind Mike Parkes (Ferrari Berlinetta) and Mike Beckwith (Lotus 23), while Arnold finished the season a class-winner.

Hugh Braithwaite snatched the lead on the last lap to win a sports and G.T. handicap race at the October B.A.R.C. meeting at Goodwood, and the Morgan year was brought to a successful conclusion at the traditional Boxing Day Brands Hatch meeting when Pip Arnold and Adrian Dence finished first and second in their class of the 10-lap G.T. race.

1963

Even as competitors were streaming away from Brands Hatch on Boxing Day, a snow storm began in south-east England which was the start of the Big Freeze, which was to last well into March, with the thermometer rarely rising above freezing point. Inevitably, many motor sporting events were cancelled, but as Britain froze, in Sydney, Australia, drivers were suffering from heat exhaustion. This was the main hazard at the Australian Grand Prix meeting at Warwick Farm, on February 10, when A. J. Reynolds and his Plus-4 finished second in the marque race supporting the main event.

The thaw in Britain had worked its way down to Oulton Park by March 19 in time for the B.A.R.C. meeting, in the first handicap race of which Adrian Dence's Plus-4 finished a clear half-lap ahead of the field, while in a later scratch race it was a creditable second, only 2½ seconds behind an Austin-Healey 3000.

On the same day, at the Hagley and District L.C.C. speed trial at Wellesbourne Airfield, Ray Meredith's Plus-4 developed an electrical fault after its first run, despite which it won its class and was only pipped by 0.08 sec by a Lotus Elite for the Marsh Cup for G.T. cars. Mike Duncan in his Plus-4 and Mike Virr in his 4-4 were other Morgan class winners.

At Sebring, Arch McNeil and William Clarens took their Plus-4 to fourth place behind three TR4s in the 12-Hours race, but the car shared by Alton Rogers and Richard Holquist retired at half-distance with a blown gasket.

Adrian Dence, Chris Lawrence and Ray Meredith did well at the B.A.R.C.'s Oulton Park meeting in April, finishing first, second and third in their class in the G.T. race, Meredith's performance being particularly noteworthy in that he worked his way through the field after stalling on the line.

This year the Spa Grand Prix became a marque championship event, with the Morgans of Chris Lawrence, Pip Arnold and Bill Blydenstein competing with their Plus-4s in the 2,001-2,500 cc class, which they were to dominate. At the end of the 36-lap, 315-miles race Lawrence and Arnold were first and second, Lawrence having averaged 101.69 mph and set a fastest lap at 105.14 mph, but Blydenstein was forced to abandon his car on the circuit with throttle linkage trouble.

Over the German border, the Nurburgring 1000-Kilometres race attracted entries from Arnold, Blydenstein and Hugh Braithwaite, and produced an excellent result after a troublesome beginning for the Morgans. Arnold's car blew up during practice when a big-end bolt sheared, and Blydenstein's distributor drive failed, resulting in a broken camshaft. Both cars were rebuilt, however, in time for the race, but all three Morgans had made unscheduled pit stops within the first 10 laps. Then things began to get better, and Braithwaite ran out the winner of his class at over 67 mph with a fastest lap at

close to 75 mph, while Arnold was runner-up.

The tiny Republic of Panama's major motor sporting event of the year was a 100-miles race on the Chane circuit, some 50 miles west of Panama City, for which the Isthmian Autosports Association entered a team of three cars, a Jaguar E-type, a Triumph TR4 and a Morgan 4-4 Super Sports, the latter being powered by a Lawrence-tuned engine and driven by B.A.R.C. member Pat Kennett, the service manager of the local Morgan agency. Kennett got away well from the Le Mans-type start, building up a useful lead in very hot weather which was soon taking its toll of drivers, while the track was soon having its effect on tyres and suspensions. After 35 laps Kennett made a quick stop to check his tyre wear, then carried on. Thoughtfully, he had provided himself with a drinking bottle in the car which kept him refreshed, and all went well until lap 47, when grabbing brakes and strange noises from the rear wheels forced him to slow, but he judged his pace carefully to come home a comfortable 38 seconds ahead of the second-placed Healey of Ramirez, having averaged 76.9 mph and shared with the Jaguar driver the fastest lap at 81.1 mph.

Meanwhile, back home in England, Adrian Dence had an excellent day's racing at the Maidstone and Mid-Kent C.C. Silverstone meeting on April 27, winning the 1,601-2,500 cc class of the G.T. race in which he set the fastest lap at 77.39 mph, then going on to score a fine win on the last corner of the marque race when the driver of the leading AC-Bristol made a slight error.

The following week P. Kerridge won the G.T. class of the Cambridge C.C.'s Duxford Sprint in his very fast Plus-4, while at the end of June Dence was back in action, at Goodwood this time, winning a race-long scrap with a TVR Grantura to finish second to an Aston Martin Zagato in his G.T. race. Other Morgan drivers were less successful, however, Gordon Spice having a waltzing time with an AC-Bristol on the first lap, while Nigel Messervy's Plus-4 tangled with a Jaguar XK 150.

The Marquis of Bath's stately home, Longleat, provided a hill-climb venue for the Burnham-on-Sea M.C. on June 30, when Ian Swift clocked a tremendous time of 48.56 secs to easily win his class. Swift was to win his class at least seven times during his season of hill-climbing, as well as do well at various sprint events.

The R.A.C. Tourist Trophy brought little reward this year to Morgan drivers Lawrence, Arnold and Dence, of whom Arnold was

Above and above right: Three Lawrencetune-prepared Plus-4 Super Sports took part in the 1963 Nurburgring 1,000 Kilometres race and two of them finished the event, competing in the 2½-litre GT class. Pip Arnold and Robin Carnegie ran their car in hardtop form and were second in class, while Rob Slotemaker and Robin Braithwaite finished just over nine minutes ahead of them to take the class victory.

The winning Morgan team of the 1961 Canadian Press-On-Regardless Rally comprising Steve Broady, Ed Russel and Alan Sands (standing).

fastest in practice at 1 min 40 secs with Dence one second slower. Arnold and Lawrence were using the then-new Lawrencetune cylinder-heads for this race, and both suffered from sticking valves. Lawrence was forced to retire after 16 laps, but it was an inoperative clutch which put out Arnold's car after an hour and a half. Dence battled on to finish in 17th place overall. However, when he returned to Goodwood for the final B.A.R.C. meeting of the year in September, he scored a fine win in the marque race ahead of Gordon Spice, Brian Kendall and Terry Sanger, all of them in Lawrence-tuned Plus-4s, which also made Adrian the winner of the *Motor Sport* Brooklands Memorial Trophy, of which this was the final round.

Dence was also in the running for the Fred W. Dixon Challenge Trophy for marque racing that season, the other leading contender being TVR driver Tommy Entwistle. Both were present for the final round at Aintree on September 28 and both were in trouble on the grid, Dence having to change the Number 3 plug after the five-minute signal had been given, while a two-inch nail was discovered in one of Entwistle's tyres with two minutes to go. However, both cars were ready for the start and Entwistle rushed into the lead while Dence became badly boxed-in by another TVR, an Austin-Healey 3000 and Gordon Spice's Plus-4.

Adrian was seething with frustration as the big Austin-Healey was faster down the straight but unwieldy through the corners, and it took him until lap 6 to find a way by, by which time the two TVRs were so far in front that there was no hope of catching them. He finished third, then had to give best to Gordon Spice in the 10-lap G.T. race in which he had been hoping for a consolation of a class win.

On the night of November 2-3 the Falcon M.C. ran their Guy Fawkes 200 Trial in which Brian Parsons won a first-class award in his 4-4 NAB 217, while later in the month only one Plus-4 was attracted to the R.A.C. Rally, and this, shared by Peter Ashbury and Brian Harper, did not feature in the results.

In marked contrast, Robin Ellis' Plus-4 was one of the entries in a G.T. race supporting the Rand Grand Prix at Kyalami, in South Africa, and after leading its class it rolled out of the race at Crowthorne, the driver fortunately not being seriously hurt.

Chris Lawrence also had a shunt at the end of the year, during practice for the Boxing Day race at Brands Hatch, and could not repair his car in time for the G.T. race. Gordon Spice had put his car on pole position, however, with a fantastic lap in 66 seconds despite pouring rain. Unfortunately, he made a mess of the start, and had to spent the race working his way up through the field, a great battle ending with fourth place overall and second in class. A slightly disappointing finish.

1964

The new season opened with a creditable first performance by the new Plus-4-Plus in the hands of Peter Morgan on the Exeter Trial, one of the events which had had to be cancelled because of the weather in 1963. January was also a good Morgan month on the Continent, where the Monte Carlo Rally included a Lawrence-tuned 4-4 Super Sports entered by Savoye, the Morgan main agent in Paris. The driver was the entrant's son, Claude Savoye, who had his brother-in-law, Etienne Girard as his co-driver. Understandably, they elected to start from Paris, and despite the extreme cold, car number 212 arrived at the start control with the hood down, and it was to remain that way all the way to Monaco, where they arrived in brilliant sunshine to claim second place in the 1,300 to 1,600 cc class behind an Alfa Romeo.

Meanwhile, back in England, some delicate use of the throttle, aided by his 4-4's good torque and comparatively large wheels, helped to give Amie Lefevre outright victory in the production car trial organized by the B.A.R.C. (South-East Centre) on January 19. Just one week later he took a further award in a similar event staged by four clubs near Salisbury, when Harry Rose, in another 4-4, earned a first-class award after being the only driver to scramble to the top of the tricky Ice Hollow climb. The two Morgan drivers met again on March 1 for the V. T. Fellowes national production car trial, and this time Lefevre finished second overall and first in his class, while Rose picked up a third-class award.

On March 31 motor racing was at long last given a permanent home in South Wales with the opening of the airfield circuit at Llandow, over 80 competitors being attracted to the first meeting, amongst them Ray Meredith's Plus-4 and Mike Virr's 4-4, which were to run in the second of the six races, for production sports cars. Meredith was so totally in command that he won the race by a lap and 13 seconds, but after chasing hard for 10 laps Mike Virr was forced to give up when his hardtop worked loose.

Right: Peter Morgan strives to maintain adhesion and motion in his 4-4 on the M.M.E.C./Shenstone/Morgan production car trial in March, 1963. Below: Tony Hollis' camera catches Cyril and Joyce Charlesworth as they tackle Tillerton on the 1964 Exeter Trial. Below right: Dixon Smith competing in an inter-club hill-climb at Shelsley Walsh in July, 1964, with his Plus-4 drop-head coupe.

A later 20-lap race for G.T. cars was to prove the most spectacular of the day for spectators. Virr was the highest-placed Morgan driver, in third place, but the real drama came in the closing stages when Meredith's car lost its exhaust pipe. A Lotus Elite was running close behind, and its driver had to take sudden avoiding action, which disturbed the line of a Jaguar 3.8 driven by H. J. Lee, whose car leapt in the air, rolled three times and was a complete write-off. Amazingly, the driver emerged unhurt.

Light rain made the Goodwood course very slippery for the B.A.R.C. meeting on April 25, and Brian Kendall had an excursion on to the grass coming out of Woodcote on one lap. He had been having a marvellous battle with John Haynes' Elva Courier, but although he recovered well to take the chequered flag the penalty put him right out of the reckoning. However, W. White and H. J. Messervy upheld Morgan honour by finishing second and third respectively.

The 1,601 to 2,500 cc sports car class at the Dyrham Park hill-climb organized by the Bristol M.C. & L.C.C. on May 18 proved to be a Morgan benefit. The fastest was the Plus-4 of Ian Swift, whose time of 37.40 secs broke the class record he had set previously in the same car, and was two seconds quicker than anyone else. Roger Middleton and Roger Bonsall duelled for second place in their Plus-4s, but although Bonsall was the quicker after the first ascents, he could not match Middleton's second run of 39.50 secs.

Jean Denton was back in action at the Billy Butlin Trophy meeting at Brands Hatch on June 14, when she won an eight-lap ladies' handicap race in a Plus-4, but at the 750 M.C.'s six-hours relay race at Silverstone in August the Morgan 4-4 Club team's hopes were dashed after a promising first hour when the gearbox failed in John McKechnie's Cosworth-engined car.

The Sports Car Club of America stage races throughout the year in six regions from which emerge regional champions in many classes of racing, who then go forward to compete in a final event for the various national championships, this year marking the inaugural American Road Race of Champions meeting. With classes C and D being combined into one race, Earl Jones' Plus-4 Super Sports was up against such cars as Cooper-Chevrolets and big-engined Specials, so an overall win was out of the question, but Jones set about his task very well to emerge production car champion in class C. The entries in class G included a 4-4 entered by 24-year-old Pat Menone, of Washington, D.C., the only woman driver to have won through from the regions, who took the big race seriously enough to arrive at Riverside several days early and take a short course at the Carroll Shelby Racing Drivers School operated from the track. However, it was all to no avail as mechanical trouble put her out on the fifth lap.

The year closed with a flurry of club events, among which the Christmas Cup trial held on December 6 by the West Hants and Dorset C.C. and the Vickers Armstrong (Hurn) C.C. is worthy of special mention. This proved to be something of a benefit for the Rose family, with Harry Rose, navigated by his wife, winning the Coronet Cup in his Morgan, while his daughter, Ann, took the ladies' award in her Ford Popular.

1965

Morgan cars did well in a typically varied Easter weekend of motor racing in Britain, a notable example being in the race for 1,601 to 2,500 cc GT cars, for the Redex Trophy, at the B.R.S.C.C.'s Mallory Park meeting. Alan House was the victor here, having hounded the leading Marcos-Volvo for three laps before finding a way past in his Plus-4 and going on to a very comfortable win. On the same day, at the South Wales A.C.'s Llandow meeting, two races became the highlights of the programme, in the first of which, a 25-lap marque sports car event, a race-long duel was fought between Brian Jenkins in his Lawrence-tuned Plus-4 and Dennis Morgan in his MGB until, after the lead had changed hands several times, Jenkins managed to hold on to take the chequered flag just in front. The other race, over 15 laps for G.T. cars, the same two drivers were to dominate, Jenkins this time working his way through the field to move into the lead in the last few seconds of the race.

Another close victory was earned by Alan House and his Plus-4 in a 10-lap race for marque and 1172 formula cars at the Maidstone and Mid-Kent M.C.'s meeting at Silverstone on May 1. The rainswept track tended to equalize the performance of the cars, and John McKechnie managed to hold his 4-4 in the lead right to the last corner, when both he and House were baulked by a tailender. Somehow Alan managed to find a gap that had not seemed to be there, drew level, and went on to cross the line just a wheel ahead.

A closely fought class battle in the Yorkshire S.C.C.'s hill-climb at Castle Howard, for the White Rose Trophy on May 15, developed between Mervyn Oldham in his Plus-4, Jim Hall in a Porsche Super

Two views of John Sheally II's S.C.C.A. H-Production 1964 4-4 racer, equipped with a fully tuned Ford 109E (1,340cc) engine. The lower picture was taken after the car had been converted from its original dark brown paintwork to its concours-winning decor of a red centre section, black wings and gold lettering and lining. Sheally later turned the car into a Plus-4 by installing a Triumph TR4 engine and Moss gearbox.

90 and David Perkins in another Plus-4, who finished in that order after the result had been in doubt to the end.

The Guards 1000 at Brands Hatch on May 22-23 was to be the longest race held in Britain since the war, with two 500-mile races on consecutive days to decide the finishing order on aggregate. The five Morgans entered included an S.L.R. to be shared by Chris Lawrence and John Spender, a normal Plus-4 for Alan House and Roy North, and a similar car for Don Jones and his co-driver. After a rolling start behind a Mustang pace car a Sunbeam Tiger went into the lead, but only briefly as Lawrence had rocketed through the field from the middle of the pack and he put the 2,196 cc S.L.R. into first place on Bottom Straight. He held his lead very confidently for 66 laps, averaging 77.18 mph, and as the car was fitted with long-range fuel tanks he was looking every inch a winner. However, it was not to be, and on the 67th lap Lawrence pulled into the pits with a broken king pin post. Despite working flat-out the repair lost Chris 21 laps before he could rejoin the race, and then he was to lose more time with brake trouble. By the end of the first 500 miles the highest placed Morgan was the House/North Plus-4 in 12th place.

On the Sunday the bright orange Mustang was again used as a pace car, the field being formed up behind in the finishing order of the previous day's race. This time a Jaguar E-type went into the lead at the start, but Lawrence, starting from the tail of the field, worked his way up steadily until he was in second place by lap 38, and suddenly he inherited the lead when the Jaguar broke a camshaft, showering oil everywhere. From that point on Lawrence and Spender cruised home to a comfortable win, covering the 189 laps of the second heat in 6 hrs 36 mins 20 secs, 64 secs ahead of the second-placed Austin-Healey 3000 of Paddy Hopkirk and Roger Mac, but of course the Saturday troubles had prevented them from finishing in the money.

The first car race meeting at Lydden Hill, Kent, took place on May 30, and the first race included the Plus-4 of John Mackay. Although they were no match for Doug Mockford's Diva, which won comfortably, a close battle for second place developed between Mackay and D. Pollard and his MGB. Pollard managed to squeeze past on the ninth of the 10 laps, and in trying to regain second place Mackay spun off at the Devil's Elbow, but such had been the pace of the first three cars that he was still able to finish in third place, having lapped the rest of the field. The MGB and the Plus-4 were joined in combat again in the third race, and this time Mackay took the lead from the start, but once again he over-did it at the Devil's Elbow, dropped back to third place, and although he managed to recover to second he was still four seconds behind the MGB at the finish, despite setting the fastest lap.

At the annual Eight Clubs meeting at Silverstone, comprising four half-hour high-speed trials and several scratch and handicap races, one of the closest finishes came in the first five-lap scratch race. The Daimler-engined Morgan of the Hon. Basil Fielding was leading the race, but being pressed very hard by M. Calvett's Ford-engined Austin A40. As they entered Woodcote for the last time the Morgan slid wide, and the A40 crossed the line a bare half-second ahead, while in a subsequent handicap event the Morgan-Daimler finished third behind a Cooper-Jaguar and a Mini-Cooper S after the handicappers had done their job well.

When the Vickers-Armstrong (Hurn) C.C. held their Wessex Slalom at Blandford Camp, on July 18, the abundance of loose grit on the large parade ground made life somewhat hazardous for the marshals. However, it was not grit which almost robbed A. Kennedy of a class win in his 4-4, but a fly, which embedded itself in the carburettor during the first run. The insect duly removed, Kennedy went on to win the class in fine style from a Triumph TR3A.

At the South Wales A.C.'s first unrestricted race meeting at Llandow, on August Bank Holiday Monday, Brian Jenkins drove a very calculated race over 15 laps for marque sports cars in his Lawrence-tuned Plus-4, working his way up from the rear of the field into second place by lap 4. He then played a waiting game until the penultimate lap, when he eased past the MGB of Dennis Morgan and went on to win by two seconds after an excellent piece of driving.

Hopes of the final of the *Autosport* Championship being a 24-hours race at Snetterton on September 11-12 were dashed when the R.A.C. decided that a circuit of under three miles was impractical for accurate after-dark timekeeping, while competitors were also worried about the cost of preparation for such a long event. So instead, the event was run in two parts, each of two hours duration, one of the races being held after dark.

Alan House paced himself and his Plus-4 very well, driving quietly but confidently in both sessions in the over-1,600 cc G.T. class. At the end of the first race he was lying in 10th place overall and third in his class, having covered 57 laps. Only 19 cars had survived to tackle

John Stapleton turns a Plus-4 into a three-wheeler at the chicane at Snetterton in 1968. Eagle-eyed Morgan enthusiasts will have identified the car as TOK 258 after re-registration.

Below: Robin Brown competing at Loton Park in May, 1966, with his ex-John MacKechnie 1964 4-4. The car was powered by a Cosworth Mark 9 1,500cc dry-sump pushrod engine equipped with twin 40 DCO Weber carburettors. Other changes in specification included a Lotus close-ratio gearbox, 6-inch Borrani wire wheels, Armstrong Selectaride shock absorbers, works bucket seats and aluminium bodywork. The car was later sold to Dr. Harvey Postlethwaite. Below right: Bruce Stapleton in action at Brands Hatch in May, 1968. This Plus-4, registered ALT 82B, was later sold to Bob Stuart, who in turn passed it on to Sir Aubrey Brocklebank.

the second race out of the 25 starters, and a further 10 cars had failed to survive pre-race practice, wrecked engines being predominant. During the second race House increased his pace and managed to put in 60 laps in the two hours to win his class at an average speed of 76.1 mph. This was sufficient to make him the *Autosport* Champion in class B.

The night of November 6-7 was very wet indeed for the Guy Fawkes Trial organized by the Chiltern, Harrow and Falcon C.C.s, but Amie Lefevre set about confirming that Morgans go well in the wet by battling through to win the Falcon Cup. But there was a special prize for him as well, for at long last someone had managed to win a premier award in this event three years in succession, a distinction he shared with Lindy Tucker. Amie was really on top form that month, for he concluded a most successful season by winning outright the 553 M.C.'s Track Mark Trial, his blue 4-4 having climbed nearest to the top of every section of the event. Finally, to round off another busy season, it was revealed that Simon Saye had finished third in his class in the contest for the Freddie Dixon Trophy.

1966

As usual, a busy programme of trials driving marked the beginning of another new sporting year, and once again Morgan drivers were prominent. There were nine Morgans amongst the 146 car entries for the Exeter Trial on January 7-8, and few had any serious difficulties, although the Plus-4-Plus of D. G. Tustin and the Plus-4 of B. Main both failed to clear Stretes Hill. It was W. H. D. Lowe's Plus-4 which emerged top of its class, although six other Morgan drivers took first-class awards. Five of the coveted gold triple awards were presented this year, marking a driver's first-class award gained in the Land's End, Derbyshire and Exeter trials, in that order, within the space of 12 months, and one of these went to Amie Lefevre. The following weekend he took the MG C.C. award in the Salisbury Trial, when once again W. H. D. Lowe was a class winner. Then, on February 6, Lefevre won his class in the Stroud and District M.C.'s Cotswold Trial after some inspired driving over a very difficult course. There seemed to be no stopping Amie this year, and he went on to win his class in both the Shenstone and District C.C.'s V.T. Fellowes Trial on March 6 and the North Wales C.C.'s Cymru Trophy Trial on April 3, a truly wonderful record.

Meanwhile, in the Sutton and Cheam M.C.'s spring meeting at Brands Hatch, on February 27, Bill Griffiths in his screenless Plus-4 JPR 247 delighted the onlookers with some spectacular, if not very successful driving during his practice run. First he tried to take Paddock Hill Bend sideways on full opposite lock, but ended up by spinning off backwards on to the grass. He stabbed his foot hard down on the throttle to spin the car back on to the course, but again ended up facing the wrong way. His sideways driving technique also got him into trouble at Clearways, where he buried his car in the bank, but undaunted he reversed out of the mud and completed his run to great applause. Obviously he learnt from his mistakes, however, because in the timed runs he set a time of 2 mins 6.0 secs to win his class after a sensible drive.

The marque race at the B.A.R.C. meeting at Goodwood on March 19 gave Chris Lawrence an absolute walk-away victory in his S.L.R. after he had lowered the class lap record to 1 min 37.8 secs, 88.34 mph, none of the other cars being able to stay anywhere near him. Brian Jenkins in his Plus-4 and Dennis Morgan in his MGB were joined in battle again on Easter Monday at Llandow, and this time it was the MG out in front, with Jenkins trying everything he knew to find a way past, but every time he seemed to have a chance he was baulked by tail-enders, and he was still a second behind at the end of the race.

A field of 32 cars for the Ilford Films-sponsored 500-miles race at Brands Hatch on May 8 included a pair of Plus-4s, one shared by Andy Pugh and Brian Kendall, who finished eighth overall, and the other by J. S. Tucker and Charles Blyth, who were classified 10th.

The honesty of Mike Bracey caused him to make a most unusual protest at the Dyrham Park hill-climb on May 7 after his Plus-4 had been credited with a time of 35.95 secs. As he had never managed to beat his previous best time of 39 secs he knew something was wrong, but the timekeepers overruled his own protest and he was awarded a class win, to his acute embarrassment. On the same day J. Backstrand produced another Morgan class win at the Castle Combe sprint organized by the Austin-Healey Club (South-West Centre).

There were two S.L.R.s present for the marque race at the B.A.R.C. Goodwood meeting on May 30, Chris Lawrence's Morgan and the Triumph-engined car of Neil Dangerfield. After setting the fastest time in practice Lawrence went into the lead on the second lap and built up a lead of 300 yards by the finish, but Dangerfield's car seemed to lose power half-way through the race and gradually dropped back. Shortly after this race a letter appeared in *Autosport* protesting about the S.L.R.'s eligibility for marque races, but as Neil Dangerfield pointed out in his reply, Chris Lawrence was in business to make Morgans go faster, and this he was doing very successfully.

Two S.L.R.s were back at Goodwood for another B.A.R.C. meeting on June 11, when Dangerfield's car was joined by the Morgan S.L.R. of Jim Donnelly as well as the very fast standard-bodied Plus-4 of Gordon Miles, who made the best start and led away from Dangerfield. But Neil was in front as they raced into Woodcote, followed by Miles, with Donnelly holding fifth place. The order remained the same until halfway through the 10-lap race, when Donnelly moved up into third place. Then Miles went into the lead when Dangerfield made a slight mistake at Lavant, and Donnelly slipped through into second position. Finally, Jim managed to outbrake Gordon at the approach to Woodcote two laps from the end and settle the finishing order of S.L.R., Plus-4 and S.L.R. (Triumph).

Gordon Miles provided the crowd at the B.R.S.C.C. meeting at Mallory Park with more excitement on July 10 with his driving in teeming rain during the marque race. After a poor start he gradually closed on the fourth-placed Chevron, whose driver then took to the escape road. Gordon then set about an XK 120 coupé, the driver of which put up a gallant fight, including opposite-lock power slides out of the chicane, until eventually the Morgan went through into third place, by now too far behind the Jaguar E-type and Sprite which had been contesting the lead.

There were mixed fortunes for Morgan drivers at the Plymouth M.C.'s Hemerdon hill-climb on July 31, when Rodney Harper recorded the fastest time of the day in 24.60 secs with his Lawrence-tuned Plus-4, but John Beer, at the wheel of David Van Horn's Plus-4 during practice, carried straight on at the final bend and made an expensive mess of the offside front suspension and bent the sub-frame. I wonder what David said? The car was repaired in time for the Taunton M.C.'s Merryfield sprint on August 21, when Rodney Harper won his class, but after setting a time 1.6 secs slower than Harper the Van Horn Morgan broke its throttle cable.

I have known for a long time that Michael Ware, the curator of the National Motor Museum at Beaulieu, has more than a passing regard for Morgans, and in researching this book I discovered why.

He once owned a 4-4 with which he competed in several events, and he scored two class wins in 1966, in the West of England M.C.'s Clyst St Mary autocross on September 18, then in the B.A.R.C.'s Blackboys Trial on November 18, Yet another name in the long list of well-known people to have owned the 'Best Sports Car in the World'.

Yet another first-class award came the way of Amie Lefevre in October in the S. Rodney Whiteley Trophy Trial, where once again he forced his car a lot higher up the test hills than most other competitors, and he rounded off a most competitive year by scoring his last first-class award of the season in the Worcestershire Production Car Trial on November 27.

1967

This year's Exeter Trial followed its usual course, with a relatively easy overnight road section to Exeter (despite fog, rain, ice and snow at various places on the routes from the Kenilworth, Colnbrook and Lewdon starting points) followed by attempts at many of the famous West Country hills. These included Tillerton, Fingle Bridge, Waterworks, Simms (perhaps the most difficult of all) before a tie-breaking test in an Exeter car park, then on to more hills at Waterloo, Meerhay and Knowle Lane before the finish at Weymouth and the prospect of a first, second or third-class award, according to the number of penalty points scored. Peter Morgan was back again with his Plus-4-Plus, and after an excellent run he emerged a class-winner.

Roger Thomas, driving Roger Bonsall's Plus-4, started his season well by winning his class and setting a new class lap record in the opening round of the Fred W. Dixon Trophy races for marque sports cars at the B.A.R.C.'s Mallory Park meeting on March 12.

On the Land's End Trial, organized as usual by the M.C.C. over the Easter weekend, Beggar's Roost proved to be one of the most difficult this year, a bank of soft shingle near the top creating immense problems, even to that Morgan trials expert Harry Rose, who failed to clear the hill for the first time since 1929. Another Morgan driver, John Hill, also failed to reach the top, although he was one of the first to clear Cutliffe Lane, a new hill that had been introduced into the trial, while Peter Morgan also had no difficulty here in the Plus-4-Plus. Crakington, Brynn Mill and the famous Blue Hill Mine, two sections of which had to be climbed, were all included before the finish at Newquay.

The North Thames Centre of the B.A.R.C. ran a slalom over a 1,100-yards course at Santa Pod on May 13, when Robin Brown in the ex-John McKechnie twin-cam 4-4 put up a masterly display during practice and went on to win his class, while his wife, Julie, took the ladies' award. Keith Davies, at the wheel of a 4-4, was a class-winner in this event, while Peter Askew finished only 0.9 sec behind him in his hardtop 4-4.

There were no fewer than 23 Morgans entered for a special five-lap handicap race at the Bentley D.C.'s Silverstone meeting on August 19, and less than five seconds covered the first three finishers. The winner was Ray Meredith, whose TR4-engined Plus-4 averaged 74.95 mph and finished ahead of the Vanguard-engined Plus-4 of Harvey Postlethwaite, later to become well-known as a designer of Formula One racing cars. Ken Davies was third in his Ford-powered Series 5 4-4, while G. Griffiths' Plus-4 was a class-winner. Although they were not amongst the winners, two of the more interesting cars were Andy Duncan's Lotus Ford-engined 4-4 and The Hon Basil Fielding's Daimler SP250-engined Plus-4, which attracted a lot of attention.

Although Alan House, driving Roger North's left-hand-drive Plus-4 in the B.A.R.C. meeting at Brands Hatch, on July 2, could not fail to win the 3,000 cc class of the marque race, being the only starter, he drove an impressive race into fifth place overall, lowering the class lap record to 60.8 secs, 73.42 mph, on the way.

Roger Bonsall had a tremendous dice with his Plus-4 against a TR4 for third place in the 15-lap marque race at the B.R.S.C.C. South-West Centre's meeting at Castle Combe, on September 9, behind the winning Austin-Healey 3000 and the second-placed Jaguar E-type. Only by very determined driving was he able to hold on to third place for 13 laps, then the Triumph squeezed by only to suffer a jammed clutch on the following lap as it went through Camp. As the TR4 coasted to a halt Roger swept by again to finish third.

The following day David Van Horn loaned his Morgan to two drivers for the Yeovil C.C.'s Yeovilton sprint meeting and was able to watch it finish both first and second in its class, Plymouth photographer John Grafton driving it to the class win, and Richard Beer using it to finish second.

On October 1 it was the turn of the AC O.C. to hold a sprint meeting at Lydden Hill, in Kent, where Morgan owners figured well in the results. J. F. Brown, in winning his class in his very fast 4-4, finished a full 12 secs ahead of the second-placed BMW, while Mike Rudd's 4-4 was third. Peter Askew recorded times of 3 mins 23.6 secs, 3 mins 6.8 secs and 3 mins 0.3 sec on his three runs to comfortably win a handicap award with his Plus-4.

The Sevenoaks and District M.C. were the organizers of the Amasco Championship meeting at Brands Hatch on November 12, when Alan House had a great fight with his Plus-4 ALT 828 in the marque race to win his class and take fourth place overall, while on November 26 he returned to the circuit for the London M.C. meeting and this time took third place overall as well as the class victory. However, he had a very lucky escape when his left front tyre exploded on his slowing-down lap. Although Alan could only finish fifth overall and second in his class in the final Amasco race at Brands Hatch, on Boxing Day, it meant that with four class wins and one second place in five races he was a worthy 1967 Champion in the 3,000 cc class.

So ended another varied year of Morgan successes in motor sport. Although the cars were no longer fully competitive in certain areas where they had shone in the past, Morgans were continuing to do well in selected events, notably in marque racing, sprints and hill-climbs, against cars with much younger pedigrees.

1968

When the Daytona Continental 24-hours race came to an end on the afternoon of February 4, the applause for the winning Porsche 907 was little more than that which erupted when a Morgan Plus-4 crossed the finishing line at the other end of the field. George Waltman had had the affrontery to enter the Morgan in the G.T. class of the race, where its rivals in the main were 7.3-litre Chevrolet Corvette Stingrays, but he obviously enjoyed the challenge and he caused quite a stir as, wearing regulation racing kit but with a red scarf flying in the wind, he plodded on steadily as one by one faster cars dropped out, and was eventually classified last of the 30 survivors out of 63 entries. The winning Porsche had covered 673 laps at an average speed of 106.697 mph whereas the Morgan completed just 339 laps at 53.69 mph. Nevertheless, bearing in mind that the little car was being lapped every other lap, it was a remarkable piece of endurance driving.

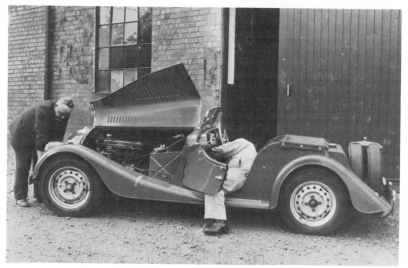

Above left: Part of the line-up for the Morgan handicap race at the 1968 Bentley D.C. meeting at Silverstone with Peter Askew's 4-4 in the foreground. Car 67 is Ian Stowe's 4-4, 82 is Mike Rudd's TR3A-engined Plus-4, 84 is Dr. Harvey Postlethwaite's 4-4 and 85 is D. J. Baker's TR3A-powered Plus-4. Above: A Fred Scatley picture showing Bruce Stapleton leading a bunch of cars through Clearways, Brands Hatch, during a 1972 production sports car race at the wheel of his glass-fibre-bodied lightweight Plus-8. The car was destroyed shortly afterwards, but an identical car was driven by John Stapleton for two seasons before it was sold to Patrick Keen.

Charlie Curtis, who was Works Chief Tester until his retirement in the early-1970s, preparing Peter Morgan's early TR-engined Plus-4 rally car, KUY 387. The white tape on the front wing acted as a marker for use in driving tests, which were often crucial in deciding rally results in those days.

Back in England, John Binns had modified the front suspension of his 1953 flat-radiator Plus-4, and was able to prove its effectiveness at the Nottingham S.C.C.'s Curborough spring meeting on March 24 by winning the event by just one-fifth of a second.

Bruce Stapleton had a very busy time on March 31 at Brands Hatch in the B.A.R.C.'s 10-lap production car race when his Morgan was one of four cars scrapping for places a long way behind the winning TVR. He finished still in the middle of the bunch, fourth overall (2 secs covered all four cars as they crossed the line) but he had won his class.

The Hagley and District L.C.C. Castle Combe race meeting on June 3 brought a class victory for David Van Horn and his Plus-4 in the 10-lap production sports car race, which finished third overall. It was a real cut-and-thrust race, with David pressing the driver of a Marcos hard for seven laps until he forced him into an error and he hit the bank at Tower. Afterwards, Van Horn had to hold off a very strong challenge from an MGB.

Two Morgans were entered for the 2-litre sports car class in the West Hants and Dorset C.C.'s Wiscombe hill-climb on June 23, David Way's 4-4 narrowly beating Tony Duncan's car for the class victory, while in the Harewood hill-climb organized by the B.A.R.C.'s Yorkshire Centre on July 21 Granville Martin looked to have won the 1,300 to 2,200 cc class with his Plus-4 and to have set a new class record. However, after the climbs his car was judged to have non-standard bodywork, which must have been a great disappointment to him.

Although the Porsche Club G.B. and the Frazer Nash C.C. joined forces to organize a race meeting at Castle Combe on August 3, the two all-comers handicap races were to provide a Morgan bonanza, Malvern-built cars filling the first three places each time. The winner of the first was James Henderson with his Daimler SP250-engined Plus-4, which had been in the lead most of the way, although under strong pressure from Mike Duncan's Plus-4, which finished second ahead of Brian Haslam's car. A fourth Morgan finished a lap behind after Brett Broughton had made a close inspection of the outfield at Quarry and had spent some time rejoining the track. Henderson and Duncan were first and second again in the second race, but this time they were followed home by Brian Jenkins and his Plus-4.

One of the favourite events for Morgan owners is the special invitation handicap race held by the Bentley D.C. as part of their Silverstone race meeting, and this year's event, on August 17, attracted 26 entries. It was to prove a really great battle, with the lead changing continuously until Robin Brown reached the chequered flag first in his Ford-engined 4-4 ahead of Brian Jenkins and his TR4-engined Plus-4; Harry Rose's similarly powered Plus-4 finished in third place. Robin's race average was 69.18 mph, but the fastest lap was set by Brian Haslam and his Plus-4 at 74.98 mph. In a later 10-lap all-comers race Mike Duncan's Plus-4 set the fastest lap at 74.60 mph.

Back at Silverstone for the B.A.R.C. meeting on October 8, Gordon Miles set a new 2,000 to 3,000 cc class lap record on the 1.61-miles Club circuit in 1 min 11.0 secs., a speed of 81.53 mph, a mark which was to stand for well over a year.

In a very different environment, David Way set a new class record of 37.59 seconds with his 4-4 to win his class in the B.A.R.C. South Wales Centre's hill-climb at Pontypool Park on September 29, while to round off another interesting year for Morgan drivers, the M.C.C. announced that their coveted Triple Baddeley award, which is only presented to a driver who has cleared every section in the classic Land's End, Exeter and Scottish Trials, had been won by Roger Bricknall and his Plus-4.

1969

Production car trials continued to provide good hunting for Morgan drivers, and in the Maidstone and Mid-Kent M.C.'s B.T.R.D.A.-qualifying Tyrwhitt-Drake event on March 23 L. F. Davis put in a great effort to finish runner-up behind a Hillman Imp, while another Morgan driven by W. H. D. Lowe won its class. A week later Harvey Postlethwaite was in action again with his 4-4, this time at the Bugatti and Ferrari O.C.'s jointly organized hill-climb at Prescott, where his time of 62.43 secs was to make him a class-winner.

A new name amongst Morgan drivers was to feature in the Castrol/B.A.R.C. Hill-climb Championship this year, that of David Way, who was to prove a vigorous competitor in his 4-4. At the end of the opening round at Harewood, on April 20, he headed the table, but his fortunes took something of a dip the following week, when he could only manage seventh place in the top-ten run-off at the B.A.R.C. South Wales Centre's meeting at Pontypool Park. However, he came back well at the B.A.R.C.'s Wiscombe Park meeting, when his climb in 48.98 secs proved to be a class-winner, while the following week he did very well indeed at the Bugatti O.C.'s Prescott hill-climb to win his class by 0.4 sec from a Porsche 904, with Andy Duncan's twin-cam 4-4 just 0.72 sec behind in third place. He went on to complete a very promising first full season of hill-climbing and take third place in the championship.

The B.A.R.C. had also been busy organizing various race meetings, at one of which, at Croft on May 25, M. Dilmot drove his Plus-4 to a well-judged class victory in a 10-lap combined production sports and G.T. race.

Just to prove that David Way did not have a complete monopoly on Morgan hill-climb successes that year, J. N. J. Upton took a very good class win at the B.A.R.C.'s Harewood event on July 20 with his 4-4, and the following week J. C. Churchill took his Plus-4 to a class victory at the Sevenoaks and District M.C.'s meeting at Sutton Valence, while Peter Binder finished third in his class at the same venue with his 4-4.

1969 was the Golden Jubilee year of the Bentley, which made the Silverstone meeting of the Bentley D.C. on August 26 even more enjoyable than usual, with a most spectacular display of these magnificent cars, of almost every conceivable type, being assembled for the occasion. Once again the special 10-lap Morgan handicap race was a great success, victory going this time to Jim Tucker and his fully race-tuned Plus-4, which overtook Adam Bridgeland's new Plus-8 on the last lap. Harvey Postlethwaite attempted to take Becketts sideways in his twin-cam 4-4, but recovered to finish the race fourth on the road, which meant that he was third in the official results because Brian Jenkins, who had crossed the line ahead of him, had incurred a penalty for jumping the start in his Plus-4 Super Sports.

On August 23, at the Lancashire A.C.'s Woodvale spring meeting, M. Smith proved that it can sometimes be beneficial to own a still rare car, because at the end of the day his Buick-engined Plus-8 had collected two separate class wins.

There must have been many occasions when a car has failed to win a race because its brakes had failed, but for a change John Stapleton had the distinction of winning his class of the production sports car race at the Guards Motor Show 200 meeting at Brands Hatch, on October 18, with the brakes of his Plus-4 jammed on! The following weekend brakes had to be used with great care at Silverstone, where

the Coventry and Warwickshire M.C. staged a sprint meeting in cold, wet and thoroughly dismal conditions, as a result of which the fastest production sports car, an AC Cobra, also set the fastest time of the day overall. Cyril Smedley displayed good pedal control in winning his class with his Plus-8, while Adam Bridgeland was third, eight seconds behind him, in his similar car. So ended another season, during which Morgan drivers had done notably well in hill-climb and sprint events.

1970

The season opened well for J. Curnow, who collected a class win with his 4-4 in the Farnborough and District M.C.'s production car trial, a qualifying round of the R.A.C. Championship, which was held in conjunction with the club's Valentine Trial at Miles Hill, Aldershot, on February 15, after strenuous efforts to clear the course of deep snow.

By mid-March weather conditions had improved considerably, enabling the Midland A.C. to stage a successful meeting at Silverstone, including a 10-lap race for modified sports cars in which the Plus-8 of Brian Haslam was a class-winner and took third place overall. The following weekend it was the turn of the Yorkshire S.C.C. to run the first hill-climb of the season in Northern England, at Castle Howard. Nigel Hargreaves made the journey worthwhile when he took his very rapid Plus-4 up the hill in 41.39 secs, which was sufficient for him to win his class, just 0.06 sec ahead of the second-placed MGB.

David Way was back in action again with his successful hill-climbing 4-4, and a time of 42.15 secs at Gurston Down gave him a class victory in the fourth round of the Castrol/B.A.R.C. Hill-climb Championship.

One of the highlights of the Mini-7 Club's race meeting at Brands Hatch on June 14 was the battle in the 10-lap modified sports car race between a TVR Vixen and Irvine Laidlaw's 4-4. Although the TVR won the race, Laidlaw spent the entire time slipstreaming the leader and trying time after time to find a way past, but the Morgan simply hadn't sufficient power to hold its rival down the straights.

During the Bugatti O.C.'s invitation hill-climb at Prescott on July 5, Andy Duncan's run in 56.58 secs with his twin-cam-engined 4-4 earned him a lot of applause, while the following weekend, at the Midland A.C.'s Shelsley Walsh meeting, he managed to break the

40-seconds barrier with the same car. However, the first sub-40-seconds time by a Morgan had been recorded earlier on by Ray Meredith in 39.41 secs in his by now ageing Plus-4. During the same meeting one driver stopped the clocks at 44.44 secs in — yes, you've guessed it — a Morgan 4-4! On the same day another hill-climb was being organized by the B.A.R.C. at Pontypool, where Dennis Parsons won his class with a time of 38.47 secs, which put him 0.19 sec ahead of a Porsche.

Adam Bridgeland's time with his Plus 8 in the Herts County A.A.C. sprint at Duxford, on September 13, was deceptively fast, and what had looked to be a quiet and very calculated run proved unapproachable by anyone else in his class, which included a very experienced driver in an Austin-Healey 3000.

This had been a relatively uneventful year for Morgan drivers, and in the main the 1970s were to be dominated by cars of much younger concept, although as the decade progressed the Morgan name was to make something of a comeback in the results lists, as we shall see.

1971

Well-known for his exploits at the wheel of a Frazer Nash, Richard Smith had changed over to a Plus-4 for the Westmoreland M.C.'s hill-climb at Barbon Manor, a qualifying round of the Shell/R.A.C. Championship, on May 22. It proved to be a successful move, for his time of 33.16 secs came close to breaking the class record, and made him a class-winner by 0.16 sec ahead of a TVR Vixen.

On the following day the South-West Centre of the B.A.R.C. ran a qualifying round of the Castrol/B.A.R.C. Hill-climb Championship at Gurston Down, where Bevel Harrison clinched the class victory with his second-run time of 43.70 secs with his 4-4, and to confirm his liking for this hill he returned to Gurston Down on June 27 to score another class win, although at the slightly slower time of 44.29 secs. Bevel made quite a name for himself this year in hill-climbing, his successes also including class wins at Pontypool on June 20 and at Shelsley Walsh early in July.

On August 15 Phil Hingley really got amongst the MGs at the Curborough sprint meeting organized by the MG C.C., his time of 43.6 secs with his 4-4 proving more than a match for all his class rivals.

John Stapleton took part in a marvellous 10-lap race for modified sports cars at Mallory Park on August 29, his Plus-8 being matched against a 4.7-litre Sunbeam Tiger and a 4.2-litre Jaguar E-type at the front of the field. During a race-long battle with the Jaguar, some spectacular driving by John had the Morgan out-cornering the E-type round the outside at the Esses, and he held on to finish in second place behind the winning Tiger and to set the fastest lap at a speed of 87.41 mph.

The previous day the Bentley D.C. had run a meeting at Silverstone with sponsorship from *The Times* newspaper, the programme including a *Times* Challenge invitation race over 10 laps in which Brian Haslam worked his Lawrence-tuned Plus-8 through the field from seventh place on the opening lap to finish a creditable third. In a later combined AC O.C. and Morgan S.C.C. race two Shelby Cobras had no real opposition and finished first and second, but third place was disputed by Brian Haslam and Cyril Smedley until Cyril made a nonsense of it on the fifth lap, leaving Brian on his own to take the class win.

Bevel Harrison was on the winner's trail again on October 3, when he picked up yet another class win in his 4-4 at the B.A.R.C.'s hill-climb at Gurston Down after never being seriously challenged, while John Gillham added to Morgan laurels by claiming another class with his Plus-8.

John Canney was second overall behind a Volkswagen and won his class at the Castle Bromwich production car trial at Coleshill and Lea Marton, Warwickshire, with his 4-4, while in a similar event on November 21 organized by the Crane Valley M.C. at Normandy Hall, near Aldershot, Ruth Atkinson was only just pipped at the post and relegated to second place in the sports car class with her Morgan.

1972

The Tyrwhitt-Drake Trophy Trial, run by the Maidstone and Mid-Kent M.C. over the North Downs, is an event in which Morgans have earned a very good record, right from its inception in 1937, and this year Len Davis maintained the tradition by winning his class.

At the B.R.D.C.'s race meeting at Silverstone, on Easter Monday, Robin Grey entertained the 7,000-crowd with a fine display of sideways driving through the corners with his Plus-8 and was rewarded with a class win in the 15-lap modified sports car race.

Although it was comparatively rare by this time to see a fully equipped road car, fitted with road tyres, competing in a hill-climb, this did not stop Alex Robinson from winning his class in the

B.A.R.C./Castrol Hill-climb Championship meeting at Prescott, in early-April, with a respectable time of 58.78 secs.

The weather was cold but the competition was hot in the modified sports car race for the Dick Protheroe Trophy at the Nottingham S.C.C.'s meeting at Croft on April 28. First there was a battle between the winning AC Cobra and a lightweight Ginetta G4 for first place, which broke up when the Ginetta was driven to the pits for a jammed gear lever to be freed. Then all interest centred on a dice between John MacDonald in his Plus-4 and the late John Gott, the famous racing Chief Constable and his equally famous Austin-Healey 3000. It was a magnificent fight, but John Gott was on his top form and he just managed to hold off the Morgan challenge to the finishing line.

Adam Bridgeland scored another class win for his collection at the Romford Enthusiasts' C.C. race meeting at Snetterton, on May 14, with his Plus-8, but Alex Robinson's car did not perform too well in the same race and finished well down the field.

Another hill-climb success came the way of a road-equipped Morgan when Bill Holt's Plus-8 recorded a time of 39.17 secs at the Midland A.C.'s meeting at Shelsley Walsh to score a class win, on July 9, one week after Ruth Atkinson and J. A. Gregson had taken their Morgans to first and second places in their class in the Rodney Whiteley Trial organized by the Airedale and Pennine M.C.

Robin Gray's Impact/Lawrence-tuned Plus-8 was one of only seven starters in a 10-lap modified sports car race on September 10 at the London M.C.'s Mallory Park meeting, but he was kept busy all the same. He spent much of the time chasing the leading Jaguar E-type, but then he had to spin the Morgan to avoid the Jaguar as it slid at the hairpin. As he took to the grass an Austin-Healey 3000 went through into second place, but Robin fought back to finish second after making up a lot of lost ground.

The combined-classes race at the Romford Enthusiasts' C.C. meeting at Snetterton, on September 17, brought a good Morgan result, despite very heavy rain. It looked as though Brian Haslam would have it all his own way in his Plus-8, but Adam Bridgeland, who seemed to be revelling in the wet conditions, had fought his way through into second place by the fourth lap, and when Brian had a quick spin at the hairpin he rushed by into first place, which he retained to the end. A supercharged Alfa Romeo had gone through into second place while Brian was spinning, but he fought back well

and repassed the Italian car, to make it Morgans first and second.

1973

Chris Lawrence was back in action again with a Plus-4 for the first round of a new championship for thoroughbred cars, sponsored by Charles Spreckley Industries, which took place at Silverstone on March 24, Lawrence celebrating his return with a class victory and second place overall behind a Jaguar XK 120.

The following day Aubrey Brocklebank was heavily engaged with his Plus-4 Super Sports in the 10-lap opening round of the Northern Sports Car Championship at the B.A.R.C. meeting at Croft, after Andy Garlick's Morgan had had to be pushed off the grid with an oil leak. The winning Lotus Elan was never seriously troubled, but Brocklebank became one of four drivers who contested the places immediately behind, and after a really great dice he crossed the line in third place.

Two weeks later the Nottingham S.C.C. ran a meeting at the same circuit, and this time three Morgans were to appear in the results. The 10-lap modified sports car race took place in falling snow, which produced some interesting challenges, and once again an Elan crossed the finishing line first, followed this time by a Clan Crusader and a Jaguar E-type. Aubrey Brocklebank had looked set for fourthplace in his Plus-4 until, trying very hard to overtake the Jaguar on the ninth lap, he spun and had to settle for a class win, and a fastest lap in his class of 69.24 mph. Aubrey had overtaken John MacDonald and his Plus-8 before his spin, but then McDonald reclaimed his fourth place overall and went on to finish second in his class behind the Jaguar after lapping at 69.38 mph, while Andy Garlick's Plus-4 was runner-up to Brocklebank's car in the other class.

The Nottingham S.C.C. were back at Croft again on May 6, when the same three Morgans were present, although this time they were less successful, MacDonald claiming a second in class with his Plus-8, and Garlick and Brocklebank reversing their previous finishing order to end up second and third in their class.

Meanwhile, Adam Bridgeland put up a tremendous effort at the Romford Enthusiasts' C.C. meeting at Snetterton to finish a bare second behind the winning Jaguar E-type in an eight-lap modified sports car race after pressing the leader all the way. When the club returned to the circuit on July 1 there were sufficient Morgans entered for the organizers to give them a race class to themselves, and they provided some quite spectacular racing with constant changes in position and a really great battle for the leading places. Eventually Malcolm Haywood was the winner in his Plus-8 followed by Peter Binder in his 4-4 and Alan Samuels in his Plus-4, while Alan Bridgeland made the fastest lap at 78.80 mph in his Plus-8.

The B.A.R.C. went to Thruxton on May 28, and so did Robin Gray, who came away with yet another class win, this time in the 10-lap modified sports car race in which he finished third overall at 87.87 mph.

Morgans featured in the results of every race for which they were eligible at the Bentley D.C.'s Silverstone meeting on August 25, beginning with a 10-lap all-comers handicap for which five of the 26 entries were Morgans. David Rutherford was never seriously challenged in this event, and he ran out a comfortable winner, 31.8 secs separating his 4-4 from the Plus-8 of Alex Robinson. In a subsequent race John MacDonald and his Plus-8 were pushed down to third place behind a Ford GT40 and a Lister-Jaguar, but MacDonald seemed to have a later 10-lap scratch race for ACs and Morgans well under control when he suffered a puncture on the eighth lap. An AC Cobra went on to win, but it was chased across the line by five Morgans, John Berry's 4-4 being second and Adam Bridgeland's Plus-8 third, and John MacDonald having the consolation of fastest race lap in 1 min 7.4 secs, a speed of 85.89 mph.

Chris Lawrence's well-known Plus-4 Super Sports was in action again at Thruxton, on September 16, when it took an easy 2-litre class win in the B.A.R.C.'s race for thoroughbred sports cars and finished third overall, only 12 seconds behind the winning 3.8-litre Jaguar XK 120.

Having made a magnificent start from the second row to lead the Modsports race at the B.A.R.C. Yorkshire Centre's end-of-season meeting at Croft, on September 23, John MacDonald threw away his lead over a Ginetta and an Elan by spinning off the track after recording a fastest lap in 1 min 15.2 secs, 83.78 mph. On the same day the Romford Enthusiasts' C.C. were at Snetterton, where Adam Bridgeland stormed into the lead of the Peter Arundell Trophy race with his Plus-8. However, before the end of the first lap Robin Gray had taken over first place in his Lawrence-tuned Plus-8 and he held on to beat Bridgeland by 9.2 secs at an average speed of 85.60 mph,

leaving an Austin-Healey 3000 in third place. Later in the day he was second in his class behind a Marcos in a combined-categories race for over-2-litre cars.

A Morgan highlight of the year occurred at the 750 M.C.'s annual six-hours relay race at Silverstone, on September 29, when there were two Morgan teams amongst the 26 entries. One of these, the Libra Morgan Grinders, was entered by the London Centre of the Morgan S.C.C. and comprised the Plus-8s of Malcolm Hayward and Bill Hopkins and the Plus-4s of Aubrey Brocklebank and Nigel Sill, supported by the Coldwell GTs of Rob Ingham-Hurst and Rob Wells. Gip Shaw had also been part of the team, but he had a slight accident during practice with his Plus-4 as a result of which he broke a finger. The team, which received 55 credit laps, was managed by Mike Rudd, who planned his strategy and tactics with great skill, and after a virtually faultless run, the only serious problem being to fit a replacement clutch to Rob Wells' car, the team worked their way up through the handicap field to finish first and collect the *Cars and Car Conversions* Trophy and associated awards.

The other team, the London Centre's Anglemog Morgans, consisted of Adam Bridgeland's Plus-8 (limited to 50 laps), the Plus-4s of Ray Jones, Frank Gillan and Allan Samuels, Peter Binder's 4-4 and the 1937 4-4 of Mary Smith, collectively receiving 93 credit laps under the handicapping and being managed by John Lindsay. During the course of the race Ray Jones' Plus-4 needed some welding work on its exhaust manifold, but for a while things went well, Adam Bridgeland lifting the team up to third place before running out of laps, but after the Plus-8 had completed its stint the other team cars were unable to sustain their position, and they had slipped to 11th position by the finish.

Robin Gray borrowed Chris Lawrence's Plus-4 for the Charles Spreckley thoroughbred-cars race at the B.R.D.C. Silverstone meeting on October 6 and had the crowd on their feet with some magnificent racing. An Austin-Healey 3000 had gone into the lead at the start, but Robin found a way past it around the outside at Woodcote and remained in front until the Healey went by again down Hangar Straight on the fifth lap. Robin kept up the pressure, and the Healey spun off at Club on the next lap, allowing Gray to regain the lead and hang on to win by just a second from a Triumph TR3 with a Jaguar XK 120 a further 0.4 sec away in third place. Robin's winning speed was 90.33 mph and his fastest lap was at 91.63

Canadian capers as a trio of 4-4 1600s driven by Bob Sterne (car 14), Dr. Stu Rulka (2) and Dave Collis (13) fight off an Alfa Romeo during a race on the Westwood track in Vancouver during 1973. Note the Plus-8 wheels fitted to the leading car.

A Graham Murrell picture during the six-hours relay race at Silverstone, in 1974, as John Lindsay, manager of the winning Vikings team, transfers the sash from Mary Smith's Series 1 to set Bob Chaplin's 4-4 on its way.

mph, a magnificent effort in a borrowed car. The following day he was back in his own Plus-8 for a World of Sport Trophy race at Brands Hatch, where he fought and won a close battle with another Austin-Healey to finish first in the over-3-litre class and second overall 27.6 secs behind John Pearson's very fast Lotus Elan.

This had been a great year for Chris Lawrence's Plus-4, which collected four 2-litre class records for thoroughbred sports cars, the first being at Brands Hatch, on June 3, when Chris lapped in 1 min 3.8 secs for a record speed of 69.97 mph; then came Brian Cutting's lap with the car on the Silverstone Club circuit on July 29, in 1 min 12.2 secs, 80.18 mph; next was Chris' lap of Thruxton, on September 16, in 1 min 42.0 sec, 83.15 mph; and finally, on October 6, Robin Gray used the car to lap the Silverstone Grand Prix circuit in 1 min 55.0 secs, a speed of 91.63 mph.

1974

One of the best performances at the Tunbridge Wells M.C.'s Urgemup production car trial on March 17 came from Carol Eales, whose 4-4 won her the sports car class at St Ives Farm, Hartfield, over 12 mud-covered sections, despite strong opposition.

John MacDonald was back in action again on the same day at Croft, his Plus-8 competing in the 12-lap Modsports race at the B.A.R.C. Yorkshire Centre meeting. Once again his phenomenal starting ability was demonstrated when he leapt into the lead, but a spin at Tower ruined his chances, and a pit stop dropped him to a lap behind the field. Despite a lap in 1 min 18.4 secs, 80.36 mph, and a class victory, he was still down in sixth place overall at the end of the race.

Robin Gray borrowed Chris Lawrence's Plus-4 again for the B.A.R.C. meeting at Mallory Park, on April 28, for a 10-lap Spreckley thoroughbred sports car race in heavy rain and became part of the best dice of the day. Three cars were in it from the start, John Harper's XK 120, Reg Woodcock's TR3 and Gray's Morgan. Harper led for the first three laps, then his engine started to play up and Woodcock squeezed past at Gerards, with Robin following him through less than a lap later. Using as much of the track as possible to avoid the spray, he closed right up on Woodcock, but as the TR3 had sufficient speed to hold the Morgan on the straights he waited until the penultimate lap before diving through on the inside at the Esses and snatched the lead. Woodcock tried hard to get back on

terms, but was baulked by back markers, and Robin went on to win at 73.55 mph and despite the conditions lowered the class lap record to 1 min 3.4 secs, 76.66 mph.

Ray Meredith shared Andy Duncan's 4-4 for the R.A.C. Hill-climb Championship meeting at Prescott, on May 5, and set the faster times, but neither of them could match the 53.14 secs climb by John Berry in his lightweight 4-4, which gave him the over-1,600 cc class.

A spin at Sear Corner ruined Robin Gray's chances in the Modsports race at the B.A.R.C. Snetterton meeting, on May 12, and he could only managed third place in the over-3-litre class with his Plus-8, although he shared a new class lap record with Chris White and his TVR Tuscan in 1 min 15.0 secs, a speed of 91.37 mph. The next round in this race series, for the Blue Circle Championship, took place at Cadwell Park, on June 2, where Gray modified the front of his car in an incident at Gooseneck after he had set a new lap record at 1 min 42.0 secs, 79.41 mph. The class winner and only finisher in the over-3-litre section was Patrick Keen with another Plus-8. Barbon Manor hill-climb was the scene of further record-breaking the same afternoon, David Rutherford's climb in 29.31 secs in his glass-fibre-panelled 4-4 being one of four new records at the Westmoreland M.C.'s event.

Four classes of sports cars were combined into a 10-lap race at the Romford Enthusiasts' C.C. Snetterton meeting on June 9, when, despite very wet conditions, the standard of racing was excellent. The leading Lister-Jaguar of David Ham was pressed hard for five laps by Patrick Keen in his Plus-8, but a spin at Russell dropped Keen back on lap 6 and the Lister went on to win by 5.2 secs from Adam Bridgeland, who won the Morgan class with his Plus-8, with Alex Robinson's similar car second and John Hewitt's 4-4 third in the class. Bridgeland also set the class lap record at 1 min 26.2 secs, 79.50 mph.

The same club was back at Snetterton on July 14, when the programme included a 10-lap race for road-going and race-equipped MG T-Register cars and Morgans. It was clear that Morgans would take the major places, but not before they had threaded their way through the very large field of T-series MGs. In the end Patrick Keen was first across the line with his Plus-8, which had led from lap 3, but a 10-second penalty relegated him to third place. The 4-4s of Rob Wells, whose car had trailed a huge plume of smoke for the whole race, and David Rutherford fought a close battle for second place on the track, Rob managing to squeeze past on the final lap to finish 0.4 sec ahead to be awarded the race, while Keen set the fastest race lap in 1 min 22.6 secs, 82.97 mph, and Peter Joiner brought his Plus-8 into fourth place. In a later race, reduced from 10 to six laps following two serious accidents, Patrick Keen won the Morgan class from Mary Smith's 1937 4-4 and finished second overall 19.2 secs behind David Ham's Lister-Jaguar.

One of the high spots of the B.R.S.C.C. North-West Centre's meeting at Oulton Park, on July 14, was the great battle between John Britten in his Plus-8 and Colin Blower in his Lotus Europa in the production sports car race, the class victory going to John by barely a bonnet-length.

The Bentley D.C. Silver Anniversary race meeting at Silverstone, on August 28, provided plenty of action for Morgan drivers, first of all in a 10-lap handicap race run in two parts, both of which went to Aubrey Brocklebank, driving the ex-John MacDonald Plus-4 Super Sports, on corrected times, while Bill Hopkins in his standard Plus-8 was second in the first race as well as on handicap, and two places behind him came David Rutherford in his lightweight 4-4. John Hewitt's 4-4 was first on the road in part two, and second on handicap, while third place was taken by Alan Kennedy in his 4-4.

Later, a 10-lap scratch race for Morgans produced a great dice between Robin Gray in his Lawrence-tuned Plus-4 and John MacDonald in his supercharged Plus-8. John led for several laps, but Robin managed to out-brake him at Woodcote and slip into the lead, but towards the end of the race his bonnet began to flap and he was black-flagged. However, he must have been concentrating very hard keeping the Plus-8 at bay because he failed to see the flag and carried on to cross the line still ahead, only to be disqualified. This gave MacDonald the race, with Patrick Keen second in the ex-Stapleton Plus-8, followed by David Rutherford in his lightweight 4-4, Aubrey Brocklebank in his Plus-4, Mike Hayward (Plus-8) and Bill Hopkins (Plus-8).

Silverstone was also the scene of a full race programme at the SUNBAC meeting on August 31, including a 10-lap Modsports race in which Robin Gray started on the sixth row after practice troubles and was on the tail of the leading Porsche 911 within two laps. On lap 3 he went ahead and began to pull away, but by lap 6 an Elan had moved into second place and was closing the gap, and two laps later the Lotus went past as Robin tried to find a way round a back marker. However, Gray fought back into the lead and went on to win by 2.6 secs after setting the fastest lap in 1 min 3.6 secs, 91.02 mph.

Few races that year can have been won by such a wide margin as the 12-lap Modsports event at the Nottingham S.C.C.'s rainy meeting at Croft, on November 10, in which victory went to John MacDonald and his Plus-8 by 1 min 31 secs. His initial battle with an Elan ended when the Lotus broke a drive-shaft, and after that he increased his lead by more than five seconds every lap until he had lapped all but two of the field, his best lap time being 1 min 24.8 secs, 74.29 mph. Three weeks later the club was back again and once again MacDonald was too quick for the opposition, his winning margin this time in a race for Modsports and special saloon cars being 32.2 secs over a Ford Escort RS 2000, after a best lap speed of 84.22 mph.

The race for Morgans at the same meeting was a very lighthearted affair, and although Aubrey Brocklebank's S.L.R. had seized in practice there was an interesting line-up, including MacDonald in his regular car, his father Iain in the 1950 Motor Show Plus-4 Coupé and Dick Smith with Chris Lawrence's Le Mans Plus-4. John MacDonald shot into the lead at the start, followed by John Hewitt in his Lotus-engined 4-4. On lap 4 the leader noticed that Dick Smith was in the pits, so he pulled in to help him. This gave Hewitt the lead for a lap, but having rejoined the race in third place MacDonald was soon back in front again and on the following lap he could have lapped his father in front of the crowd, but sportingly moved over and delayed his pass until they were both out of sight. All this allowed Andy Garlick (Plus-4) and John Hewitt (4-4) to close up with their battle for second place, and MacDonald's lead over Garlick was down to 4.2 secs at the end of the race, with Hewitt a further 1.2 secs away in third place. Although John MacDonald's winning average speed was a modest 69.13 mph, his fastest lap had been in 84.23 mph.

Morgan successes during 1974 had included five new lap records, beginning on April 28 when Robin Gray lapped Mallory Park in his Plus-4 in 1 min 3.4 secs, 76.66 mph; on May 12 he used his Plus-8 to take the Snetterton class record at 1 min 15.0 secs, 91.37 mph; then on May 27 John Northcroft drove round Castle Combe in his Plus-8 in 1 min 24.6 secs, 78.30 mph; Robin Gray took another record when he was timed at Cadwell Park, on June 2, at 1 min 42.0 secs, 79.41

mph; and finally John Britten went round the Brands Hatch Club circuit, on September 8, in 1 min 0.2 sec, 73.18 mph.

1975

Brilliant driving by Robin Gray prevented a clean sweep by Jaguar-engined cars in the Jaguar D.C.'s Silverstone meeting on March 22, despite a terrible start, which dropped him down to eighth place at the beginning of the Modsports race. But he recovered well, and by lap 4 he was in amongst the E-types and on the leader's tail. By the end of the lap he had found a way through, and he then fought off a determined counter-attack to take his Lawrence-tuned Plus-8 across the line the winner by 0.4 sec, having made the fastest lap in 1 min 6.0 secs, 87.71 mph. In a later race for the Classic Car Championship Aubrey Brocklebank took his Morgan S.L.R. to second place in the class for G.T. cars.

Two days later Gray was at Mallory Park for the B.R.S.C.C. meeting, where he won his class but had to settle for second overall behind an Elan in the Modsports race. The club was also in action at Croft that afternoon, where John Britten fought and won a battle with a V-12 E-type Jaguar for victory in a production sports car race in which Chris Alford was a class-winner with his 4-4. Over the Easter weekend Britten also had a comfortable win, by 18 seconds over a Lotus Europa, in a similar race at Rufforth, while Alford again won his class, this time beating a TR6 to the line. Chris Hopkins took his Plus-8 to fourth place in his class at the same meeting.

On April 20 Robin Gray seriously miscalculated the amount of fuel he would need for the 10-lap Modsports race at Mallory Park, for he ran dry with three laps to go having looked a sure winner despite a strong challenge from an Elan. His fastest lap was in 51.0 secs, a speed of 95.30 mph, while Chris Cooke took fourth place overall in his 4-4. Chris Alford scored a good class win in the production sports car race, and his fastest lap in 1 min 1.6 secs, 78.90 mph, was a new class record.

Gray had ample fuel on board at Silverstone, on April 27, when he won his class and finished third behind two Elans in the 10-lap Modsports race at the B.A.R.C. meeting. However, three weeks later, on May 17, 'Rain Stopped Play' in the 750 M.C.'s six-hours relay race after two-and-a-half hours' racing. By then the heavy rain and poor visibility had caused the track to become littered with shunted cars and it was proving altogether too hazardous for marshals and drivers alike. After a meeting of team managers the race was halted and it was decided to base the results on the positions at the time of abandonment, which gave a class win to the Middlesex Polytechnic Libre Morgan team of Rob Wells and Bryan Harvey in 4-4s and Bill Hopkins and Charles Morgan (driving when the race was stopped) in Plus-8s.

Conditions were a lot better at Brands Hatch the following day when Robin Gray and his Plus-8 won the over-3-litre class of the B.A.R.C.'s 10-lap Modsports race, finishing third overall behind two Elans but well ahead of a V-12 E-type, his fastest lap of 53.6 secs, 83.28 mph, equalling the class record.

Co-promoted by the London C.C. and the Romford Enthusiasts' C.C., the Snetterton meeting on June 8 included another popular race between Morgans and T-series MGs which again proved a runaway success for the Morgans, Robin Gray (Plus-8), Chris Cooke (4-4) and Patrick Keen (Plus-8) taking the first three places. In the over-2,500 cc class Myke Bluston was third behind Robin and Patrick, while in the under-2,500 cc class Chris was followed by Rob Chaplin and Leigh Sebba, both in 4-4s.

Robin Gray just beat a cloudburst at Snetterton on June 15 when he lowered the Modsports class lap record to 1 min 14.6 secs, 92.51 mph, in winning his class and finishing second overall behind an Elan, while on July 13, at Brands Hatch, the main Morgan interest centred on Chris Alford and his 4-4 and Plus-8 driver Bill Hopkins, who finished third overall behind an Elan and a Jensen-Healey in the production sports car race. Chris was a class-winner once again and he shared a new lap record at 1 min 3.6 secs, 70.19 mph with Doc Griffiths and his MGB.

On the same day Robin Gray went to Oulton Park for the Modsports race at the B.R.S.C.C. Midland Centre meeting, his Plus-8 holding on to win from John Evans' very powerful Elan by the narrowest of margins (the two drivers were given identical times) as well as equalling the lap record of 1 min 8.2 secs, 87.31 mph.

The August Bank Holiday meeting at Silverstone was to produce yet another class win for Chris Alford in the Britten 4-4, while Chris' boss John Britten was second overall in his Plus-8 behind the very fast Radio Luxembourg-sponsored Elan.

The Bentley D.C. Silverstone meeting proved as popular as ever with Morgan driver, Aubrey Brocklebank setting the ball rolling by taking his S.L.R. to a victory by 8.4 secs over the Plus-8 of Mike

Above: Every Morgan enthusiast's dream. This is how Bryan Harvey discovered a car which was to become a successful competition model. Above right: The same car with the conversion almost completed. Note the modest size of fuel tank.

Two markedly different Morgans competing at the B.M.R.M.C. meeting at Donington in 1978 with Terry Garland's almost standard 4-4 four-seater temporarily ahead of Pat Keens' far from standard Plus-8, which went on to win the race. (Photograph by Graham Murrell.)

Hayward in the opening handicap race, while in the second handicap event P. Hornby's Plus-8 was just pipped by one second by an Aston Martin DB4, but set the fastest lap at 1 min 15.0 secs, 77.18 mph. As usual the Morgan S.C.C. was granted a 10-lap scratch race, from which only one of the 25 cars entered retired. The winner was John Berry in his Rutherford-built 4-4 which, with its special frame and glass-fibre body must have been just about the lightest 4-4 around at that time. He had an easy win from Patrick Keen's turbocharged Plus-8, followed by Alan Kennedy in his well-known 4-4 and Bill Hopkins in his Plus-8. A. L. Stirling (Plus-4), Hopkins, Berry and Keen were the four class-winners.

Having blown up the racing engine of his Plus-8 in the previous round of the Modsports contest and lost valuable championship points, Robin Gray was anxious to defend his class lead at the B.A.R.C.'s Mallory Park meeting on September 21, so he installed a standard engine from a crashed Rover and drove a quiet and sensible race into fourth place overall, 48.8 secs behind the winning Elan, but most importantly first in the over-3-litre class at an average of 86.54 mph. This put him into an almost unassailable position.

On the same day the Nottingham S.C.C. ran a six-race meeting at Croft, where Tony Palmer and his 4-4 could only finish second in class in the Modsports race, but then had a great race in the thoroughbred sports car event to take a comfortable win over Ian Giles and his Plus-8, with A. J. Dunn third in his Plus-4, and John MacDonald's Plus-4 further behind. Early in the race Tony had a spirited dice with Dick Smith and his Plus-4 Super Sports, which ended when Dick's throttle spring snapped as he went into Tower, leaving the throttle wide open and sending him into the banking, where fortunately only the car suffered injury.

Robin Gray had a Lawrence-tuned engine back in his Plus-8 for the Modsports race at Brands Hatch on September 28, when practice times suggested he would have a close battle with Simon Packford's Davrian, but Packford made a bad start, leaving Ed Reeve in a supercharged MG Midget to just beat Robin into the first bend. But Robin showed the superior power of his car on the bottom straight and went through into the lead, and although Reeve fought back gamely the Morgan was still 0.8 sec ahead as they crossed the line, having averaged 80.11 mph.

Although the production sports car race at the B.R.S.C.C. meeting at Snetterton, on October 5 provided a runaway victory by

half a minute for the winning Elan, a real battle was fought for the subsequent places. John Britten had had to start from the back of the grid in his Plus-8, having practised out of time, but he had soon worked his way near the front to harrass a pair of 5.3-litre Jaguars, and he slipped through into second place when their drivers made a mistake. But then John in turn made an error, which let the Jaguars through again, but on the last lap one Jaguar spun off and the other overheated, so once again the Morgan was back in second place, where it finished ahead of Bill Hopkins, whose Plus-8 managed to grab third place from the surviving Jaguar. Meanwhile, Chris Alford was very busy cementing his claim to the championship by easily winning his class in his 4-4 and setting a new lap record at 1 min 29.4 secs, 77.19 mph.

The season ended, therefore, with a fine Morgan double, Robin Gray being announced the winner of the over-3-litre class, nine points ahead of his nearest rival in the Miller Organs Modified Sports Car Championship, and Chris Alford being declared the B.R.S.C.C. Production Sports Car Champion, having only twice failed to win his class in this contest, and being the holder of three new lap records at Mallory Park, Brands Hatch and Snetterton.

1976

Anyone who enjoys close racing, with the leading positions changing lap after lap, must have been delighted with the Modsports event at the Midland A.C.'s Silverstone meeting on March 6, when Robin Gray in his Lawrence-tuned Plus-8 and Mark Hales in his Turner fought a magnificent race-long battle, victory finally going to Robin, who swept back in front on the last corner to win by a length at 80.89 mph. A fortnight later he was back for a similar race at the Jaguar D.C.'s meeting, and this time was locked in combat with a Jaguar E-type. He delayed his challenge to the last lap, but when the two cars came up to a back marker at Woodcote Robin had to take the outside line, and he failed by just 0.2 sec to secure another win.

The following day he moved on to Mallory Park, and was more fortunate, taking the lead in the first round of the B.R.S.C.C.'s Modsports Championship when the leading Elan had throttle-linkage trouble two laps from the end. He then resisted a strong attack from a Marcos, and after setting the fastest lap at 91.35 mph he won by the margin of 1.4 secs.

Chris Alford had exchanged Britten's Minster-tuned 4-4 for a

Cyril Charlesworth, with his wife Joyce acting as 'bouncer', tackling Blue Hills Mine with his Plus-8 on the 1975 M.C.C. Land's End Trial. (Photograph by Tony Hollis.)

Below left: Bruce Stapleton competing with Morris Stapleton Motors' brand new Prodsports Morgan Plus-8 at the Eight Clubs meeting at Silverstone in March, 1977, when he set a new lap record which was to stand for a long time. (Photograph by John Gaisford.) Below: Another success for the Morris Stapleton team, this time by Bill Wykeham, who also collected a lap record on the way to a race victory at Donington in 1978. This Chris Davies photograph shows him leading a TVR.

similarly prepared TVR 1600 for the B.R.S.C.C.'s production sports car race at Snetterton on March 28, but the 1975 champion found some tough opposition from Chris Hampshire's 4-4 before scoring a narrow class victory. The overall race promised an exciting battle between the Plus-8s of Bill Wykeham and Charles Morgan and two TVRs behind Chris Meek's winning Europa, but Charles ran into trouble at the bridge and Bill could only finish a distant fourth. The same afternoon Robin Gray found some tough Porsche opposition at the B.A.R.C.'s Silverstone meeting and could only finish second in his class, and he had a similar result, finishing third overall, at the B.R.S.C.C. Northern Centre's meeting at Rufforth, on April 17. The next day the same club moved on to Croft, where Tony Brewer and his 4-4 were second in class behind Chris Alford's TVR in the Direct Tapes production sports car race, in which John Britten and Bob Stuart finished second and fourth overall in their Plus-8s behind the winning Europa.

Robin Gray's Plus-8 was a bare car's length behind Dave Bettinson's Caterham Super Seven, fourth overall and third in class in a close-fought Modsports race at the B.A.R.C. Snetterton meeting on May 16, but two weeks later, what had promised to be another close-finishing victory, at the B.R.S.C.C. Oulton Park meeting, turned sadly wrong. He spent the 10-lap race slipstreaming Brian Murphy's E-type Jaguar, then challenged on the last corner, drawing level on the outside. But the combination of a wet track and the wrong line was too much for the Plus-8, which smashed into the Armco barrier, wrecking the car's front end. Luckily, Robin was not seriously injured, but it was to be some time before he and his car were fit enough to race again.

The B.R.S.C.C.'s busy race programme included meetings at Mallory Park on June 20 and at Oulton Park on June 26, where on both occasions Chris Hampshire and his 4-4 had to give best to Chris Alford's TVR in the £2,001 to £3,000 class of the production sports car race, while in the overall order John Britten was second to Chris Meek's Europa Special at Mallory Park, and finished third at Oulton Park.

No fewer than 23 records were broken the same day when the Hagley and District L.C.C. staged a hill-climb at Loton Park, and David Rutherford came close to making it 24 when his first run in his lightweight 4-4 was within 0.83 sec of the class record, and his second run looked set to beat it when he ran off at Keepers. However, his earlier climb had been quick enough to give him the class victory.

On July 4 he journeyed to Snetterton for a rare race appearance at the Romford Enthusiasts' C.C. meeting where he was never seriously challenged in John Berry's lightweight 4-4 until Myke Bluston put in a late effort in his road-going Plus-8 to finish 2 secs behind. Bob Stuart's Plus-8 crossed the line fourth, 1.8 secs behind a Dutton, which had been in all sorts of trouble through the Esses nearly every other lap. John Berry then used his own car for a combined-classes race for cars of special historic interest and was contesting the lead with a Rover Special when he ran out of fuel on the penultimate lap, having forgotten that this was a 12-lap race, whereas the earlier event had been over 10 laps, which indicates the extent to which drivers go to keep their cars' weight to a minimum.

David Rutherford was back in more familiar surroundings on July 18 when he competed in the Morgan S.C.C. sprint at Curborough, where he won his class by just 0.1 sec in a time of 36 secs, and was only 0.4 sec slower when he competed with the car in a second class to score another victory. Ray Meredith was second in Mike Duncan's BDA-engined 4-4, Mike himself being just 0.1 sec slower for third place.

For several months Charles Morgan had been gaining useful racing experience with his Plus-8, and on July 25, at the B.R.S.C.C. meeting at Cadwell Park, he demonstrated his progress by finishing the production sports car race in second place behind Chris Meek's Europa and ahead of the best-placed TVR.

In perfect conditions, seven class records were broken at Shelsley Walsh, on August 15, when the Morgan S.C.C. combined their annual *concours* and gathering with the hill-climb. Over 150 Morgans were in attendance, and Andy Duncan set the seal on a successful day by setting a new record time of 37.02 secs to win his class. Just one week later another hill-climb record fell to a Morgan when David Rutherford managed a remarkable time of 61.29 secs at Loton Park to take a comfortable win in a combined modified and limited production sports car class at the Hagley and District L.C.C. meeting.

At the 40th anniversary Bentley D.C. meeting at Silverstone, on August 28, the first all-comers handicap race became a Morgan benefit, the marque taking the first four places, led by Bob Nicholls in his turbocharged Plus-8, who was chased across the line so closely by Charles Morgan in his works Plus-8 that they were credited with identical times. Malcolm Hayward in another Plus-8 was only 0.8 sec further behind, and fourth was the Plus-4 S.L.R. of Aubrey Brocklebank. Charles also set the fastest lap at 1 min 17.0 secs, 75.18 mph. The end of the three-months drought which England had been enduring coincided with the Morgan S.C.C.'s 10-lap scratch race, which Robin Gray led from start to finish. He was followed across the line by Bruce Stapleton, Peter Garland and Charles Morgan, all of them in Plus-8s. Stapleton then took part in another all-comers handicap race, which he led all the way to win by just 1 sec from a 3.5-litre Alvis Silver Eagle Special.

The following day Robin Gray moved on the Mallory Park, for the B.R.S.C.C. meeting, where he resisted a strong late challenge from a Jaguar E-type to take a class win after setting a fastest lap in 52.4 secs, 92.75 mph.

Morgan interest in the West Essex C.C. Snetterton race meeting on October 10 centred mainly on a 10-lap combined-classes event, which provided an overall win for David Ham's Lister-Jaguar. For Morgan drivers it was a race of seconds, Rob Wells being runner-up to Ham in his Plus-8, while Bryan Harvey took second place in the 2,000 cc class with his 4-4 and Brian Yates was second in the 1,600 cc class with another 4-4. Luckiest Morgan driver of all, though, was Bob Stuart, who escaped unhurt from his road-going Plus-8 after rolling it up the bank at Russell on the penultimate lap.

The 10-lap production sports car race at the B.R.S.C.C. meeting at Oulton Park, on October 16, provided yet another easy win for Chris Meek and his Elan, but there was a fine battle for second place between Bill Wykeham in his Plus-8 and Rod Gretton in his 3-litre TVR, which scraped home ahead of the Morgan by 0.4 sec. Behind them another battle between Tony Brewer in his Britten 4-4 and Gerry Brown in his MGB ended at Old Hall when they became involved with a back marker, all three cars crashing quite heavily. Tony was lucky to escape unhurt, but Brown required hospital treatment.

Although Morgan drivers failed to win a championship this season, they finished the year with honour, Chris Hampshire being runner-up to Chris Alford (TVR) in the £2,000 to £3,000 class of the Euro-Burgess Southern League Production Sports Car Championship, and Tony Brewer and his 4-4 being runners-up to Alford in the Direct Tapes Championship, while despite his early-season crash at Oulton Park, Robin Gray still finished third in the

B.A.R.C. Modified Sports Car Championship.

1977

There were mixed fortunes for Morgan drivers at Silverstone during March, Rob Wells and Chris Stapleton having to give best to a Europa and a TVR 3000M in the production sports car race on March 20, but having a fine battle in their Plus-8s for third and fourth places, which was resolved on the last lap when Chris' car was baulked by a back marker, enabling Rob to build his lead to 14 secs across the line. The following weekend, Mary Lindsay took her Plus-8 to a 13-secs victory in a seven-lap scratch race at the Eight Clubs meeting, but Gordon Dennis found his Plus-8 heavily handicapped in a subsequent race and could only managed fifth place, while Patrick Keen and his Plus-8 took one of the major prizes in the first of the 20-minute high-speed trials.

At the Easter Monday meeting at Castle Combe Robin Gray made the best start in the second round of the B.R.S.C.C. Modsports Championship, but he left the track briefly at Quarry first time round, which allowed two Elans through, and he only regained one place on the last lap when one of the Lotuses caught fire. He also won his class and set the fastest lap time of 1 min 11.8 secs, 92.26 mph.

The Silverstone Production Sports Car Championship was staged at several circuits, the second round being at Brands Hatch, on May 1, when Charles Morgan in his Plus-8 chased Chris Meek's Europa hard to finish a good second, and Bruce Stapleton might well have finished third but for a last-lap spin, which dropped him behind a TVR. In the next round of the contest, at Oulton Park on May 19, it looked as though Bill Wykeham had finally got the measure of the Meek Europa with his Morris Stapleton Plus-8 until it broke its fan belt and retired from the lead on the fifth lap. The two drivers met again at Brands Hatch on June 5, when Meek had a comfortable win by half a minute over Bill, who spent most of the race fighting off another Europa until it crashed at Paddock, letting Rob Wells' Plus-8 through to third place. In the smaller class Tony Brewer's 4-4 finished third behind a TR7 and a Ginetta.

The Lotus-Morgan battle continued at Silverstone, on July 4, when Charles Morgan managed to lead until the eighth lap, when the Europa swept by and went on to win by 7.2 secs, while the previous day Bill Wykeham's car continued its insatiable appetite for fan belts by consuming one on the second lap of a Modsports race at the B.M.R.M.C. meeting at Donington, having led the race initially until being pushed out of the lead at Red Gate. Patrick Keen missed a gear at this spot, but he recovered well and had worked his way back up to second place by half-distance, to finish behind a Jaguar V-12 E-type. Patrick went on to win a 10-lap race for Morgans, 11.6 secs ahead of John Berry in his lightweight 4-4, with Chris Cooke third in another 4-4 and Gordon Dennis fourth in his Plus-8. Four days later an evening meeting at Donington brought a great win for Patrick Keen in the 10-lap Modsports race over a pair of Jaguar E-types to reverse the results of the previous meeting.

The following day Bill Wykeham's Plus-8 ate yet another fan belt, this time at Castle Combe, where it had been leading for three laps after a daring overtaking manoeuvre at Camp on lap 2, but things went better for him at Brands Hatch, on July 24. He was shown a black flag on the second lap when his exhaust started to flap in the wind, but apparently he failed to see it until lap 7, by which time he had built up a useful lead in his class; he then made a quick stop for the offending pipe to be wrenched off, rejoined having lost only one place and went on to finish second in class and third overall.

The Golden Anniversary of the Nurburgring was celebrated on the weekend of August 13-14 with a programme of 12 races, all but two of them for cars, and each divided into two five-lap heats, one on each day. Unfortunately, in the first event in which three Morgans featured, two were written off when Andy Garlick's Plus-4 and M. Lucassen's Dutch-entered car collided on the North Curve and Andy was taken to hospital with concussion. It was then left to John MacDonald to uphold Morgan honour, which he did by winning the first heat after the leading Porsche had left the track. However, the following day he had engine problems and had to limp round for the entire race, but even so was able to claim a class win overall.

The following weekend, at Oulton Park, Rob Wells and Bill Wykeham in their Plus-8s were matched against Chris Meek's Europa Special and Colin Blower's TVR 3000M once more, and things went well until the penultimate lap, when Bill, having led most of the way, spun at Lodge and dropped to fifth place. Meek slipped through to lead while everyone else slowed to avoid the gyrating Morgan, and Rob was just beaten into third place by 0.4 sec by Blower.

It was a similar story the following day at Mallory Park, when Rob Wells took over the lead from John Kent's Europa on the second lap and stayed in front until he spun off on the last lap, allowing the Europa through to win, closely followed by Blower's TVR, with Bruce Stapleton in third place with his Plus-8. However Rob claimed the fastest lap at 1 min 4.3 secs, 75.58 mph.

The Bentley D.C. annual Silverstone meeting took place on August 27 and included an all-comers' race involving some strange handicapping which resulted in Phil Hornby (Plus-8) being awarded fourth place as the highest Morgan finisher although his car had been 20th across the line at the finish. In fact, the first three Morgans to finish were the Plus-8s of Peter Garland (first) and Rob Wells (third) and the 4-4 of Alan Kennedy (fourth), and they were followed by D. Morris' Plus-8 (sixth), Mary Lindsay's Plus-8 (ninth) and Brian Yates' 4-4 (13th).

A 10-lap Morgan-only race was much easier to follow and was won by Chris Cooke and his 4-4, nearly 12 secs ahead of Bruce Stapleton's Plus-8 with Rob Wells' Plus-8 a further 0.4 sec away in third place amongst the 11 finishers out of 16 starters. Next came another all-comers' race in which Leigh Sebba drove his 4-4 very determinedly to snatch second place to an Elva Courier, just 0.8 sec ahead of a Le Mans Aston Martin, while in a final scratch race Bill Wykeham finished second to a Lister-Jaguar in his Plus-8, with Mary Lindsay's similar car ninth.

The following day Rob Wells and Bill Wykeham moved on to Snetterton to finish second and fourth in another round of the Certina Watches production sports car contest, split by Colin Blower's TVR. Victory went to Chris Meek's Europa again after a controversial incident on the third lap when the Lotus literally pushed Bill Wykeham's car off the track and into the fields, and then cut across the track to bump Rob Wells' car off as well. That no protests were lodged is an indication of the sporting attitude which generally prevailed in this class of racing.

The next day Rob had his revenge when he won a championship race over 10 laps at Silverstone and Meek's Lotus ran out of track at Copse, leaving a TVR to take second place. The two met again at Donington, on September 11, when Wells was barged off the track at Redgate and later ran into the sand at Old Hairpin in his efforts to make up the lost ground. Bob Stuart then took up the Morgan challenge, but lost his third place when his Plus-8 boiled on lap 7. Meek went on to win, and again Wells decided not to protest, although an MGB driver decided to challenge Meek's driving, but

John MacDonald, photographed by Graham Murrell at Silverstone as he steers his Plus-4 one-handed through Woodcote during the 1978 Bentley D.C. meeting.

Below left: John Millbank on the same day in his mildly tuned and essentially road-going 4-4 chasing an Aston Martin. Below: Peter Morgan looks slightly bemused as he discusses with Chris Cooke the latter's highly modified 4-4 which won the all-Morgan race at the Bentley D.C.'s 1978 Silverstone meeting. (Photograph by Graham Murrell.)

had his protest turned down.

A week later the battle was rejoined at Snetterton, and at Riches on lap 6 Rob Wells' car was elbowed off the track yet again. The Lotus had been chasing the Plus-8s of Wells and Wykeham and Blower's TVR, and having passed the TVR as Blower was searching for a way through back markers it hit Wells' car, causing it to spin, and Rob had to walk back to the pits. Next time round Blower pulled into his pit, conferred with Rob, and withdrew from the race, while with some superb driving Bill Wykeham managed to out-wit Meek and hold on to the lead at the chequered flag, though the two were credited with the same time. Several protests flew around afterwards, but apparently none was upheld.

The final round, on October 1, would decide the outcome of the Silverstone Production Sports Car Championship between Chris Meek and his Europa and Howard Johnson in his Austin-Healey Sprite, the two starting from pole position and the third row, respectively. But it was not to be Meek's day, and he pulled off with ignition failure on the first lap while Johnson drove steadily to finish second in his class to take the title. Rob Wells had a good race to finish second to Colin Blower's TVR and seventh in the championship, while Bruce Stapleton was fifth in the race in the other Plus-8.

By now protests were thoroughly marring this previously enjoyable type of racing and things got so bad at Donington on October 2 that 16 drivers, allegedly tired of Meek's constant questioning of the legality of their cars and of his own driving tactics, refused to race if he was allowed to start, but it was all smoothed out at a meeting before a B.R.S.C.C. official, the protests were withdrawn, and the race took place, Meek emerging the winner from Wykeham, but it was clear that the R.A.C. would have to step in and restore some order to the production sports car scene.

The final round of the Certina series took place at Donington on October 30, but neither Wykeham nor Wells was present and Meek's race ended in mechanical failure, which meant that once again he was runner-up in a championship, while Bill and Rob were fifth and 10th respectively.

1978

Aleybars was another sponsor's name to be linked with a production sports car championship, and the first round, at the B.R.S.C.C.

Castle Combe meeting, on Easter Monday, was to prove to be a two-car race from the start, between Colin Blower's TVR and Bill Wykeham's Plus-8, which finished 3.3 secs behind it. Anthony Palmer, the only other Morgan driver, fought and won a six-car battle for fifth place by half-distance, then was kept busy defending his hard-won position.

The next Aleybars round, at Donington on April 9, was to be a memorable race for Charles Morgan. Drama began for him on the front row of the grid when he noticed a leaking fuel line a few minutes from the start, but he managed a repair in time and he shot off into the lead, only to be outbraked by Blower's TVR and Wykeham's Plus-8 on the approach to the Park Chicane. By lap 4 the two leaders were hard at it, first one then the other taking turns to set the pace until, on lap 9 with one to go, the TVR passed the Morgan on Starkey's straight, Bill tried to counter-attack under braking into Park, the two cars touched and they both spun off. Charles Morgan, who had been keeping in touch, was able to slip through to claim his first ever race win in his Plus-8, and Colin recovered first to claim second place in front of Bill, who had set a new class record at 1 min 28.0 secs, 80.07 mph.

A week later, for the next championship race at Silverstone, Charles Morgan came close to claiming a second victory. He had led from the start, then Blower's TVR came through on the inside at Woodcote on lap 2, but in trying to regain the lead at Copse Charles ran wide on to the grass and was unable to make up his lost ground, despite a new lap record at 1 min 7.0 secs, 86.40 mph. Bill Wykeham came home a comfortable third, and fourth was Anthony Palmer, who gave a fine display at the wheel of his Plus-8 in holding off a determinedly driven Lotus Europa Special.

Morgan Plus-8s were to take the first three places in a 10-lap D.B. Motors-sponsored race at Silverstone, on May 1, in the order Charles Morgan, Bruce Stapleton and Rob Stuart, but not without a strong challenge from Colin Blower's TVR. Colin had been pressing Bruce hard for second place when the Morgan spun at Becketts on lap 4, but a few laps later the TVR spun at the same spot and dropped two places. Bruce's second place was accompanied by a new fastest lap in 1 min 6.73 secs, 86.75 mph.

Perhaps the most exciting Aleybars race of the season came at Snetterton, on May 7, when Bill Wykeham's Plus-8 and Colin Blower's TVR alternated in the lead for eight of the 10 laps, hotly

Peter Askew competing in his Modsports 4-4, now sporting a full-width front apron, at the Bentley D.C.'s Silverstone meeting in 1979, when he was photographed by Fred Scatley.

Bryan Harvey seems shy of Graham Murrell's camera as he waits in the Silverstone pit road for his next stint in the 1976 six-hours relay race.

pursued by Charles Morgan's Plus-8. Then, as the first two cars were baulked by a back marker, Charles tried to pass them at Riches, failed, and tried harder at Sear, only to spin, and delay Bill Wykeham. This allowed Colin back into first place with the TVR, and he was followed across the line by Bill and Charles. However, Bill had his revenge at Croft the following week, when he led the TVR from start to finish to win by almost 2 secs.

The new D.B. Motors round, at Oulton Park on May 20, proved disastrous for Morgan drivers, Charles having an argument with the railway sleepers at Old Hall while trying for a fast practice lap, which put him out of the race, and Bruce Stapleton having a similar accident at the same spot when challenging for second place in the race, which was won by Blower's TVR.

The following day there was a Motortune-sponsored race for Porsches at the Aston Martin O.C.'s meeting at Brands Hatch, to which several other makes of car were admitted in order to make up the numbers. Amongst them was a Plus-4, which had been brought all the way from Holland by Michael Lucassen, and he made the journey well worthwhile by leading all the way to beat the second-placed Porsche 356 by 16 secs, a fine achievement, even though the driver of the best-placed Porsche received more prize money.

The Whit Monday meeting at Oulton Park included another Aleybars race for production sports cars over 61 laps for a total distance of 100 miles, and Rob Wells of Libramotive, who had worked wonders on Charles Morgan's wrecked car to have it ready in time, was rewarded with a drive as Charles could not be present himself. The race turned out to be a comparatively quiet affair, John Kent moving into the lead with his Europa Special when Colin Blower made a refuelling stop in his TVR around half-distance. Behind them, Anthony Palmer and Rob Wells had been leading the rest of the field in their Plus-8s, and towards the end of the race Blower joined them following his quick stop. Both Wells and Blower passed Palmer, their battle for second place finally being won by Bob, although his Plus-8 was too far behind the winning Lotus to threaten its first place. Poor Bill Wykeham's race ended in front of the pits shortly before the end, although he was classified sixth in class.

Six class records were broken on June 18 at the B.A.R.C. hill-climb at Loton Park, one of the most interesting battles being in the marque sports car class where the record first went to a Porsche Carrera, then was passed to the Plus-8 of Peter Garland, who improved on his second run to leave the figure at 62.71 secs. On the same afternoon, another D.B. Motors race at Silverstone brought a repeat of the first round with Morgans in the first three places after a tough battle. Charles Morgan led for the first half of the race, then Colin Blower (TVR) and Bruce Stapleton (Plus-8) went by and the order remained the same until the last lap. Going into Woodcote Blower seemed to have the race in his pocket, but Stapleton left his braking extremely late and a surprised Blower spun off into the sleepers, allowing Charles Morgan and Anthony Palmer to finish second and third behind Stapleton, who was the first to commiserate with Blower after the race. Colin's car was not badly damaged and was in action again the following week at Brands Hatch, where once again Morgans finished in the first three places in the order Bill Wykeham, Charles Morgan and Anthony Palmer.

A B.M.R.M.C. meeting at Donington, on July 1, included a special Morgan race for which 14 cars arrived on the grid, one driven by Nils-Erik Norsher, from Denmark. Patrick Keen (Plus-8) made a slow start from the front row through missing the lights, which let Alan Kennedy and David Rutherford through to lead in their 4-4s, but the Plus-8 was up into first place by lap 3, ahead of Rutherford, while Peter Garland was making excellent progress through the field having started on the back row because he had practised out of session, and he went on to finish third, 5 secs behind Rutherford.

Meanwhile, down at Castle Combe, the next round of the Aleybars Championship had developed into a three-car race with the Plus-8s of Bill Wykeham and Charles Morgan and Colin Blower's TVR. By lap 4 Blower had managed to pass both Morgans, but Bill soon fought back in front again and the lead changed twice more before Colin made a final vain effort to retake the lead on the last lap before settling for second place. Charles finished a long way back in third place, having spun at Camp on the last lap, while Anthony Palmer drove well to overcome a 10-second penalty for a jumped start and finish fourth.

The next time the production sports cars were in action again was on August 13, for the D.B. Motors race at Mallory Park, when Charles Morgan led from start to finish to beat Blower's TVR by 6 secs, with the Plus-8s of Bruce Stapleton and Anthony Palmer next across the line. The following weekend, at the B.M.R.M.C. meeting at Silverstone, all races were reduced from 10 to six laps following a

Rob Wells driving his Libra Motive Racing Plus-8 to a convincing victory at Thruxton in April, 1979, with his hood bulging under the pressure of air through the partly open side screen.

Two months later Rob Wells was in action again with MMC 11, this time at Donington. This is the car with which Charles Morgan won his 1978 Production Sports Car Championship, and which by 1979 had covered over 72,000 miles.

tragic accident resulting in the death of two marshals on the first lap of the Modsports race, and in the re-run race Chris Cooke finished third overall in his special-bodied lightweight 4-4, while Patrick Keen and Norman Stechman were second and third with their Plus-8s in the over-2,000 cc class. In a later Porsche-Morgan challenge race a great battle developed between Cooke in his 4-4 and Charles Morgan, who took the lead in his Plus-8, Chris's final effort to get past bringing the crowd to their feet as he spun his car in the final yards and crossed the finishing line on the grass travelling backwards, just 0.7 sec behind! A Porsche Carrera RS just edged past Patrick Keen's Plus-8 for third place, and David Rutherford's class-winning 4-4 was fifth.

Morgans contested four of the nine races at the Bentley D.C. Silverstone meeting on August 26, including the first handicap event which was led home by Alan Kennedy, having his first drive in his ex-David Rutherford lightweight 4-4, followed by an AC Cobra and Peter Garland in his Plus-8. The Morgan S.C.C.'s 10-lap scratch race attracted 17 starters and was led throughout by Chris Cooke, whose 4-4 finished with a margin of 12 secs over Peter Garland's Plus-8, which finally won a race-long battle with David Rutherford's twin-cam lightweight 4-4. Alan Kennedy (4-4), Norman Stechman (Plus-8) and John MacDonald (Plus-4 Super Sports) ran nose-to-tail most of the way before crossing the line in that order. Terry Garland later emerged the winner of a confusing handicap race involving 26 cars, while John Millbank led a Porsche 356 across the line by 0.5 sec for second place, and in a final scratch race Patrick Keen finished second in his Plus-8 to the winning AC Cobra, while David Rutherford's 4-4 was fourth behind a second Cobra.

On the same day at Donington the D.B. Motors race, over 10 laps, provided Charles Morgan with a runaway victory in his Libramotive-prepared Plus-8 (MMC 11), ahead of Anthony Palmer in his Plus-8, which went into second place when Colin Blower had a huge spin in his TVR at Old Hairpin on the penultimate lap before recovering to finish third. Bruce Stapleton was fourth, despite an ignition problem, after a fine drive through the field after a spin at Coppice on the first lap. He had cured the problem in time for the next round, at Silverstone, two days later, but again it was Charles Morgan who scored the victory, after losing the lead to Blower's TVR on lap 2 and regaining it three laps later. This time Bruce Stapleton earned third place.

The Donington Racing Club held their inaugural meeting on September 3, which included a 10-lap race for production sports cars in which Bill Wykeham and Anthony Palmer and their Plus-8s had to give best to Blower's TVR, after they had led it initially. On lap 8 both Wykeham and Blower spun at Park, and Palmer moved into second place before the TVR got going again, but as the two Morgans entered Park for the last time they ran into trouble, and Blower seized the opportunity to slip through into the lead as they sorted themselves out to finish 2 secs ahead of Wykeham with Palmer a close third. Earlier on Rob Wells had ended up in the sand at the chicane after a battle for fourth place.

Charles Morgan finished a full 14 secs ahead of Blower's TVR in the next D.B. Motors round, at Thruxton on September 10, having led all the way, the TVR taking Bruce Stapleton's Plus-8 on the last lap, which in turn was almost caught on the line by Anthony Palmer's car. In the course of his runaway win Charles set a new class lap record at 1 min 35.45 secs, 88.85 mph.

Two weeks later, at Silverstone, Blower led for three laps until he spun at Becketts, which let Charles Morgan through for another victory, while Colin took no less than 3.3 secs off the lap record in his climb back to second place, while Bruce Stapleton and Anthony Palmer were only 0.44 sec apart at the finish in third and fourth places. The next day Charles continued his winning run with another victory over the TVR at Cadwell Park, this time with Bill Wykeham taking third place.

The highly popular 750 M.C.'s six-hours relay race, held on this occasion at Donington on October 7, produced a magnificent result for Morgan drivers, the Anglemog Saxon team and the Anglemog Viking team each scoring 264 laps, one more than the third placed Chanton 750F team, the Saxons narrowly winning the handicap challenge award. As this event so typified the enjoyment to be derived from a major success at club level I have drawn on the words which Andy Downs and Bob Northover, who managed the two Morgan teams, wrote afterwards for the Morgan S.C.C.'s *Miscellany*. They will be found in the next chapter, amongst other items from the M.S.C.C. archives.

On October 21 night racing returned to Britain at Snetterton, when a two-hours race was divided into two parts, the second taking place in darkness, the 22 entries being divided into modified saloon, production saloon and production sports car categories. A failure of

Bill Wykeham competing in a Donington G.T. Championship race in the Plus-8 which Morris Stapleton Motors built to Group 4 specification for the 1979 season. (Photograph by John Gaisford.)

The same car taking part in the World Championship of Makes six-hours race at Brands Hatch in August, 1979, with Bill Wykeham taking over from John Spero as the team mechanics refuel the car, clean the screen and check tyre temperatures as manager Mike Wykeham looks on.

the marshals' telephone system brought the first race to an end after 35 minutes, but the night race ran its full distance, and in the final order Bill Wykeham and Bruce Stapleton were placed third overall and had won their category, while Anthony Palmer was placed second in the category, all of them in Plus-8s.

The following weekend Snetterton provided the scene for a runaway victory in a members' handicap race organized by the Combined One Make C.C. for Norman Stechman and his Plus-8, while a long way behind Mary Lindsay and her Plus-8 were beaten by only 0.6 sec into second place by a Porsche 914S.

It had been a very good year for Morgans in the production sports car field, and when the points were totted up, Charles Morgan was the overall winner of the D.B. Motors Championship, and Bruce Stapleton was sixth overall and third in his class, while in the Aleybars Championship Bill Wykeham was second overall and a class-winner, with Charles Morgan taking third place in the class.

1979

For the new season D.B. Motors were to share joint sponsorship with *Cars and Car Conversions* for one production sports car championship, while the C.A.V. name was linked to another. The opening round of the D.B./C.C.C. contest took place at Thruxton on April 1, when Rob Wells in his Libramotive Plus-8 and Colin Blower in his TVR had an exciting battle for the lead, their positions changing constantly until eventually Rob managed to cross the line 0.3 sec ahead.

The same drivers dominated the C.A.V. race at the B.R.S.C.C. meeting at Snetterton, on Easter Sunday, Rob never being seriously challenged this time and winning by 4 secs, while at the D.B./C.C.C. round at Brands Hatch a week later the same finishing order persisted for the third time, the gap being 1.83 secs.

Charles Morgan encountered clutch trouble during practice at Oulton Park for the Bank Holiday Monday meeting on May 29, and Rob Wells and his mechanic Andy Adamou worked in pouring rain to effect a temporary repair. Charles was handed back the car for the race with a strong warning to use the clutch as little as possible, but his steady drive was rewarded when Colin Blower made an excursion on to the grass on lap 7 and Charles was able to slip through to an unexpected victory.

On June 17 Rob Wells had another easy win in a D.B./C.C.C.

round at Silverstone, ahead of John Kent's TVR, while Malcolm Paul and Bob Stuart fought a real battle for third place, Malcolm getting the verdict by 0.4 sec at the end of an exciting race.

An interesting experiment took place at Donington on July 21-22 when the Historic S.C.C. and the B.A.R.C. combined to organize a meeting sponsored by *Thoroughbred & Classic Cars* magazine, who also staged a *concours d'elegance* to run alongside it. In the race for historic sports cars Michael Lucassen had an easy win in the 1,651-1,700 cc class with his Plus-4 Super Sports, and the following day he took a second victory, at 71.74 mph, in a race for road-going production, vintage and P.V.T. sports cars.

In the next round of the C.A.V. Championship, at Cadwell Park on July 22, Charles Morgan was a comfortable class winner and finished sixth overall in a race in which production sports cars competed against Modsports cars and special saloons. He then went on to Snetterton, on July 29, when he celebrated his birthday with another easy win, averaging 82.13 mph and finishing 16.6 secs ahead of the field. But the following weekend the Plus-8 which he had shared with Rob Wells and which had proved so reliable blew up at Silverstone, and for the Mallory Park round on August 26 Charles was lent Malcolm Paul's car, which he used to good effect, finishing second to John Kent's TVR after a long scrap to maintain his challenge in the championship.

When a Plus-8 lined up on the starting grid at Brands Hatch on August 5 for the ninth round in the World Championship of Makes it was the first time that a Morgan had appeared in a long-distance international race since 1968. It was the Stapleton Motors car, and had been built to the specification worked out by Bruce Stapleton and Bill Wykeham and homologated into Group 4. John Spero joined Brian Classic and Bill Wykeham to share the driving, Bruce Stapleton having to step down at the last moment because of a family tragedy. Mike Wykeham acted as team manager and Bruno Pericardi was technical adviser. The car ran like clockwork in the race, apart from one very alarming moment when Bill Wykeham heard a sound like a gunshot followed by a rumbling brake pedal as he descended Dingle Dell. But an unscheduled pit stop failed to diagnose the cause, and so the drivers continued, using high gears as much as possible and with the minimum of braking. Strangely, their times continued to fall, so the 'Easy' sign was held out and the car came home 18th of the 32 starters and eighth in Group 4, having

The Stapleton brothers' racing Plus-8 gleaming in the rain on display at 'MOG 79' and making a vivid contrast with the Le Mans replica 4-4 alongside it.

'MOG 79' was also one of the rare occasions when Charles Morgan's Plus-8 was at a standstill long enough to be photographed. The neat spare wheel cover is an ideal place for delivering the Morgan message!

beaten four Porsches and a BMW amongst the finishers. It was a magnificent effort, and it must have given the team invaluable experience should they decide to pursue their thoughts of a return to Le Mans during the 1980s.

At the Bentley D.C.'s Silverstone meeting on August 25 the programme, as usual, began with a handicap race in which Malcolm Paul's Plus-8 finished a close second to the winning Lister-Jaguar with Norman Stechman's Plus-8 in third place. The Morgan S.C.C.'s 10-lap scratch race was for the Morris Stapleton Trophy, and it was Bruce Stapleton in his specially developed Plus-8 who was soon setting the pace. Peter Askew, making a racing comeback after an absence of eight years, kept his Modsports 4-4 in close contact during the opening laps, but then Bruce steadily forged ahead until he was about half a lap ahead on the last lap, but rather than win his own trophy he pulled up short of the line to allow Peter to cross the line first, 11.4 secs ahead of Peter Garland's Plus-8, with Malcolm Paul in third place. D. J. Hodgson was the winner of the three-wheeler class which was incorporated into the race.

Mrs. Vivien Morgan, Charles' wife, gained a very creditable third place and set the fastest lap in 1 min 16.4 secs, 75.77 mph, in a 10-lap all-comers' race later in the meeting, and in the final event John MacDonald and his supercharged Plus-8 had the crowd on their feet when, having pulled out a comfortable lead, he eased off only to find an AC Cobra closing fast, and in the end he won by just 0.9 sec, with Norman Stechman third in his Plus-8. The following month, Peter Askew went to Goodwood for the Combined One Make C.C.'s challenge sprint and with his 4-4 set the fastest time by a member of the Harrow and District M.C. to claim the Wimsett Trophy.

Meanwhile, back at Silverstone on August 27, Rob Wells, driving a Plus-8 borrowed from Bob Stuart, scored a narrow but useful victory over Malcolm Paul's Plus-8 in another round of the D.B./C.C.C. series, with John Kent's TVR chasing them hard to the line after an earlier spin at Becketts, while the following day, at Mallory Park, it was Charles Morgan's turn to borrow a car, this time from Malcolm Paul, as his own engine had blown up at Silverstone the previous day. Again he used it well, to finish just 0.5 sec behind John Kent's winning TVR in the C.A.V. Championship race, while Steve Cole was a close fourth in another Plus-8, behind Tony Hill's TR7. The next important date for Rob Wells was September 9, when he scored a decisive win at Mallory Park in his borrowed Plus-8 over Colin Blower's TVR, with Malcolm Paul's Plus-8 in third place in the D.B./C.C.C. race.

The final round of the D.B./C.C.C. Championship took place at Silverstone on October 7, when Rob Wells needed only one point to become Class A Champion. His race began well as he romped into the lead, but he suddenly lost all his oil pressure on lap 4, so he pulled off the track and waited until the rest of the field went by for the last time then limped across the line to collect the necessary point for finishing. The cause of the trouble had been a broken rocker-arm.

Two weeks later the final round of the C.A.V. Championship took place at the B.R.S.C.C. Midland Centre's championship finals meeting at Mallory Park, although all the classes had already been decided, and appropriately each class would fall in the race to the new champion. Charles Morgan ended his season in fine style, winning easily at 86.47 mph and equalling the class lap record at 88.04 mph, but Malcolm Paul was unable to recover from a bad start and could only finish fourth.

The Plus-8 which Charles Morgan and Rob Wells had shared for the two championships had served them very well indeed, Charles being the C.A.V. Champion in Class A and finishing third overall with 48 points, while Rob was D.B. Motors/C.C.C. Champion in Class A and second overall with 31 points. A worthy record.

Icy conditions greeted competitors for the traditional Boxing Day meeting at Brands Hatch, where the entry included the Plus-8s of Bill Wykeham (in Patrick Keen's car) and Malcolm Paul for the production sports car race. Bill had some very interesting moments in his race with a TR7, which went ahead on the last lap to win, while Malcolm drove a sensible race into third place to conclude another very good season for Morgans.

To all those whose exploits have gone unrecorded in this chapter — and I know there must be many of them — I can only apologise and hope that they will appreciate the difficulties of keeping track of so many cars, drivers, clubs, venues and events in which Morgans of one type or another have featured. Long may they continue to do so as this great sports car moves into the 1980s.

Chapter 3

The Morgan Sports Car Club

Any motor club which has been in existence for a long time has probably suffered its setbacks and perhaps its near-collapse in its early years. The Morgan 4-4 Club, as the Morgan Sports Car Club was once known in its formative years, was no exception. However, with the enthusiasm and even on occasions the financial assistance of a few of the more devout members, the Club staggered its way through its early crises to become, today, one of the largest one-make clubs in the world, with a membership of almost 1,200.

As the Club grew, so did its reputation in all forms of motor sport, and in the hey-days of rallies, sprints, driving tests, etc, hardly a week passed without the Club Secretary receiving invitations to enter teams in some event or another.

In order to link the membership, a club magazine was founded, this taking the form of a monthly newsletter called the *Miscellany* with a larger quarterly edition produced under the title *Motoring and Morgans*. Unfortunately, in those early days it proved quite a struggle, and it was no fault of the editors, of whom there have been many over the years, that editions failed to appear at their planned regular intervals. The problem was a shortage of printable material, for it was scarcely worthwhile sending out a one-page newsletter. But gradually the membership responded and in return they can now look back on more than 10 years of regular publication, while the quality of the production has increased as well, the *Miscellany* now looking a very professionally produced magazine, complete with illustrations.

The membership of the Club is divided into full, associate and overseas members, while following an Annual General Meeting of the Club on April 30, 1955, family membership became available under which the benefits of membership were extended to a member's immediate family on payment of the appropriate subscription.

As the membership increased, so did the complaints about the long distances which some members had to travel in order to attend the Noggins and Natters held in the Midlands. To overcome this problem, Richard Upshall, with the committee's blessing, organized a meeting in the London area late in 1959 with the idea of forming a London Centre. However, the project was short-lived, due to lack of support, and it was not until October 1965 that a committee was formed at an inaugural London Centre meeting held at the garage premises of W. Griffiths, in Willesden. This time it was a great success, and the London Centre, now one of 20 covering nearly all the U.K., has never looked back. Each Centre has its own Secretary and can organize social and competitive events independently of the main Club, while all Centre activities are open to any M.S.C.C. member, regardless of where they may live, visitors from one Centre always being most welcome at others.

An important Morgan milestone was the company's Golden Jubilee, which the Club celebrated on July 30, 1960 at Beaulieu Motor Museum with a rally and *concours,* the latter being judged by Mr. Acock of Bowman and Acock, Peter Morgan and Michael Sedgwick, at that time the Curator of the Museum. In those days the museum was a small one, housed in various outbuildings surrounding Palace House, and a far cry from the impressive National Motor Museum and its attending complex, which was opened in 1972 and attracts so many thousands of visitors every year.

The first attempt to change the name of the Club was made in August 1962, when a member from Canada proposed that the name be changed to the Morgan Owners' Club, which seemed to echo the thoughts of a number of home-based members, mainly Plus-4 owners. However, when the committee decided to hold a postal vote of members, a large majority opted to keep the original name, and the subject was not raised again until 1968. Members were invited to air their views through the pages of the *Miscellany,* but opinion seemed to be evenly divided, so the question was deferred again for 18 months. Then, in November 1969, a postal referendum took place in which 317 of the 451 voting papers sent out were returned completed. To the question whether or not members wished the Club's name to be changed, 195 replied 'Yes' and 122 'No'. To the subsequent question, which of three names would members prefer in the event of a change, the scoring was: Morgan Car Club — 121 votes; Morgan 4-Wheeler Club — 39 votes; Morgan Sports Car Club — 136 votes. The remaining 21 papers were either spoilt or unanswered. The Club was renamed from January 1, 1971 as The Morgan Sports Car Club.

For the 60th Anniversary of the Morgan Motor Company a commemorative meeting was staged jointly in June 1970 by the Morgan 4-4 Club and the Morgan Three-Wheeler Club (in its own Silver Jubilee year) at Prescott, the weekend comprising a speed hill-climb, a *concours* and a cavalcade up the hill. As far as possible, every year in the company's history was represented in the procession, which was led by the oldest known Morgan survivor at the time, a 1913 Runabout. Perfect weather helped to make it a marvellous weekend, at which the largest number of Morgans ever assembled in one place were gathered together, over 100 three-wheelers and well over 500 four-wheelers being present. As Peter Morgan remarked, 'How pleased father would have been'.

The next landmark for the Club was the formation of the 4-4 Series 1 and Plus-4 Registers in mid-1972 to provide, 'a means for owners to contact each other, a source of advice, data and information, help in obtaining spares, etc.' John Orton was the first Series 1 Registrar and Tim Cree the first Plus-4 Registrar. This was the birth of the Club's comprehensive spares and advisory service for members which now embraces a Series 1 Registrar and Technical Adviser, a Plus-4 Registrar and Technical Adviser, a Used Spares Registrar and a Librarian.

In 1973 I had the privilege of representing the Morgan Motor Company and the Morgan Sports Car Club in a Drive into Europe which was organized by a joint committee of officials of several leading car clubs, under the overall direction of Lord Montagu of Beaulieu to mark Britain's entry into the Common Market. It began at the Horse Guards Parade, in London, on January 6, where the Prime Minister inspected all the participating vehicles, and the route took us through Folkestone and Ostend to Brussels (where Jacques Elleboudt, the local Morgan agent, was one of many who clamoured to take a close look at my 1938 Le Mans 4-4), then on to Ghent and back home again via Ostend and Folkestone, two days later. It was a magnificent experience, with wonderful hospitality shown to us all the way, and a crowd estimated as between 250,000 and 400,000 turning out in Brussels to see the cavalcade of historic British cars. The only sour note was that we were harrassed by a crowd of anti-marketeers in Britain, and the Morgan was one of five cars to be sabotaged during a refreshment halt (I only just made the Sealink cross-channel ferry, and lost hours on the other side stripping down the fuel system to discover that sugar had been poured into the petrol). But this apart, it was a most enjoyable occasion, and I was honoured that my car, together with a three-wheeler, was chosen to represent Morgan on this historic event.

The 25th Anniversary of the Club was celebrated by several functions during the summer of 1976, a year which also marked 40 years of production of four-wheelers. The first event comprised a hill-climb, *concours* and cavalcade at Harewood, towards the end of May, then in July the Swedish Morgan O.C., also celebrating their own 10th Anniversary, sent a large contingent to Britain to coincide with the M.S.C.C.'s Curborough sprint meeting. Next came a special display of Morgans at the Biddenden Spectacular, in Kent, on August 7, where Peter Morgan was present, and where the guest of honour was to have been the Club's first Chairman, Dick Pritchard, who unfortunately had died some time earlier. Finally, there was a combined event with the Morgan Three-Wheeler Club at Shelsley Walsh, later in August, which attracted more than 200 Morgans to a hill-climb and *concours,* including a contingent from the Dutch club, who also donated some of the *concours* prizes.

In 1978, David Stretton-Smith put forward the idea of MOGAID, which is an international register of club members who are willing to assist any other member who breaks down in their area. Each member is issued with a list of names, addresses and telephone numbers which he can call upon for assistance if it is required. It is a splendid idea, which other one-make clubs might do well to copy.

The major annual gathering of the Club is entitled MOG, followed by the last two numerals of the year in which it is held, hence MOG 79, MOG 80, and so on. So far the gatherings have been staged at different locations around the country, with the appropriate local Centre being responsible for organization, which usually means arranging a *concours d'elegance*, gymkhana events and all the facilities necessary for a large gathering of members and their cars. As I write this, a major effort is being put in by a special joint committee of the M.S.C.C. and the Three-Wheeler Club to make MOG 80, at the National Motor Museum, Beaulieu, an event worthy of the 70th Anniversary of the Morgan Motor Company.

In the previous chapter I dealt at some length with the wide variety of events in which Morgans and their drivers have achieved competition success. Most of these were organized by other clubs, but the M.S.C.C. itself also has a considerable history of event organization, from races to production car trials, and from sprints to driving tests. But if members were asked to pick out one event which best illustrates the intense pride of Morgan owners when they challenge cars of other makes, I think many of them would name the 750 M.C.'s annual six-hours relay race, in which Morgans have achieved a fine record. Two events, in particular, remain in the memory of many Morgan enthusiasts, and I can do no better than quote the reports which appeared subsequently in the *Miscellany*, because in each case they were written by people right in the middle of the action.

The first event took place at Silverstone on August 11, 1962, when the Morgan team consisted of John McKechnie and his 4-4, Ray Meredith and Bob Duggan in their Plus-4s, and two more Plus-4s driven by Chris Pickard and Brian Redman, Pickard's being a standard Lawrence-tuned car, and Redman's a standard production Plus 80 with small brakes, but with 15-inch wheels and a 4.1:1 rear axle. Everything went well in practice except that both the Pickard and Redman cars lost oil through the breather cast into the petrol pump, which could easily be blocked-up. This is how Adrian Dence recalled what was to become 'the win that never was' in his article headed *An Inside Report:*

Practice was held on the Friday before race day, all drivers putting in some useful lapping except Bob Duggan, who practised in the morning of race day. The whole team went out in this last practice session, fastest lap going to Ray Meredith in 1 min 17 secs. This he considered could be improved upon with slightly less traffic. The other practice times ranged around the 1 min 21-22 secs mark, which was not terribly encouraging from Chris' and Bob's points of view. Bob was not too happy about his Cinturas, and Chris' car was not motoring as fast as a Lawrence-tuned car should. On the other hand, 1 min 22 secs is a highly creditable time for a 4-4, these cars possessing far less punch than the 2-litre model, as all Plus-4 owners must know. Brian is to be congratulated on pushing his old Plus-4 round in 1 min 21 secs, a time that must have placed a considerable strain on his inadequate brakes.

In order to make the best use of our handicap, the Team Manager decided that our best chance of success stood in sending Ray out first in order to get a good start, followed by the rest, who would circulate as fast as was consistent with safety and, most important, with as few pit stops as possible. It was anticipated that John and Ray would return the fastest lap speeds, so our handicap included a maximum of 120 laps between these two drivers. Accordingly, Ray's car was placed on the start with John as number 2. So far as the pit work was concerned, it was decided to leave the complicated maths involved in a handicap race of this kind to the organizers, and concentrate on calculating exactly how fast our drivers were going, and keep them informed of their lap speeds and number of laps. The temptation of trying to speed our drivers by signalling a slower lap than they had in fact covered was considered, but refrained from!

As 1 pm came nearer excitement mounted, and the prospect of six hours of racing in front of us produced something of the atmosphere to be found in the Le Mans 24-hours race. Five minutes before the start Tommy was still fussing over Ray's engine and to anyone who doesn't know Tommy, clad in Persil white, Morgan-emblazoned overalls, the prospect for the Morgans might have looked doubtful. However, all was well and the bonnet strap was finally tightened.

Two minutes to go, drivers on their spots, 24 cars lined expectantly across the track, the starter counts off the last seconds, the flag is up — two — one — down — the Six-Hours is on! Suddenly, all the cars are gone, except Ray's. Over-enthusiasm with the throttle has flooded the engine. A few seconds of desperate churning on the starter, John grabs for his crash helmet, Tommy and the Team Manager leap off the pit counter, a quick push, and he's off, the last two cylinders quickly joining in. Hardly an auspicious start, the only consolation being that six hours is a long time.

The field comes roaring through, Wrottesley's Lister accelerating fiercely in the lead. Ray obviously has not been flustered by his bad start as a standing lap in 1 min 20.3 secs demonstrates. For the next 10 laps he is baulked by slower cars, but thereafter he really starts motoring in earnest, most laps being completed in well under 1 min 17 secs. Three or four slower laps while he deals with Eric Brown's XK 120 of the Jaguar A team and once again lap times come tumbling down, the Morgan really sounding wonderful. A broad grin from Ray as he accelerates out of Woodcote ahead of an E-type, having out-cornered this co-called sports car. It was amusing to see Eric Brown accelerating out of Woodcote for lap after lap with the tail hanging well out, just collecting the big XK in time to give the thumbs-up sign to his pit.

Sixty laps after the start we are well placed and Ray is going like a train. The fuel board is shown to Ray, who gives a thumbs-up. Already most teams have changed cars and the Team Manager realises that the longer Ray can keep going the better. After 70 laps and 113 miles, Ray signals he is coming in. A quick pit stop and John's 4-4 is continuing the race. This really was a superb drive by Ray at an average of approximately 76 mph, putting us well up on handicap; fuel consumption — 12 mpg.

It soon became obvious that although John's car was lapping at a creditable speed (1 min 22-23 secs) and sounding marvellous, the greater the number of laps of the 120 maximum that Ray could cover — if you see what I mean — the greater would be our chance of winning. Accordingly, after 22 laps, John was called in and Chris went out with his Super Sports to settle down for a long spell. Meanwhile, Ray had a snooze and Tommy had a look at his car, which was still perfect, thanks to meticulous pre-race preparation by the Regal Garage racing department, Bromsgrove.

Chris settled down to lap in 1 min 20 secs, which was not too bad a time as the car sounded distinctly flat past the pits and had nothing like the bite of Ray's Tommy-tuned car. Surprisingly, after a mere 11 laps, Chris signalled he was coming in, the temperature gauge registering hot, so he anticipated trouble. Undue play in the dynamo bearings necessitated quick removal of the dynamo from my Plus-4

before Tommy reassessed that no breakdown was imminent with the original dynamo. A faulty temperature gauge was found to be the only trouble — it was an electrical type which when broken registered boiling!

Occasional glances at the track made sure that Brian in his elderly Plus-4 was still circulating, and returning to the pits I was amazed to find him keeping up a steady 1 min 20-21 secs. The 4.1 axle in his car had an appreciable effect on acceleration, and Brian changed into top long before the other Plus-4s. He was reaching 5,500 in top down the straight before braking for Woodcote, then from 100 to 50 in about 50 yards — quite a feat for drum brakes.

After a very praiseworthy drive lasting 46 laps, Bob Duggan took over after a total of three hours of racing, and soon he was lapping around the 1 min 20 secs mark, a time which, although not as fast as Bob had done, was explained by his tyres, which were not at their best in the dry. Our position in the race (by courtesy of *Autosport*) was second and gaining on the Jaguar B team, for which Fowles' XK120 was motoring steadily.

Having calculated that there were 28 laps of the 120 joint maximum to cover, Ray was woken up and asked if he would mind joining battle again. After Bob had covered 46 laps he was brought in and the maroon, wire-wheeled car once more upheld Morgan honours. After 26 laps, an observer informed us that the Morgan's undertray was likely to detach itself but, Tommy having satisfied himself that it wasn't, Ray was allowed to continue for a further two laps, despite the threat of the black flag.

The change-over between Ray and Chris Pickard, who had been brought out to finish the innings, was accomplished without incident, and out he went. By this time the two-laps start we had had on the nearest team — the Jaguars — was beginning to tell, and we were about half a lap in the lead. However, although we had thought that the Lister-Jaguar had done its full allowance of laps it was wheeled out and obvious preparations for a change in the Jaguar B pit were made. John McKechnie discovered that they had about half an hour of running time left with this car — which they sent out at approximately 6.30 pm. Chris Pickard, at this time with half a lap lead, was circulating regularly in 1 min 21 secs with occasional laps at 1 min 20 secs and one or two in 1 min 19 secs when the road was clear. The next team, the Lotuses, were about five laps behind, and being caught by the Jaguar A team, so were no menace to us, but

Above: The official badges of the parent Morgan club, before and after the name change. Above right: Not all M.S.C.C. competition activities are intended to be taken too seriously. At this field day the idea was to balance the car (in this case a Plus-8) on the see-saw keeping both ends of the planks clear of the ground for 10 seconds. If you think this sounds simple you should try it! Below right: 'El Patron' raising a laugh as he speaks at the M.S.C.C. annual dinner and dance in 1978. Beyond Peter Morgan are Arthur and Stephanie Neal, the Club Chairman and his lady, while in the foreground are the author, who was after-dinner speaker that evening, and his wife Janet.

then a very quick pit stop sent the Jaguar B team's Lister-Jaguar out to make up nearly a lap in 30 minutes. There was nothing we could do except wait for Wrottesley to have his usual shunt or spin, but he didn't; he drove very well and caught and passed Pickard to win the race for the Jaguar B Team.

Or did he? A few days later, Geoffrey Kramer, who had organized the lap-scoring team for the event, wrote a most apologetic letter to the Club in which he stated that after all the lap-scoring papers had been rechecked, certain errors had been noted (which had not been detected during the auditing on race day) and that in fact the Morgan team had won the event after all. The problem had arisen because key members of his regular lap-scoring team had been unavoidably absent, and their replacements had been found wanting for such a difficult lap-scoring assignment.

The motoring Press were informed of the changed results, and all teams were sent corrected results. However, the Jaguar D.C. protested that the amended results had been delivered outside the stipulated time limit of seven days, and therefore the original results should stand. A meeting of the concerned parties was arranged at the R.A.C. in Pall Mall, but when the Morgan contingent arrived, they were told by the hall porter that he knew of no such meeting, and so they went on their way. In fact the meeting was taking place, in the competitions department, but no-one had informed the porter! The upshot of all this was that the Jaguar remained the officially published winners, although the organizers had no doubt as to which team had really won. If nothing else, the upset prompted a tightening-up of lap-scoring arrangements, and no similar trouble has occurred since.

The other 750 M.C. Six-Hours relay race with fond Morgan memories had a much happier ending, as indicated in the previous chapter, for in 1978 the only query after the race at Donington was which of the two Morgan teams had won, the Anglemog Saxons or the Anglemog Vikings.

The Saxons team comprised Terry Garland, John Millbank, Bob Chaplin and Mike Duncan in 4-4s, Dave Saunter in a Plus-8 and Peter Evans in a Plus-4 Super Sports, all under the management of Andy Downes. The Vikings comprised Mary Lindsay, Pat Keen and Norman Stechman in Plus-8s, Andy Kennedy in a 4-4, John MacDonald in a Plus-4 and Andy Garlick in Patrick Keen's Plus-4, with Bob Northover their manager. First, here is how Andy Downes described the event to *Miscellany* readers:

The mist on the circuit was thick enough to postpone practice for an hour or so, but race afternoon promised to be fine. When practice finally got underway only three laps per car were required and all the Morgans completed this formality without mishaps. All too soon it was time to ensure that the first car was on the grid. Having decided to run Peter Evans' Plus-4 Super Sports to start with I rode with him on to the track and affixed the team sash to the bonnet. When Peter asked me how I wanted him to run, I told him to go out and enjoy himself. Having installed my timekeepers in pit 22 it was suddenly midday and the race was on.

Peter made a fine start, and from the onset was lapping quicker than he had ever done before at Donington. The other Morgan team were ahead of us on the road, but we had a more favourable handicap and the race was still young. On his eighth lap Peter's hard driving resulted in a spin, and this was repeated three laps later, but after that his driving was all I could have wished for — smooth, safe and consistent.

My tactics were simple — six hours, six cars, therefore one hour apiece. After 35 laps the first hour had passed and Peter came in to hand over to Dave Saunter in the Plus-8. The sash was quickly transferred, and Dave tore down the pit road, tyres squealing.

At the first hour, on the handicap, the Saxons lay eighth. Dave gave his stint all he'd got and lapped well under his best times on previous Donington visits. His nickname 'spinning Saunter' didn't seem applicable and after 70 laps the two-hour board brought the second stint to an end. Dave came into the pit-road at a phenomenal speed, locked all four wheels and slid to a halt exactly where I wanted him.

Another fine sash change saw the red 4-4 of John Millbank take up the challenge. With Dave's driving and the handicap beginning to unwind we had pulled up to fourth place, one third of a lap behind the Classic Sports Car Team and one lap ahead of the MG T Types. In his first six-hours race John's drive was faultless in every respect, and he took us to half-way without a single problem. Things were better than I could have hoped. John came in after doing 35 laps in his hour.

The standard 4-4 4-seater of Terry Garland went swiftly away for the fourth hour, this also being Terry's first six-hours. A fuming John Millbank stalked through the pit, having been dangerously nudged by a Porsche whilst completing his last lap. Damage turned out to be minimal, and John's face positively beamed once he learned that the Saxons had moved into second place in front of the 750 Motor Club. With the Vikings leading the Morgans were one-and-two.

Meanwhile, out on the tarmac, Terry showed himself a model of consistency and looked the part, peaked open-face helmet and goggles. When Terry came in at four hours, the Vikings had managed to increase their lead to over two laps.

Bob Chaplin in the 2-litre 4-4 left the pits, wheels spinning and tyres shrieking, and he soon had the bit between his teeth. At four-and-a-half hours Bob was going like a train. Then, ten minutes before he was due in, I had a visit from the Clerk of the Course. Apparently one of his observers reported that car 22C was consistently trying too hard whilst in close racing company. The report went on, 'on at least eight consecutive occasions he has exited from Red Gate with two or more wheels on the grass!' Initially the Clerk wanted me to bring Bob in for a caution, but he relaxed this request when he learned Bob's stint was almost up.

For the last hour Mike Duncan was the man upon which everything hinged, after one fifth and final sash change. Mike soon got into the groove, whilst Dave took up the position of reserve car in the pit garage. When Mike went out we had actually displaced the Vikings from their premier position. However, we didn't know this until half-way through the final hour. The positions at five-and-a-half hours were given at ten-to-six, and these showed us with a slender lead of one sixth of a lap from the Vikings. With five minutes to go a Morgan one-two looked on the cards, but we knew Mike had to stay ahead of Pat Keen's Plus-8 Modsports car to give Saxons victory. Pat, however, had other ideas, and he gained on us at the rate of over 13 seconds a lap!

When the flag finally came out we didn't know who'd got it, although I suspected that the Vikings had run out worthy winners. As the handicap results came over the Tannoy the cheers in pit 22 drowned out the announcement that our victory had been a scant 3 seconds. It was only afterwards we learned of the drama behind Mike's apparent trouble-free final session. With 15 minutes to go he out-braked a Midget into one of the corners, and instead of backing off the Midget kept coming and rammed the 4-4's offside. An astonished Mike Duncan glanced at his crumpled running board,

decided nothing was amiss, and pressed on without detriment to his final lap time!

And now, here is the Viking team's viewpoint as seen by Bob Northover:

Early morning fog meant that practice was delayed so that everyone was limited to only 3 laps practice when it finally cleared. However, this was enough for several problems to arise. Pat Keen's Modsports Plus-8 had a recurrence of a season-long problem — the oil left the engine in favour of the catch tank — and his mechanics set about trying yet another cure. Mary's road-going and much-raced Plus-8 needed new front brake pads. Alan, who was driving his blue Modsports car rather than the lightweight gold car seen at the Bentley Drivers' Club meeting, needed a tyre change. All in all the mechanics were kept busy in the horrifyingly short interval before the race started.

Arthur Neil was once again wearing the Assistant Team Manager's hat (and what a very odd hat it is, too!) and he was left to cope with all this excitement while I withdrew to the timekeepers' lair to try to persuade the handicapper to be more generous. He was unmoved by my pleas, but our handicap in truth seemed very fair at 47 credit laps over the scratch team of Porsche 911s.

When the flag dropped at noon Pat Keen led off for the Vikings in his black Plus-8. Everyone had their fingers crossed that a new oil breather mod would overcome the difficulty encountered in practice. The crossed fingers worked, because Pat survived his 20-minute stint and managed to pack an indecent number of laps into that short time. Alan Kennedy then took the sash and set off for a half-hour session. There was some doubt as to how long Alan's car could run since he only has a 4½-gallon tank and with a highly tuned twin-cam engine that obviously wasn't going to last long. However, our calculations were about right and Alan managed the half-hour with petrol to spare. He certainly had his fair share of excitement in that time as an engine blow-up in another team had liberally annointed the racing line with oil. Alan discovered this when his car refused to obey commands at the chicane and charged at the retaining wall. Thankfully, Alan regained control just in time to avoid contact.

Andy took over the sash from Alan, and had to cope with a track that was still very oily, and this in a car that he had never raced before. Despite these difficulties, Andy was circulating very consistently until caught out by the chicane, when he spun at the exit. Horror of horrors, the car stalled and would not restart. For what seemed like days, poor Andy sat in the middle of the track, while we in the pits went frantic. Finally, the Plus-4 sprang into life again and in fact a later study of the time sheets showed that only one minute was lost. It seemed much longer!

Unknown to us in the pits 'TOK' was running well, and Andy brought it in just before 1.30 pm to hand over the sash to Pat. Meanwhile, we had discovered that after one hour we lay fourth on handicap. Pat's car ran without problems for another 20 minutes, despite the fact that he had to patch a puncture in his slicks before going out. At about a quarter-to-two Norman took over the sash in his cream road-going Plus-8 to turn in a perfect hour's racing, lapping very quickly and consistently without any drama. For the first time in the race we could relax a little in the pits while Norman, who is in his first season of racing, reeled off a string of laps at 1 min 35 secs. To cap it all the handicap positions after two hours showed us to be in the lead! That put paid to the relaxed atmosphere in the pits; now everyone could sense the possibility of victory.

We held the lead at 2½ hours and still held it at 3 hours, when none other than the Anglemog Saxons were in second place. By this time John MacDonald had taken over the running and was maintaining the pace. However, the clutch in the Plus-4 was finding the task of handling power (the car developing 135 horsepower at the back wheels!) more than it could cope with and John was forced to come in at about 3.30 pm. Alan followed, and this time he had a less slippery track. He completed his share of the driving and then handed over to Andy.

Meanwhile, the MacDonald Plus-4 was having its clutch sorted-out, and when Andy came in John took his Plus-4 out again. Almost immediately the clutch ceased to function and John was circulating stuck in third gear for much of the time. Despite this he managed to lap very quickly, even producing a lap of 1 min 33 secs! Even with all the extra change-overs that we had had to make we still held the lead at 4.30 pm, although the Saxon team was closing fast.

Throughout all this drama poor Mary had been secreted right inside the pit with her Plus-8 as a precaution in case a car came to change-over before the next team member could be brought round from the paddock. She finally got the opportunity to get on to the track at just 5 o'clock. As always, Mary lapped consistently quickly, and she seemed to be suffering no ill-effects from being cooped-up in the pits for so long.

In the five-hour handicap positions the Saxons led by one third of a lap, and there was frantic calculations going on in the pits to try to work out how we could regain the lead. After much agonizing I took the decision and Mary was brought in to hand over the sash to Pat for the final 20 minutes. Pat had to catch and overtake the Saxon team twice to regain the lead on handicap. He was lapping about 10-15 seconds quicker than Mike Duncan, and it seemed possible. As time slipped away he overtook the Saxon car once to a roar from the Viking pit. It was unbearably exciting, and I aged years in those last 20 minutes. Then at 5.59 pm, the two Morgans corssed the line 3 seconds apart, with the Saxon car ahead.

At Red Lodge Pat swooped past, and the Vikings pit erupted. We had done it! But, had we? The flag came out before the Morgans reappeared, and we all gradually realised that the race was judged on whole laps completed within six hours. So the 3-second gap at 5.59 pm determined it — the Saxons had won. We could not have been beaten by a better team.

I hope you agree that these recollections from Club members reveal the essence of the friendly rivalry which exists amongst the competition-orientated membership of the M.S.C.C. It is because of their enthusiasm that officials of the Club, past, present, and I am sure in the future, are willing to put in so much hard work over long hours, and at times their own financial support, to ensure the Club's continuing well-being. Through their efforts they have forged it into the substantial organization it is today, respected throughout the motor-sporting world and the means through which so much Morgan fellowship is generated.

Chapter 4

Morgan clubs around the world

To own a Morgan is to own an international calling card. If a Morgan owner visits another country, with or without his car, and spots another Morgan, he will invariably seek out its owner, and often the resulting discussion becomes the beginning of a lasting friendship. If he visits a country where he already knows the address of a Morgan owner, and if he has the time, he will make a particular effort to make contact, just to talk Morgans and compare notes.

Morgan ownership is rather like drug addiction, and once hooked the addict has little chance of being cured. How many times have you heard these familiar words, 'I used to own a Morgan (Moggie), and I wish now I'd never sold it'? Current Morgan owners are hearing them all the time. Through this particular addiction, Morgan owners have sought each other out in many parts of the world, and as the circle widened have formed themselves into an exclusive club. Some remain very small, but others have grown into large and very active organizations.

In this chapter I list these clubs — and in some cases individual owners — and offer in each case a brief history and a run-down of their activities. I also offer a contact name and address of a club official (usually the Secretary) in case you are a resident who would like to join the club, or are a visitor from another country who simply wants to make contact. In some cases I have explained the methods adopted by clubs in awarding trophies and staging events in case they may be of interest to other Morgan clubs.

I think the very essence of the justification for forming a Morgan club is epitomized by the wording which is printed inside the register of members of the Morgan Owners Group — Great Lakes. It reads:

'The Morgan Owners Group was established in 1965 to promote the Morgan automobile and to provide technical advice and social companionship for those fortunate enough to have found their very own, world's last true sports car.'

Morgan Owner — Andorra
The small country of Andorra, rather like Monte Carlo, is a customs-free principality, and at the last count its modest car population included just one Morgan. This is a 1978 4-4 two-seater, which belongs to Mr. H. K. H. Dale, an Englishman who works and lives for most of the year in Andorra.

The car was ordered with over £1,000 worth of extras, including green all-leather upholstery, green hood and tonneau cover, green sidescreens and chrome wire wheels with knock-off hub-caps, and was collected by its owner while he was spending part of the year in England. Mr. Dale will be only too pleased to meet and talk Morgans to anyone visiting Andorra, and he can be contacted c/o Credit Andorra Bank, Andorra La Vella, Principat d'Andorra.

Morgan Owners Club of Australia
The club was founded in August 1958, 10 members attending the first meeting. Early meetings were informal gatherings at members' homes, but by 1960 increasing membership caused the meeting places to be changed to various halls or club premises in the Sydney area. That year the club joined the Confederation of Australian Motor Sport (C.A.M.S.), which is the representative of the F.I.A. in Australia.

By 1963 the membership had grown to 44, by 1968 it was 82, and at the end of 1976 there were 126 fully paid-up members. The club fought and won a five-year battle with C.A.M.S. as a result of which all Australian clubs with at least 40 members, and which had been in existence for at least four years, were granted full membership with voting rights; hitherto clubs with less than 100 members had only been granted associate membership, with no voting rights.

In 1970 the club joined the Council of Veteran, Vintage and Thoroughbred Motor Clubs (C.V.V.T.M.C.), an organization which brings together about 30 clubs in the Sydney area and stages a static annual display of between 500 and 700 vehicles and motorcycles at Warwick Farm race course, including a *concours*.

The magazine *Morgan Ear* is issued monthly and covers all aspects of the club's news and events. Meetings are held on a regular basis, including state and inter-state monthly gatherings. An annual inter-state rally is held, as is a week-long camping rally, and the club stages all the usual type of speed events and its members also compete in open events and regularly collect honours in these. The club awards are presented at the annual dinner-dance held in late-September. These include prizes for the highest social points scored during the year, which are awarded on the following basis at each qualifying event or meeting:

Attendance at club runs		100
Attendance at club meetings		100
Attendance at club socials		100
Introduction of new full member		50
Introduction of new associate member		25
Punctuality at all club functions		25
Apologies for absence from club function		25
Cleanliness of car on club runs:		
Outside	10	
Under bonnet and front end	5	
Inside	5	20
Friends at club functions (3 per person)		9 (max)
Friends on club runs (5 per person)		5 (max)
Driving a Morgan on club runs		9

(Any member competing in, or assisting another member to compete in, an open event with an M.O.C.A. competition licence on the same day as a club event is granted attendance and punctuality marks.)
Penalty marks are also awarded as follows:

Member leaving without excusing himself	20
Member passing club captain on a club run within the first half-mile, unless directed to do so	50

The club address for all correspondence is: The Morgan Owners Club of Australia, Box No. A.422, P.O. Sydney South, New South Wales 2000, Australia.

Morgan Sports Car Club of Austria

The club was formed in 1977 and has 28 members, one of whom lives in Switzerland. Between them they own 13 Plus-8s, 14 4-4 two-seaters and four-seaters, and a 1935 JAP-engined Super Sports three-wheeler. There is also a 1952 Plus-4 in the country undergoing complete restoration, and it is hoped that its owner will join the club when the work is complete.

The club holds a five-day rally each year, and in 1978 this was based on the town of Velden, beginning with dinner at the leading hotel followed by a trip to a disco. The second day involved some lighthearted competitions then a visit to a private beach club, followed by two days of convoy runs to various places of interest with entertainment by local town officials. The climax on the fifth day involved a *concours* in which the Morgans were joined by Ferraris, BMWs and a Panther J72 and paraded through the streets, bedecked with flowers and with a lady model assigned to each car, led by Mario Andretti's Lotus 78, with his son in the cockpit. After judging by Niki Lauda, Ronnie Peterson, Mario Andretti, Colin Chapman, Rolf Stommelen and Nina Rindt the rally ended with an evening firework display, dinner, the prizegiving and finally live entertainment.

All Morgan visitors to Austria are assured of a warm welcome, and anyone interested in joining the club should write to Dr. Hans Schmolzer, Roseggerstrasse 15/1 Stock, 8700 Leoben, Austria.

Morgan Club of Belgium

In the summer of 1973 Dr. Albert De Mey and Patrice Libiez met in the latter's home, along with two other Morgan owners and two Jaguar owners, with the idea of forming a Morgan club in Belgium. From this modest beginning the club had grown to 65 members by 1978.

Members meet on the second Wednesday of each month at the

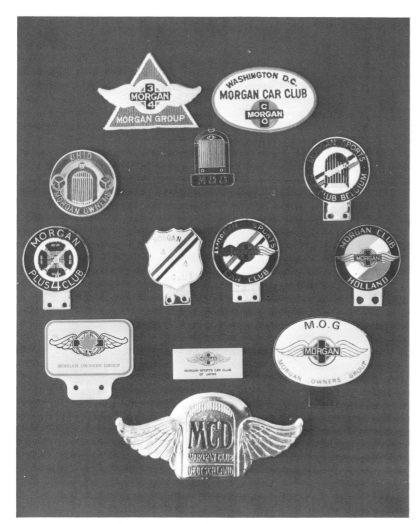

Here are just some of the badges which Morgan club members throughout the world carry on their cars.

Morgans on parade in Austria for the five-day rally based on Velden in August 1978.

Almost ready for the start of the Balloon Rally in Belgium.

A well-attended gathering at Piper's Farm in Canada.

N. E. Norsker photographed this gathering of Morgans at the Danish club's meeting in May 1977.

Three months later members of the club were upholding the reputation of the marque at the Djurslandring races.

Cafe Delta in Brussels, when owners of other sports cars are also welcomed, as are any Morgan owners who happen to be in Brussels on that date. The club tries to organize five events each year, comprising a social run with a visit to a place of historic interest. The main rally of the year must be unique in the Morgan club world, being held in conjunction with an international hot-air balloon meeting. The balloons are lifted off from the market place in the town of Saint Niklaas, the first one carrying a trophy. The Morgan owners then follow this balloon in their cars, and the first one to reach it when it lands claims the trophy. The idea is not as dangerous as it might sound, due to the slow progress of the balloons, and the event has the co-operation of the local police.

There are four three-wheeled Morgans within the club membership, one of them being an F Super, which was found, absolutely complete, after it had been stored for 30 years with only 12,100 kilometres on the clock. There are also four flat-radiator models in the club, one of which is used by its owner as everyday transport. Because of the poor condition of some Belgian roads most modern Morgans have a rear-suspension modification involving the fitting of telescopic shock absorbers by the Brussels Morgan man, A. Starmet, which improves the ride greatly.

Club membership is open to all Morgan owners or enthusiasts, and anyone interested in joining should contact either the Treasurer, Dr. Albert De Mey, 9 Av Cdt Vander Meeren, 1070 Brussels, Belgium, or Reggy Luyex, Kluishof, Prekerijdreef 4, B-9090 Stekene, Belgium.

Morgan Club of Canada

The golden era for Morgans in competition in Canada was the Fifties, when they competed with great success at the Harewood Airport circuit and on the unpaved hill-climbs at Rattlesnake and Hockley, and dominated the ice races at St. Mary's Lake. On the rallying side they were less successful, perhaps because these were sometimes about 1,300 miles long and held in temperatures around −40 degrees C. However, in November 1961 a team of three Plus-4s won the team prize in the Press-on-Regardless Rally.

The first attempt to form a Morgan club occurred in 1962, when 18 Morgan owners met at the Jolly Miller Tavern, in Toronto. However, Alan Sands, then 'between Morgans', was concerned that the proliferation of one-make clubs in Canada was sapping the sports-car movement, and he persuaded the Morgan owners to stay with their existing general-purpose sports-car clubs, and the idea of a Morgan Club of Canada faded for five years.

Then, in 1967, Doug Price was driving his Plus-4 when he spotted two Morgans parked at a kerb. A quick U-turn and a short wait, and he met Ian Campbell and Ken Miles, as a result of which the first post-1962 meeting was held at Alan Sands' farm, Piper's Hill, where, with the unexpected publicity boost from Radio CFRB, 12 Morgans were assembled for the meeting. The next few months were spent locating other Morgan owners, and by 1968 some 25 cars had been traced, including five three-wheelers. Contact was made with the Great Lakes Group, in Detroit, and joint meetings were arranged and an effort was made to form a group in Vancouver.

As with so many clubs, interest waned during the formative years, and whereas some 36 cars were on the register in 1974, two years later, when Reg and Audrey Beer staged a barbeque, there was only one Morgan present apart from their own. Most of the others were rotting in garages under the pretext of undergoing restoration. The club then decided to take action, and another meeting was held at Piper's Hill Farm for a 'Spring tune-up'. A mixture of Plus-4s of older members and 4-4s and Plus-8s of younger and more recent owners turned up, enthusiasm was rekindled, and 10 cars were present for the next barbeque. By 1978 club membership had risen to 89, events had become well supported, and at last the club had become a viable movement.

The newsletter, published irregularly and called *The Blurb,* covers an area from the Arctic Circle to the Great Lakes and carries an illustration of a pig driving a Morgan. This has its origins in the fact that Toronto is sometimes unkindly referred to as Hogtown, and that the M.S.C.C. often chooses a name for its centres appropriate to its location, hence Taffmog for South Wales, Hopmog for the hop-growing area of Kent and Hogmog for Canada. Despite the long distances involved, many Canadian members manage to attend the national meeting of the American clubs at Luray each year, and some even collect prizes.

Potential members, or anyone wanting to talk Morgans in Canada, should contact either the Secretary, Doug Price, 95 Willingdon Blvd, Toronto, Ontario M8X 2H8, or Mrs. Audrey Beer, PO Box 137, Bolton, Ontario L0P 1A0, Canada.

A fleet of Morgans from the French club assembled in Paris for a national meeting.

Below left: After spending the winter on studded tyres, this immaculate Morgan drop-head coupe is now ready for the much more pleasant conditions of a Finnish summer. Below: One of two wire-wheeled Plus-8s in the German club taking part in the annual slalom at Bad Gandersheim for the Morgan Cup donated by Peter Morgan.

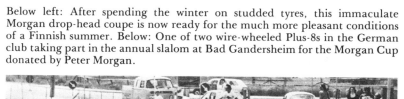

Morgan Club of Denmark

The club was founded in October 1973 at a meeting held at the home of an owner, at which six Morgans were present. Since then the membership has grown to 34, which is thought to represent three-quarters of the total of Morgans in the country. In addition to normal social gatherings and competitive events, including race meetings, in Denmark, members of the club, known as Danmog, also compete in events held by the Swedish club.

The club is open to all Morgan owners and enthusiasts, who should write to the Secretary, Nils-Erik Norsker, Nytorv 3, 1450 Copenhagen K, Denmark.

Morgan Owner — Finland

Until recently the only Morgan in Finland was the Plus-4 Drop Head Coupe owned by Nick Marschan, so it is not surprising that there is no Morgan club in that country. However, Mr. Marschan is a member of the M.S.C.C., as well as belonging to the Sports Car Club of Helsinki, which covers all makes and has approximately 100 sports cars within its membership.

The Plus-4 has Chassis Number 6851 and Engine Number C.T.80080, and was purchased direct from the factory in 1969. The car is absolutely standard, but was supplied with four extra 72-spoke wire wheels for use with winter tyres. Recently, a 1972 Plus-8 was imported into Finland.

Nick Marschan will always be happy to talk to other Morgan owners should they happen to be in Finland. His address is Bertel Jungs väg 8, 00570 Helsinki 57, Finland.

Morgan Club of France

This club was founded in 1973 by Patrick Boisvieux and another Morgan owner who lived in Paris, and from this humble beginning and an initial lack of interest by other owners it has grown steadily and now has more than 40 members throughout the country. Because of the large distances involved in attending meetings, the club has been divided into five regions, each of which runs its own events, including concours and rallies, although the club has organized a national meeting.

One member, Jean Christophe Frot, of Paris, is a regular visitor to M.S.C.C. 'MOG' gatherings in England, and has never been placed lower than third in class in concours events there, which is particularly praiseworthy for a car used as everyday transport. Other members have attended the Balloon Rally in Belgium.

The club has a full range of regalia and issues the magazine News irregularly. Membership is open to all Morgan owners and enthusiasts and visitors are always welcome at club events. Anyone interested should contact the Honorary President, Jean Christophe Frot, 20 Rue Daguerre, 75014 Paris, France.

Morgan Club of Germany

The Morgan Club of Germany was founded in 1970 by six Morgan enthusiasts at a meeting in Frankfurt, where a committee was elected, the first President being Nick Borsch. Slowly the club grew in numbers and in 1972 Pius Kuhlmann took over as President, who in turn was succeeded in the post by Jurgen Bell in 1976. In 1975 the club adopted a formal constitution and was registered as an association by the city of Essen. Potential members join as guests for a year, then can be granted full membership at a General Meeting after having been proposed by two sponsors, and if elected can display the official club badge on their Morgan. Total membership had risen to 47 by 1976 and to over 200 in 1979.

The club is divided into four regions — North, Central, South and Berlin — each organized by a section leader, who arranges monthly meetings to enable members to meet each other and cultivate friendships. Sharing experiences and technical tips and the restoration and rebuilding of Morgans are recurring popular topics, and the success of the club in helping to forge friendships is to be seen in the number of private meetings which take place in members' homes.

The club has had its own magazine, the Morgan-Post, since 1975. Its first editor was Heiner Giersberg, from Berlin, who handed over after one year to Reiner Wandert, who originated the magazine's current illustrated style and presentation. Pressure of work caused him to pass on the editorship to Helmut Kuhlemann, who has made the magazine an interesting, informative and colourfully presented source of information for members.

Between 60 and 70 per cent of members' cars are Plus-8s, about 15 per cent are 4-4 four-seaters and the remainder are 4-4 two-seaters or no longer totally original machines. Two flat-radiator Drop Head Coupes are owned by club members, but are in need of rebuilding, and the only registered three-wheeler is a 1934 Super Sport with a

A carefully posed photograph by Kentgens depicting two distinctly traditional forms of power in Holland.

A pair of photographs by Kentgens recaptures the battle between Michael Lucassen (car number 11) and English visitor Andy Garlick (14) during the historic car race at Zandvoort at Easter in 1977.

water-cooled 998 cc Matchless engine, owned by Eberhard Schirdewahn, from Delmenhorst.

The club's membership also includes Morgan drivers from Holland, Belgium, Switzerland and Austria, so it can claim to be truly international. Anyone interested in joining or visiting the club should contact Jocken Patzwaldt, Annastrasse 26, 565 Solmgen, West Germany.

Morgan Owners — Greece

There are about seven Morgans in Greece, and although one of the owners attempted to start 'Greasemog' it was all to no avail. Most of the cars appear to be uncared-for and are being used only as runabouts, the only exception being the Plus-8 of Ian Marsh, who is a member of the M.S.C.C.

On one occasion he passed a Plus-4 on the road with a lady driver, stopped her and tried to reason with her about the general condition of her car, and in true Morgan tradition he offered to assist in its restoration. Although he was allowed to do certain work, proper restoration was refused.

Although disappointed by this, he is a true Morganeer and would be delighted to talk to any owner visiting Greece. Letters should be addressed to Ian K. Marsh, c/o American Express I.B.C., 17 P.O. Box 67, Athens, Greece.

Morgan Sports Car Club Holland

This club was formed in April 1972 through the enthusiasm of one man, Hans Dee, who at the time of writing is Treasurer. The first meeting was attended by 15 Morgan owners, but the club has since gathered momentum and has become one of the most active in Europe, with a membership of over 100. Of the original 15 members, 14 still have the same car.

The club organizes two big events each year, one in May, the other in October, comprising driving tests, sprints, concours, social get-togethers and, last but not least, good food. In addition, the club usually organizes a summer event abroad, for example in 1976 21 Dutch Morgans were present at the M.S.C.C. weekend at Shelsley Walsh, in 1977 the club attended the historic car races at the Nurburgring, and in 1978 a contingent went to the 'MOG 78' meeting at Ragley Hall. As in nearly all large countries, the club has local centres, which organize monthly noggins and natters.

Although most Morgans in Holland are stored for the winter due to the salt on the roads, the club always holds a New Year's cocktail meeting arranged by the Dutch Morgan agent, who also happens to be the proprietor of the Dutch National Automobile Museum, so the surroundings are ideal.

A quarterly magazine is called *Fatamorgana* and its editor, Dick de Bruyn, excels in obtaining material from all over the world for inclusion in it. Membership is open to all Morgan owners, as well as 'sympathizers', although the basic rule of the club is, No Morgan, No Vote. All membership inquiries should be addressed to Dick de Bruyn, Jasmijastraat 5, Puttershoek, Holland.

Morgan Owners — Hong-Kong

Although there is no official Morgan club in Hong-Kong, partly because of the strict governmental regulations relating to the formation of clubs, and partly because the majority of Morgan owners travel overseas a great deal and are often transferred to other countries, at the last count there were some 17 Morgans in the colony.

The very bad conditions of roads tend to restrict the usage of cars, and have necessitated the introduction of various modifications aimed at curing steering-wheel shake, one such alteration being the fitment of a small shock absorber into the steering. Another hazard for Morgan owners is parking, and it is best to leave your car in a multi-storey car park hidden beneath a specially made nylon cover, otherwise a parked Morgan will immediately attract a crowd, many of whom will be not content just to look, but will clamber all over the car and have their photographs taken with it.

The Hong-Kong-based Morgan with the most interesting history is 'Betsy', the 1953 flat-radiator Plus-4 four-seater which took part in the first Macau Grand Prix in 1954. Its present owner, Dick Worrall, bought the car in late-1967, sold it in April 1970, regretted doing so, then bought it back again in July 1973. When the silver anniversary of the Grand Prix was celebrated in November 1978, the Morgan was the only known survivor of the original race, and Worrall was invited to take part in a six-lap classic car race, along with other entries from Hong-Kong, Japan and Macau itself.

Although 'Betsy' set the fastest practice time, the Morgan and the only other post-war car, a TR3, were forced to start from the back of the grid, but the Morgan worked its way through the field until it was

The first meeting of the Hong-Kong Morgan Owners Club, which was held at Jack Tucker's Outward Bound School in the summer of 1975.

Below left: 'Dinger' Bell photographed by W. R. Worrall with 'Betsy' on the starting grid for the first Macau Grand prix, which was held on October 31, 1954. Below: G. Bernardi's 4-4 after its arrival at Knebworth House for 'MOG 79', having been driven from Milan with the owner's 11-year-old son in the passenger's seat. (Photograph by John Trenchard.)

lying second to a supercharged eight-cylinder Alfa Romeo after four laps. These two cars then dominated the race, the Morgan being just over 3 secs behind the Alfa at the finish. The following month 'Betsy' was declared best car in a *concours* for post-1945 cars at the Hong-Kong A.A.'s annual Driver of the Year show.

Despite the lack of a club, a list of Morgan owners and of literature held by them is maintained, and any Morgan owner moving to or passing through the colony is assured of a warm welcome from Dick Worrall, c/o Royal Hong-Kong Police Force, Headquarters, Arsenal Street, Hong-Kong.

Morgan Owners — Italy

The most enthusiastic Morgan owner in Italy must be G. Bernardi who, accompanied by his 11-year-old son, drove over 2,000 miles in his 4-4 to attend 'MOG 79' at Knebworth House, his car signwritten boldly to publicize the round trip. Needless to say he picked up the 'Furthest Distance Travelled' award, and while attending the function he expressed an interest in setting up a Morgan club in Italy, and a wish to receive any Morgan owner who happened to be in Milan. But take your own interpreter as he cannot speak English! He can be contacted at Via Valvassori 83, Milan, Italy.

Morgan Sports Car Club of Japan

It is very doubtful whether any Morgans were imported into Japan before World War Two, and after the war import of foreign-made cars was prohibited until 1958. When this ban was lifted a very few Morgans were imported, but the one or two to be seen in Tokyo in the early-1960s were owned by U.S. servicemen or by British college lecturers.

In 1967 Mr. Toshio Takano was appointed Morgan distributor in Japan and he took delivery of four new cars, but few people knew about the Morgan car at that time and it took several months to sell them. Now, as nearly everywhere else, orders for new Morgans far outnumber the availability.

In late-1972 Masahiro Naito took delivery of a 4-4 two-seater after a two-year wait and was so impressed with his car that he contacted other Morgan owners and formed the Morgan Sports Car Club of Japan. For the first meeting, in December, there were 18 members, and by 1978, by which time the club had staged 34 events from touring rallies and hill-climbs to gymkhanas, sprints and races, the membership had grown to 80. National meetings since 1977 have been well-supported and joint meetings are held each year with the Tokyo Auto Club Sports and the Japan British Automobile Society.

It is believed that about 12 three-wheelers survive in the country, the rarest known being a 1937 barrel-back model with a lowered body and an air-cooled Matchless engine, which is owned by Yutaka Ando, while the rarest four-wheeler is a 1938 Coventry Climax-engined 4-4 owned by Masahiro Naito, the club's President.

Article 2 of the club constitution says: The object of the club is to enjoy auto sports through the Morgan cars, promote friendship among members, observe traffic rules while trying to improve driving skill and retain the spirit to endure to every difficulty experiencing with an automobile 'Morgan.' Anyone agreeing to support these words can be admitted to the club, and any Morgan enthusiasts visiting Japan are assured of a warm welcome. All enquiries should be addressed either to the President, or to the Secretary, Mrs. Yoshiko Naito, 4-16-16 Kajinocho, Koganeishi, Tokyo 184, Japan.

Morgan Owners — Luxembourg

A recent survey lists 19 Morgans — eight Plus-8s, seven 4-4 two-seaters and four 4-4 four-seaters — in the principality of Luxembourg. In May 1978 six Morgan owners held a social meeting, since when interest has increased steadily, a variety of mainly social events have been organized by Georges Leurs, and the list of owners or people interested in the marque has grown to 32. Because of this growth of interest Georges Leurs hopes to create a formal club in the near future, and meanwhile he would be most interested to hear from any Morgan owner visiting his country. His address is Rue du Parc, Bertrange, Luxembourg.

Morgan Owners — Papua New Guinea

Although it has no official Morgan club, Papua New Guinea can claim four Morgans, three Plus-8s in Port Moresby, the capital, and an early-1970s 4-4 four-seater in Lae. Another Morgan owner, Garrett Thistlewait, still lives in Port Moresby, but his 1937 4-4 is now in Melbourne, Australia.

A recent arrival from England is a very fast Plus-8 belonging to Rod Paris. This is a very early example, which has been greatly modified and now features a five-speed ZF gearbox, a supercharger and numerous other engine and suspension changes. Rod used to

A quartet of Morgans, one still carrying a British number plate, assembled for a club gathering in Luxembourg.

Below left: The Morgan Sports Car Club of Japan insist that for their sprint meetings cars must run in standard road trim, and to set a good example the club's President, M. Naito, took part in this event with a suitcase on the luggage rack! Below: Several members of the club pose with their cars at one of the well-attended meetings.

drag-race this car in England, where he regularly recorded 0-100 mph in 6 seconds and a top speed of around 158 to 160 mph.

Although the weather in Papua New Guinea is ideal for sports-car driving the roads are not meant for Morgans, mostly being in a poor state of repair and only a few of them, mainly in built-up areas, being made-up. Should any Morgan owner visit the country they will find a warm welcome from Bob Bell, PO Box 5142, Boroko, Nr. Port Moresby, Papua New Guinea.

Morgan Sports Car Club of New Zealand

This club began in 1971 as a result of a chance meeting of Morgan owners on the road, held its first meeting at Easter 1972, and then was run informally for three years until becoming officially established in 1975. On its formation the total membership of 35 represented 80 per cent of Morgans in the country, while at the time of writing the number has risen to 75, which represents 100 per cent membership. There is a club magazine, *Borrowed Time* (the title was copied from an article on Morgans by Peter Garnier in *Autocar* in September 1965) which is published monthly.

Club members include Terry Waterfield, who has a very potent Plus-4 which develops 118 bhp and holds a New Zealand sports car class record at 129 mph, and Bruce and Ian Utting, who were first and second overall in their Plus-8 in a novel Country Gentleman's hill-climb in which the results were decided on combined times for travelling both up and down the hill. Another club member, John Rock-Evans, put both the club and the *marque* on the map in 1978 by appearing in the Mastermind competition on New Zealand television and answering questions on the history of the Morgan Motor Company. He reached the semi-finals before failing on the question: 'Has the Morgan Motor Company ever produced a model, other than the Plus-4-Plus, which could be classed as an enclosed vehicle?'. (They did, but can you name it?) Another keen owner collected his car, a 1977 4-4 four-seater, in England and drive it to South Africa, all without trouble, before shipping it the remainder of the journey.

Membership of the club is open to all Morgan owners or 'Morgan nuts', and details can be obtained from the Secretary, Lloyd Gleeson, 101 Grahame Street, Thames, New Zealand, to where any visiting Morgan owner is also invited to make contact.

Morgan Owner — Peru

Just before the outbreak of World War Two three Englishmen each imported a 4-4, but because of the war they had to return to England, leaving their cars behind them. One of these has disappeared, but the other two were found by Mr. A. Gardillo, who is now in the process of restoring them. The only other known Morgan in the country, a 4-4 two-seater, was imported new in 1963.

Mr. Gardillo, who is a member of the M.S.C.C., would be delighted to meet any Morgan owner who visits Peru, and can be reached at Luis Felipe Villaran 395, San Isidro, Lima 27, Peru.

Morgan Owners — Sicily

Six Morgans have been traced in Sicily, two 4-4 four-seaters, three 4-4 two-seaters and a Plus-8, the owners of which are all known to each other. Although they do not meet on a regular basis, or have an official club to link them, they offer each other the usual Morgan mutual assistance whenever necessary.

In 1974 strict exhaust regulations came into effect, and at the same time a 35 per cent VAT was applied to cars of over 2,000cc, so the owner of the Plus-8 counts himself very lucky to have bought his car just before these rules came into effect. Anyone visiting Sicily and wanting to talk Morgans should contact Mr. R. Bonomo, Via Alcide de Gasperi 203, Palermo, Sicily.

Morgan Owners — Singapore

Although there is no official Morgan club in Singapore, the five known Morgan owners keep in regular contact with each other. The earliest of their cars is a pre-war 4-4, which is owned by an English couple who really cherish it. A New Zealander owns a 1954 two-seater, there are two four-seaters, dating from 1963 and 1964, and an Indian Singaporian keeps a 1969 two-seater in excellent condition.

Several local factors affect the ownership of Morgans and certain other cars in Singapore, one being a rather strange government taxation system which increases tax on all cars over 10 years old (regardless of condition) and almost doubles it by the time the car is 15 years old. As a result old or interesting cars are reduced to an absolute minimum. The weather is also a major influence, for it rains on average once every day and at most other times there is very hot sunshine. This has led to hood modifications by Morgan owners,

Left: The very first meeting of the South African club, which was held on July 4, 1971, with all seven cars illustrated in *concours* condition. Below left: The membership gathers together again to pose for an up-to-date photograph for inclusion in this book. Below: This four-seater owned by Ronnie Wilson is believed to be the only open sports car to be allowed into a game park, and to prove the point here it is parked in front of the guest house. (All photographs on this page by Ronnie Wilson.)

one arrangement being to provide a sedanca hood position, with the top folded back from the screen halfway and fastened to the hood irons. Another way of avoiding being drenched by one of the sudden rainstorms is to drive the car with the hood up, but with a zipped flap for the rear window which can be operated from inside the car.

The five Morgans have proved very popular in Singapore, their owners being approached almost weekly by people offering to buy their car. Any visitor wishing to meet a local Morgan owner should first contact Mr. W. J. Lawrence, PO Box 57, Tanglin Post Office, Singapore 10.

Morgan Owners Group of South Africa (SAMOG)

Morgan owners in South Africa seem to be independent-minded individuals, so much so that they do not see the need for a formal Morgan club. Nevertheless, they have formed themselves into an association so that the 30 or so cars spread throughout this large country remain identified and are well looked after. The group was started by Angela Heinz, a really adventurous kind of woman whose hobbies include flying her own aeroplane and selling Morgans and motorcycles, and who is a familiar sight to the Police in Johannesburg driving her very potent Plus-8 into town with her plaited pony tails streaming in the wind. In the days of free import of Morgans into South Africa she acted as the official agent, but now import regulations make it virtually impossible to get a new Morgan into the country.

Her first gathering of Morgan owners was held on July 11, 1971, at her oil executive husband's prestigious house in a select Johannesburg suburb, where seven Morgans were gathered together. Since then, broadcaster Ronnie Wilson and his wife Colleen have organized a number of social events, including drives to gracious old mine managers' homes on the Golden Reef, barbecues, and so on, and recently Ronnie was chosen to be Chairman of SAMOG. As a result of a letter asking him for details for inclusion in this book he arranged a special gathering of Johannesburg-based cars at the Jukskei Motor Museum for a photographic session, which drew approximately a third of all Morgans known to be in South Africa.

The group do not believe in subscriptions, but the newsletter which Ronnie Wilson puts out from time to time is financed out of small 'fines' which owners incur if they ever turn up for a gathering with an incomplete or otherwise sub-standard car (member Alan Robertson was fined a few cents for driving his car straight from the body shop before the headlamps had been refitted, and Alan Gerhardt was similarly penalized for arriving without a grille), all money collected this way going into a Golden Hubcap 'kitty'.

In motor sport the Morgan name is upheld in South Africa by former MG owner Steve Spencer, who now races a particularly fast Plus-8, and by John Frewin, from Middleburg, who is a keen rally competitor. South Africans are great travellers, and several owners have made the pilgrimage to Malvern, while conversely a warm Morgan greeting awaits anyone visiting South Africa, where Ronnie Wilson can be contacted at 29 Macay Avenue, Blairgowrie, Randburg 2194, Transvaal, South Africa.

Morgan Owners Group of Sweden

The formation of this group came about as a result of a chance meeting of two Morgan owners in the car park of a sports car exhibition in Gothenburg, in April 1966. When Arne Holmström, now Chairman of the group, parked his 1952 Plus-4 Drop Head coupe he was approached by the other Morgan owner and in the ensuing conversation they discovered that they knew of 10 Morgan owners in Sweden, and so the idea of forming a club was born. The first meeting was held at the Gothenburg home of one of the owners on January 11, 1967, a provisional name of Morgan Register of Sweden was proposed at a subsequent meeting a few weeks later, but in April that year the changed name, allowing the use of the letters M.O.G., was adopted.

The first competitive event tackled by the members was a club race at the Dalslandsring, run by the Gothenburg Sports Car Club, and in July 1967 nine members took part in a two-week holiday to England with their cars, the nine Swedish-numbered cars attracting a great deal of attention throughout their tour, which included a factory visit at Malvern, where they were warmly greeted by Peter Morgan.

The following month, when the first officers and committee of the group were elected at a meeting at Gränna, membership had grown to 20, and with the help of an active competition programme, including hill-climbs and rallies, and a good social calendar, membership has grown steadily ever since, the most recent count being 61 members, who own 75 Morgans between them. The club issues its own magazine and has two sub-sections covering the North and South of the country. The club's Secretary is Johan Wikström,

Above left: Swedish club members' cars parked in the paddock for the Omberg hill-climb in 1970, when they were photographed by Gunnar Andersson. Above: The tables are turned as Gunnar Andersson is photographed competing on the hill in his 1962 4-4. Left: An impressive line-up of Morgans with an occasional interloper at a well supported Swiss club meeting at Pfister.

Tjärblomsgatan 6 B, S-417 18 Gothenburg, Sweden.

Morgan Club of Switzerland

Following a gathering of Morgan owners in July 1976 the Morgan Club of Switzerland came into being the following June, since when the membership has grown from 45 to 92. Each year the club organizes a race, two two-day get-togethers which include a gymkhana, treasure hunt, etc., as well as monthly regional gatherings.

Nearly all the cars of club members are extremely well kept and original, and most have covered quite a low mileage, very few of them being used as everyday transport, especially during the winter months, when salt can remain on the road for anything up to six months at a time. About 80 per cent of the cars within the club were manufactured between 1966 and 1976, and of these 60 per cent are Plus-8s, 20 per cent 4-4 two-seaters, 10 per cent Plus-4s and 10 per cent 4-4 four-seaters. There are also five three-wheelers (two V-twins and three F-models). The rarest car in the club is a pre-war 4-4, believed to date from 1937. There are also known to be a Plus-4-Plus, a Plus-4 Super Sports and five other three-wheelers in the country, the owners of which are being encouraged to join the club.

Although the club has very detailed rules, which fill a 12-page booklet, nobody seems to take them too seriously. The club facilities include technical advice and the supply of cheap parts, while the club magazine *Mcs ORGAN* is edited by the Secretary and issued three times a year. It is a good-quality production, with photographs, and contains a lot of useful information. A Morgan register is being compiled which, it is hoped, will contain full details and specifications of every Morgan in Switzerland.

The club and its members are always happy to receive visits from Morgan owners from other countries, who should first contact Frank Friedli, M.C.S. Sekretariat, Breitensteinstrasse 39, CH-5417 Untersiggenthal, Switzerland.

Morgan Car Clubs in the U.S.A.

Although as many as 11 clubs for Morgan owners have been recorded in the United States of America, the following six which have supplied me with information on their history and activities would appear to be the most active.

Morgan Car Club — Washington D.C.

Claimed to be the largest and oldest of all the Morgan clubs in the U.S.A., the Washington D.C. club was founded in 1959 by a small group of owners in the area, has grown to a membership of over 350 and is now run on a national basis. The club holds monthly meetings and competitive events including autocross, rallies, *concours d'elegance* as well as social gatherings.

In 1971 the first MOG (Morgan Owners Gathering) was held to coincide with the inaugural Pocono 500 at the Pocono International Raceway, a venue which the club used for the next four years before moving to Luray, Virginia, in 1976. Morgan owners travel hundreds of miles to attend these gatherings, and Mr. and Mrs. Peter Morgan were present for both the 1972 and 1978 events.

When the club was formed, club racing was just beginning in the U.S.A., and most of the venues were within easy striking distance of Washington D.C. A club team of Morgans, called Team Revel, competed at all these events, but the showcase was the 1.2-miles road circuit at Marlboro, which was to prove an ideal training ground for future stars like Mark Donohue, Peter Revson and Bob Tullius. A highspot of the club's early days was when 50 Morgans attended the Patuxent Naval Air Show and associated sprint meeting.

When the economic conditions of the mid-1960s caused most of the convenient road circuits to be closed, the club turned its attention to rally and autocross events, its autocross and sprint teams nearly always finishing amongst the top three whenever they were entered. The club issues a monthly magazine, aptly named *Rough Rider,* which is edited by Edmund (Ed) Zielinski and is of good quality with technical bulletins, a swap-and-sell column and news of club activities, and is illustrated by photographs by the club's President, John H. Sheally II.

Morgan owners the world over are always welcomed, and should contact Ed Zielinski, 616 Gist Avenue, Silver Spring, Maryland 20910, U.S.A.

Morgan Plus-4 Club of Southern California

This is the second oldest Morgan club in the United States, having been formed shortly after the Washington D.C. club, and is also one of the most active. Regular meetings are held in the rear of the Pizza Parlor near Los Angeles International Airport, where it is not unusual to find more than 40 enthusiasts present. Two meetings are

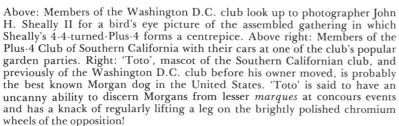

Above: Members of the Washington D.C. club look up to photographer John H. Sheally II for a bird's eye picture of the assembled gathering in which Sheally's 4-4-turned-Plus-4 forms a centrepice. Above right: Members of the Plus-4 Club of Southern California with their cars at one of the club's popular garden parties. Right: 'Toto', mascot of the Southern Californian club, and previously of the Washington D.C. club before his owner moved, is probably the best known Morgan dog in the United States. 'Toto' is said to have an uncanny ability to discern Morgans from lesser *marques* at concours events and has a knack of regularly lifting a leg on the brightly polished chromium wheels of the opposition!

held every month, one a general business meeting (the other is a board meeting) which is really a euphemism for a social gathering each month which is the pre-assigned responsibility of a member, a good balance being maintained between social events, rallies and slaloms, with an occasional wine-tasting tour, baseball game or picnic thrown in. All events are well supported, despite the large distances often involved.

The President and officers adopt parliamentary procedure at their board meetings, business being conducted in a reasonably formal fashion, the size of the group permitting good delegation of responsibility. Particularly impressive is the role of Spares Chairman, which is filled by a member who manages a very sizeable inventory of Morgan spares. (At the December 1978 meeting I was privileged to be extended Honorary Membership of the club in recognition of my 'extensive contributions to The Cause', an honour I was delighted to accept.)

For many years in the past an annual social event was held, often at a place called the Sky Ranch, but recently this has given way to something more ambitious linked to the historic car races which take place at Laguna Seca, near Monterey, towards the end of August. Thanks to the dedicated efforts of some of the Northern California members, notably Goodman Loy, the historic races have become a focal point of Morgan activities on the annual-meet level, and although the event may lack the organization and activities of the Luray event (there is no *concours,* for example) it offers a most relaxed and enjoyable atmosphere in which the social side is sometimes supplemented by a competitive event, such as the rally hosted by the Northern club in 1978.

The historic races at Laguna Seca that year became one of the most significant events in recent U.S. Morgan history when three Morgans, one a rare SLR, competed in different events. In the fifth race, Brian Howlett, a past President of the club, driving a 1962 Plus-4, utterly humiliated two Porsches to win the most exciting race of the series, ensuring that the Morgan name would be imprinted on Southern California motor racing for some time to come. There is now a speculative plan to augment the Laguna Seca event, which is becoming more popular each year, with a spring meeting, possibly based on Reno, Nevada, and involving a Monte Carlo-style rally organized by Morgan clubs in the region.

Visitors to California who would like a warm Morgan welcome should contact the club's President, Norman Kear, 1130 South Vermont Avenue, Los Angeles, California 90006, U.S.A.

3/4 Morgan Group of America

A group of 15 Morgan owners from the New York area who attended the first MOG event at Pocono, Pennsylvania, decided to form their own club, membership of which has since grown to approximately 60. Most live in the North-Eastern United States, but the club does have members from as far South as Virginia and as far West as Chicago, while the Easternmost member is Peter Morgan, who was presented with Honorary Membership of the group by the President, Harry J. Carter, when he visited the U.S.A. in 1977.

As its title infers, the club caters for both three and four-wheeled Morgans, and as a registered corporation it has comprehensive articles which extend to 12 typed pages, of which the following sets out clearly the objectives of the group:

'The purposes for which this corporation has been organized are to promote fellowship and extend acquaintanceship among Morgan car enthusiasts by means of social gatherings and discussions to promote interest in the ownership and enjoyment of the operation of such cars by means of such activities as, but not necessarily limited to, rallies, *concourses d'elegance,* autocrosses, gymkhanas, races, time trials, technical workshops, meets, noggins and tours; to engage generally in any causes or objects similar to the above-mentioned in order to promote the welfare of the membership and for 'maintaining the breed' (which phrase shall be deemed to mean the promotion or the preservation, and of the regular use, of the three-and-four-wheeled Morgan cars which were originally designed by the late H. F. S. Morgan and by his son Peter H. G. Morgan and which were, and are being, produced by the firm which they built, the Morgan Motor Company Limited of Pickersleigh Road, Malvern Link, Worcestershire, England).'

The club membership owns a fine assortment of models, but the rarest car is the 1938 4-4 T.T. Replica owned by Jack Artley. The club magazine, *Morganeer,* is published montly and like some other American club journals, the back cover is left blank apart from the words First Class printed on it in large letters. The member's name and address is then typed on the cover, which is then stamped and posted, thereby saving the cost of envelopes — an idea that other clubs might care to adopt.

An assembly of cars of the 3/4 Morgan Group Limited at Hyde Park, New York, on the occasion of a Hudson River Antique Auto Association event. (Photograph by Harry Carter.)

Ohio Morgan Owners gathered in Columbus for what they term their spring meet and *'unconcours'* in 1976. The 1947 4-4 Series 1 drophead coupe in the foreground belongs to Paul Schodorf.

Any Morgan owner or enthusiast visiting the area can contact Harry J. Carter at 37 Hawthorne Place, Summit, New Jersey 07901, U.S.A.

Ohio Morgan Owners

This is an informal regional group of Morgan owners dedicated to keeping their cars on the road by sharing technical information, trading spare parts and getting together two or three times a year for various Morgan-related events. It was started in 1973 when three Morgan owners invited all 15 known owners in the area to an initial picnic meeting in Columbus, Ohio, to which 10 of them responded. Mainly by word-of-mouth contact, membership had risen to 72 at the last count, who own 82 Morgans between them, all but 20 of the members having become fee-paying since 1978 in order to finance expanded mailings and various club activities.

Ohio developed a good population of Morgans in the early-1970s when Don Simpkins' M.M. & M. Imports, of Derby, brought many cars into the U.S.A. when they were not as fashionable as they are today. He now runs Morgan Fab Industries (Morgan Restoration Shop) in Buford, Georgia, but he probably handled half the cars now owned in Ohio.

The group have always been well represented at national Morgan events sponsored by the Washington D.C. club, laurels having been won by Walt Squires' 1971 Plus-8, Jerry Boston's 1961 Plus-4 Drop Head Coupé, Jim Besst's 1958 4-4 Roadster, George Brokaw's 1961 Plus-4 Drop Head Coupé, Charles Miller's 1970 4-4 Roadster and Bob Burrows' 1963 Plus-4 Roadster. The group also participates in local classic and vintage car shows and sports car rallies to promote the *marque,* and a typical recent season included combined events with Jaguar, MG, Triumph and Austin-Healey clubs involving rallies, sports car shows and swap meets.

Facilities for members include the group's own car badge, lists of all Morgan spare parts available in Ohio together with lists of recommended parts suppliers and specialist shops for mechanical, body and upholstery work. On the members' roster there are 35 Plus-4 Roadsters, 13 Plus-4 four-seaters, 10 4-4 Roadsters, four 4-4 Competition Roadsters, six Plus-4 Drop Head Coupés, seven Plus-8s, three three-wheelers and two 4-4 Series 1 Drop Head Coupés.

Interesting cars which have or are being restored include Jim Besst's 1932 Family Model three-wheeler, Bob Burrows' 1949 4-4 Series 1 Drop Head Coupé, Dutch Junge's 1928 Super Sport three-wheeler, Dick Nelson's 1955 dual-spare (long-nose) Plus-4 Drop Head Coupé, Winn Rosch's 1934 three-wheeler and 1964 Plus-4-Plus and Paul Schodorf's 1955 Plus-4 four-seater Drop Head Coupé. An interesting newcomer is Bruce Edwards' Issis Imports 1978 Plus-8 propane-powered Roadster.

It is not necessary to be a Morgan owner to enjoy membership of this group, the unofficial President of which, Robert T. Burrows, can be contacted at 7080 Westview Drive, Worthington, Ohio 43085, U.S.A.

Morgans of Philadelphia (MOPS)

This club was formed on March 13, 1977 when 25 enthusiasts responded to an advertisement in the city newspaper and within two years the membership had almost reached 40. Monthly gatherings and visits to local auto shows are held, and in the autumn the club hosts a gymkhana which is well supported by other clubs. In a recent event the crowd were treated to President Gus Spahr's *concours*-winning 1932 Aero three-wheeler doing very well while competing against a field of 4-4s, Plus-4s and a Plus-8.

There are some interesting cars amongst the membership, and Alex Smith, who used to work for a local Morgan dealer back in the days when the cars could be imported legally, has one of the few Plus-4-Plus models in the U.S.A. Fellow member Bob Lehr, who is also Vice-President of the Washington D.C. club, has a right-hand-drive Plus-4 Super Sports which was probably the last Super Sports to be imported into the U.S.A. and is one-of-a-kind in that it is not entirely aluminium-bodied. Factory correspondence indicates that in 1967, when the car went into production, the supply of aluminium was low, and rather than wait the owner elected to have his car built with steel. Bud Bernard's 1967 Plus-4 is a perfect example of a Morgan transition car in that it has the rear treatment of the 1959-66 Plus-4 with other features, including the locked glove box, of a 1967, and was one of the first 1967s to enter the United States during that last year of legality.

A 1966 Plus-4 Super Sports has been undergoing restoration since 1971 by Dick Larrick, who is so fanatical about detail that some of his restored parts may soon need restoring! Jim Schrader's 1964 Plus-4 has a TR transmission with overdrive to go with its TR engine, this neat conversion having been done before he bought the car. In

This 1966 Plus-4, which has recently been completely restored, belongs to the registrar of the 'MOPS' (Morgans of Philadelphia) club.

A few of the members of the Morgan Owners Group — Great Lakes at the third Mid-West meet at Harbor Springs, Michigan, in 1978.

addition to his multi-award-winning 1962 Plus-4 club member Dick Smith has the last Drop Head Coupe to be imported into the U.S.A., a *concours*-condition early-1968 car. Alex Knight's 1933 barrel-back three-wheeler Super Sports should be back on the road by now, and Peter Gunshor's 1975 4-4 four-seater is a recent addition to the club strength.

Membership of MOPS is decribed as 'open to anyone who is tolerant enought to put up with the inexplicable affection they have for Morgans, and the driving pleasure they bring them', and a monthly newsletter, *MOPS Mania,* is supplied to all members. More information regarding participation may be obtained from the Club Registrar, John Moffatt, 93 Runnymede Avenue, Jenkintown, Pennsylvania 19046, U.S.A.

Morgan Owners Group — Great Lakes

This group began informally in 1964 or 1965, its principal founders being Don Frante and the late Jack Markley, longtime Detroit Morgan enthusiasts, who would get together with about 10 other Morgan owners when the mood struck them to socialize a little and discuss their mutual Morgan interests. By chance meetings on the road and by word-of-mouth new members were attracted, but the group remained informal under the unofficial presidencies of Don Frantz and Pat Kobielski until it was decided around 1970 to bring some organization into the club, with the payment of modest dues, the preparation of a calendar of events and the regular mailing of notices to members.

This led in 1975 to the official incorporation of the Morgan Owners Group as a Michigan non-profit corporation, and the club had grown to a membership of more than 65 by 1979, most living in the Detroit, Michigan and surrounding Great Lakes area of the Mid-West, but some from all over the country and even as far away as Australia. More than 75 Morgans are owned by the membership, including three-wheelers, pre-war 4-4s, a Plus-4-Plus and what is probably the only 1976 4-4 presently in the United States.

A full calendar of events includes monthly meetings at a local restaurant and at least one other monthly function. In the winter events tend to be mainly social as few members are willing to expose their cars to the harsh Michigan weather. The outdoor season begins in the early-spring with the annual English day road rally held in conjunction with the Austin-Healey, Jaguar, MG and Triumph clubs, followed by the spring car clinic, a gathering with a technical emphasis to inspect members' cars and prepare them for summer driving, which includes an English day at the Waterford Hills S.C.C.A. track and various picnic and cross-country outings.

Highlight of the year is the annual Mid-West meet, a weekend affair held at a northern Michigan resort and involving competition events such as a road rally, a *concours d'elegance* as well as a banquet and a lot of good northern air. The first of these was held in 1976, when it was felt that the long journeys to national meets discouraged many local members from participating, and that the club had grown large enough to support such an event alone. They have proved a huge success, usually with over 30 cars attending. The annual awards banquet is held each October, when the election of officers also takes place.

In addition to sponsoring activities, the club also puts out publications of interest to Morgan owners, including event notices and general news in the monthly *Flexible Flyer*. The club is also putting together a technical manual of hints and suggestions on how to maintain the Morgan car, based on the experiences of members and other Morgan owners. This is a very active and enthusiastic group, and anyone requiring more details should write to the Morgan Owners Group, Webb Drive, Farmington Hill, Michigan 48018, U.S.A.

Morgan Owner — U.S.S.R.

The only known Morgan in the U.S.S.R. is the pre-war 4-4 which was featured in my companion book on the Flat-Radiator Morgans. Naturally, the owner does not use the car during the winter months, and he stores it in a novel way by winching it up and suspending it in the roof space of his garage, above another car. He would be most interested to hear from other Morgan owners, and his name and address are G. Michailow, Lenin Str 121-58, Riga 225012 ind, Latvia, U.S.S.R.

Chapter 5

Morgan memorabilia

For this chapter I have assembled a collection of interesting odds and ends, which have come to light in the course of my research for this book. They include the funny, the serious, the rare and the famous, but in no way are the items meant to tell a complete story. They only have one thing in common, namely that they all refer to Morgans or Morgan enthusiasts and I hope that they will contribute to the enjoyment of readers of this book.

The birth of a racing Morgan

It is every Morgan Maniac's dream to discover a Morgan rotting away in a garage or breaker's yard. This is what happened to Bryan Harvey when he discovered the following car in a lock-up garage: 1964 Morgan 4-4 Series 5, Chassis No. B.1034, Engine No. S.367979.

He managed to trace the owner and bought what at first appeared to be a bargain — a Morgan for £250. It turned out in the long run to be a shambles and not such a bargain after all. Nearly every moving part was either seized-up or broken, including things like the rear axle and steering column. The wheels were off an old Volvo, and were only put on to keep the car off the ground; the owner of the garage in which it was found had taken the Morgan wheels away so that the owner could not move the car until he paid some rent. Needless to say the rent was not paid! It was known that the car had stood under piles of rubbish for at least eight years and had never been maintained or protected against corrosion during this time. At first glance the bodywork appeared quite sound, except for two wings which were damaged, but when it was dismantled the metal was so

thin through rust and all the edges had broken away; a new body was certainly needed.

The original idea was to rebuild the car to its standard specification, but as it was dismantled it was realised there was not much worth saving. It was then decided to develop a competition car from the remains. From then on the idea was to have a competition car that could be used on the road. During the construction this idea was dropped, but not before some road wheels had been purchased, which later were changed to 13in. racing wheels fitted with 9in. and 7in. low-profile slicks. The old engine went for a song and a racing Ford crossflow engine was bought. This was a highly tuned engine bored to 1,760cc with twin 40 DCO Weber carbs, and a dry-sump arrangement with belt-driven oil pump. A 2000E Ford gearbox was purchased to replace the old push-and-pull gearbox of the early 4-4s and later during the car's development close ratios were provided for the top three gears to stop the rear wheels locking up when changing down at high speeds. The original chassis was strengthened under the doors and at the back of the engine compartment. Then a spaceframe was designed and fitted, which incorporated the roll-cage, and a glass-fibre body was made by Rutherford Berry, along with the wings, and this was fitted over the spaceframe and fixed to the chassis, the wings being widened an extra 3in. from the widest available from Rutherford Berry to cover the extra width of the racing wheels.

The front suspension remained the Morgan 'old faithful', but Spax shockers were fitted because of their adjustment advantage and the oil charger removed and grease nipples fitted to the top. Three leaves were taken out of each rear spring, leaving only two, and Koni shock absorbers fitted for their stiffness. The chassis at the rear was braced to stop any flexing, and a tie-bar was fitted between the rear axle and the spaceframe to stop tramping of the rear wheels under heavy braking. The brakes were standard 4-4, but the fronts were modified slightly to fit into the smaller rims of the wheels; they proved to be adequate for the much lighter car.

A four-gallon aluminium tank was fitted as it was thought this would be sufficient for most races, but it proved to be a problem while competing in the six-hour relay races. A deeper radiator was fitted to give more efficient cooling and an oil-cooler fixed below this. An aluminium bonnet was made to measure by the factory and constructed and fitted in a day, the original steel cowl being used as it was felt something from the old car should be fitted. The interior and bulkhead was panelled with aluminium, which proved a nightmare, each piece being tailored three or more times before it all came together, then the floor was covered from below with thicker aluminium. A glass-fibre spoiler was attached to the front wings, but this was later changed in design and blended into the wings. A design was worked out for the paintwork to incorporate the roundels and the car sprayed in two-tone metallic blue.

Bryan then used the car successfully in competition for three years, after which time he decided to sell it. It was bought by its present owner, Peter Askew, who decided to fit it with a 1,650cc Cosworth all-steel pushrod engine, which delivers almost 165 bhp and was supplied by Dave Rowe Racing, of Hornchurch, Essex.

Peter has had quite a few teething problems with the new engine, but thinks that he has now got it sorted-out. In addition he has altered the starter system, and has had a new front-end spoiler made. He informs me that he thinks he has plenty of racing years ahead of him ('life begins at 40', he says). He is also bringing up his children in the correct manner. Lee, his six-year-old son, has already laid claim to the car, so any would-be buyers can try their hand at building their own. Bryan and Peter may give you permission to take a few dimensions.

Eric White recalls his specially built Plus-4 Super Sports four-seater — EMJ 266E

From the word go it was a super car. Its performance was superb, its petrol consumption frightening — it was a good thing I had a tame

petrol station. But it did go well. The only near-calamity was a burst oil-cooler. By luck I was only doing a short run of four miles and stopped before the engine seized. I was pushing on far too fast to notice the gauges. One of the advantages of being a Morgan agent was that I could phone for a new element and a can of oil to be brought out by one of the boys, so a quick roadside changeover was done and we were away. The sump was then removed and the bearings checked. No damage was evident, but the big-ends were changed just to be safe. Here a problem cropped up as one big-end bolt had bottomed and torn the threads of the big-end. This was cleaned up, but as the rods were balanced a failure could have been a big problem. However, the bolts torqued-up alright and they were then drilled and wired just to be safe. No problems ever occurred from this.

I ran this car for seven years until the Plus-8 came along. I always felt it put up a very good show compared with an '8' and it is a car I really would love to have kept. However, it did go to a very good home. I sold it to Roger Williams, to whom I had promised the car after I had only had it four months. At the time of writing this, 12 years after the car was born, we are giving the bodywork a full rebuild, so it is looking just as new. The mechanics of the car do not need any attention and the engine runs as sweetly as the day it was built. One thing I do recall is that the clutch slipped from new, but I got used to letting it bite for a second before putting on the power, and so it rarely gave me trouble. Eventually I had the engine taken out and a competition clutch fitted (Daimler Dart cover, etc.) which made all the difference and then I really could use the power to the full without any problems.

Successor to the Plus-4 — Eric White's four-seater Plus-8 — XMJ 84L, later 23 HEW

I took delivery of XMJ 84L in July 1972. I had been pressing very hard for this right from the introduction of the Plus-8 in that the first car after the introduction car each dealer received was ordered as a 'four-seater for me'! At that time I really didn't realise what a favour I was asking. About three years later a four-seater Plus-8 wooden body frame was shown to me propped up in the corner of the works — mine! Also about this time there was talk of the new Rover box, etc, and possible problems with getting Moss parts, so it appeared best to try and get that combination. This left the frame standing for

Chris Lawrence and Robin Gray with just a small collection of the many trophies which they have won over the years in a variety of Morgans.

about a year, and from time to time I asked that it be pruned if the growth of leaves and boughs got too great.

About June the car was really on its way and I received a number of photos of its production as well as taking a number myself. I was lucky in that it was started just ahead of the show cars, which meant that it went through very quickly (when the show cars get started they have to go through with priority over the normal production).

The car was finished in black leather and was fully trimmed in leather *everywhere* not in *most* places, as with normal leather trim. The engine was the high-compression big-carb, large-bore silencer set-up, which was probably the best series built. Paintwork was in the original Westminster Green, which I had grown so fond of on my Super Sports-engined Plus-4.

Except for initial troubles with solder from the petrol tank getting in the pump during the first 1,000 miles, the car has behaved beautifully. I did find, however, on a Silverstone test day, that as I suspected it was very much more of a handful when driven on the limit than a two-seater. As a high-speed tourer, though, it is just my car and not swapable for anything.

After a year on number plate XMJ 84L I obtained 23 HEW (my initials Hugh Eric White) and this is the registration number it has run on ever since.

Chris Lawrence's recollections of the build-up to Le Mans 1962

I took the car out to Le Mans for the test days and I cheated. I do not think that I have ever told this to anybody before, but I put a 2.2-litre engine in it, a really good sprint, 10-lap engine, one of the old ones. In fact it was the 1959 Freddie Dixon Trophy engine. Basically speaking it was worn out, very loose, but it went like nobody's business. We had a 2.9 axle, but that engine pulled about 5,400, which we only got in the race by slipstreaming as the 2-litre which we used would only pull 4,900. We had fitted a very smart hardtop. We had drawn it up and had had five or six goes at it between 1960 and 1961, making one hideous thing after another, but in the winter of 1961 we got it right. Mind you the 4-4 body helped a lot; the back of a Plus-4 was much more difficult because it was higher. We had this very pretty hardtop made for us in aluminium by Williams & Pritchard.

I had a very funny incident during the test weekend. On the Saturday it was nice and dry and we were all out practising. The car went very well and everybody was looking a bit sideways at it, then on Sunday morning it was absolutely pouring with rain, stair-rods straight down, and nobody wanted to go out. Everybody was just standing around staring at it. I thought . . . this, I haven't come all this way to stand here. I wanted to know how the car went in the rain, so I went out. I used to fancy myself a bit in the wet so I had a real go. I was having a lovely time all by myself, when after about eight laps I began to close slowly on a huge cloud of spray in front of me. Of course, the conditions were so bad that I really couldn't tell what it was at all. I genuinely hadn't any idea, but I wasn't really bothered and I got quite close to it. The trouble was that the closer I got the faster it went, whatever it was. We did another four laps like that, apparently going faster and faster. There was no way I could really tell as it was impossible to see pit signals in those conditions. Eventually, whatever it was stopped, which immediately rather switched my concentration off and I had the most monumental spin on the next lap. It was, in fact, Walt Hansgen in a Cunningham 'E' type, who was the only other bloke who went out the whole morning. He had seen someone closing on him and had gone faster with me chasing after him. When he stopped I switched off my concentration as I came out of Indianapolis, I just lost it towards White House where there is a rise where you lose a lot of 'g'. I went for what appeared to be miles, spun it three times and ended up in a ditch. I didn't hit anything solid, but I had buckled the oil filler a little bit on a fence post, that was all. I really didn't damage the car at all and was able to drive it back to the pits. However, it taught me a very valuable lesson.

Although we did not normally drive the car on the road to continental events, we did drive it to Le Mans and back. Le Mans is a mammoth undertaking, especially when you get down to the details of running a car for 24 hours. We usually carried the car in a special caravan, which we had built with one end like a horsebox. The car went in it and we lived in the caravan when the car was removed. However, for Le Mans we had to take so much gear for 14 people to live for a week that the caravan became full, so we elected to drive the car there. We also drove the second car, which was built by Peter Morgan at the factory and was the prototype of the Super Sports. It was an exact replica of the actual race car and was 170 GWP; this later became my S.L.R.

Two views of the present-day power unit of the famous Lawrencetuned Morgan TOK 258, a car with an enviable competitions history.

One of the things that the Le Mans organizers had said in 1961 was 'This is a 1939 car on to which you have grafted disc brakes. Please take it away; it is not in the spirit of the race'. It was, in fact, a new car which Richard Shepherd-Barron had built, which was painted blue and registered XRX 1; this became Pip Arnold's number. However, in 1962, after the test day, they sent a very nice letter saying how nice it was to see the new Morgan, but would we please change the colour from red to green? So it went back to the factory to be repainted whilst we prepared the engine. We had a new gearbox and, of course, we had to prepare the new 2.9 axle. It was a huge 3HA Jaguar axle, not like the 7HA which the car normally had; it weighed almost as much as the rest of the car! All the work was finished in good time and we were not forced to rush anything. And the race? Just magnificent!

Another entry for the record book?

The Guinness Book of Records lists Stirling Moss as the most successful racing driver. Stirling won 167 races, 11 of which were shared. but there is a Morgan driver who must surely merit a mention as well, even if he could never displace Stirling Moss. His name is George Beatty Sterne, or 'G.B.' as he is popularly known.

Although not that well known in the U.K. 'G.B.' enjoys justifiable fame on the North American continent. He started racing in 1954, at the age of 42, and it was not until 1956 that he had his first win. During the next 19 years 'G.B.' won no less than 400 trophies, before he retired from racing in 1975, every one of them in a Morgan.

The Morgans he used in his career were: 1954-56 Plus-4; 1957-59 Plus-4 four-seater; 1960-62 Plus-4 four-seater; 1963-65 Plus-4 Super Sports; 1966-68 Plus-4 competition model; 1969-72 Plus-8; 1973-75 4-4 '1600' competition model.

In 1956 'G.B.' wrote to the Morgan Motor Company asking to become the Canadian West Coast agent. At first the Company refused, but after repeated attempts 'G.B.' got the agency which he held until he retired from active business at the end of 1976. His son, Bob, took over the business, and is still running it.

Bob also raced the same car as his father from 1970-75 and won a total of 90 trophies. He retired from racing at the same time as 'G.B.' to concentrate on the business interests of the family. Throughout 'G.B.'s' racing career his wife, Lydia, played a big part in the racing team; she attended nearly every race, helped in the pits, and of course did nearly every other job over the years, including lap-scoring, timing and flag marshalling, as well as having several races.

Sheila Hancock, former (and future?) Morgan owner

The following is an extract from a letter I received from the well-known actress Sheila Hancock, during the course of researching this book, which I think typifies the deep bonds which are forged between Morgan owners and their cars. She was writing about her 1969 4-4, which carried the number plate VYL 364G:

'It was a four-seater . . . I bought it from Peter Morgan himself when I saw it at one of the motor shows in London . . . I loved it with a passion, and in fact, truthfully, I wept when I sold it, which I had to do as my family grew — as you probably would agree, it is not the perfect family car. However, my husband has promised me faithfully that when I am a very old lady he will buy me a two-seater to spin around the lanes in.

I think the thing I liked most about the car was that it is the sort of car that brings a warm smile to everybody when you pass. MGs bring out aggression in other drivers, whereas Morgans seem to bring out gentleness and it is always lovely to suddenly shoot off from the lights with that marvellous acceleration in what looks like a very old car. I suppose it is a show-off's car, but I was deeply fond of it and miss it to this day. Another interesting fact is that I never got a parking ticket the whole time I had my Morgan, although I used to park it in the most extraordinary places. I think even Traffic Wardens were kindly disposed towards it!'

A special type of 'Mogwoman'

As far as I have been able to discover there is only one woman in the world who restores Morgans professionally. Her name is Penny Bates and she has her restoration shop in Philadelphia, U.S.A.

Penny got tired of paying to get her cars fixed so she set about learning to carry out her own repairs. Slowly she developed her knowledge and skill and by 1978 had passed the necessary tests to carry out State Inspections (similar to the M.O.T. in England).

In June 1978 she teamed-up with Rob Schmidt to form Pen-Rob Classic Cars. However, Rob has since moved to California and Penny has taken over the whole show. She specializes in British-made cars and at the time of writing she had enough work to keep her busy for at least a year.

Penny is very petite, only 5 feet 2 inches tall and weighs 105 pounds. She has a B.A. degree in Art and still makes use of a potter's wheel and sells her creations at craft shows. She has also won trophies for canoe racing and horse riding, and to relax she plays guitar and sings folk. As one of her friends said of her, 'She's quite a gal!'

Ten ways to recognize a fellow Mogman

The assumption that the typical Mogman is a rugged and healthy physical specimen as a result of his constant exposure to sunshine and fresh air is totally fallacious. He is, rather, invariably debilitated, and can easily be recognized by the following characteristics of poor physical condition:

Characteristic	Probable Cause
1 He wheezes	Lungs overtaxed by constantly inflating leaky seats
2 He has rheumatism	Driving for prolonged periods in wet clothing
3 He has frostbite	Obvious cause (colder locations) One hand may be unaffected if he smokes a pipe when driving
4 His teeth are yellow	Head-on collisions with flying insects (not an infallible sign for owners of later models)
5 He is getting bald	Worry (where will next replacement part come from?)
6 He is hard of hearing	Obvious cause (especially if engine exhausts to side)
7 He is hunchbacked	Sitting in bad seats
8 He squints constantly	Automatic reflex to keep dust from eyes on rough roads
9 His left shoulder droops	Strain from carrying large pails of wood preservative
10 He is covered with bruises	Giving wrong answers to wife's question 'You love the Morgan more than me, don't you?'

As to treatments for the above maladies, none are known except the selling of the causative vehicle. However, as most owners also show pronounced mental aberrations, this is perhaps no solution, it being recognized that ownership is terminated only by death, either from any of the above, or the rigours of upkeep. (Hilton White)

Extracts from a report in the *Washington Post* newspaper on the MOG 8 meeting in America:
'The car bottoms out in a two-inch pothole. Morgan fanatics call it 'keeping in touch with the road'.'
'The ride is like being dragged naked in a coal scuttle backwards over gravel by a cantankerous mule.'
'My theory of autocrossing a Morgan is this. You spit every half-hour. If it is blood you know you're bleeding internally and we try to get you to hospital.'

Allegedly overheard at one of the hill stages of the Land's End Trial: 'The only way you will get a comfortable ride in a Morgan is if you have been neutered.'

Non-member John Dexter to a lady driver of a Plus-4: 'Madam, are you in the club?' Lady driver: 'I hope not'.

Overheard in the car park of the pub where the HOPMOG centre of the Morgan Sports Car Club were holding one of their monthly 'Nogging and Natters': 'Don't take any notice of them old cars, dear, they're only plastic kits put there by the pub owners to attract the would-be boy racers.'

Seen on the rear of a Plus 8 'Running in. You are invited to attempt an overtake'.

The easiest way to describe a Morgan's suspension is that if you ran over a penny you could tell if it's heads or tails.

Jim Goodall nearly created a strike at the Motor Show one year. It appears that he started to screw up a few wood screws on the Morgan stand. He was seen by a union man who demanded to see his union card because he was doing a carpenter's job. It took a lot of talking to avert a strike by the carpenters who were employed to erect the stands.

Alleged to have been said by an enthusiast when describing the remains of a Series 1 which he had found in a derelict barn. 'Oh no! its not a runner, but if you whistle the woodworm get up a fair turn of speed'.

Whilst being interviewed for a B.B.C. radio programme, Peter Morgan was asked about famous people who owned Morgans. He spoke of the car which was owned by Brigitte Bardot. The interviewer then asked 'Did you ever have direct contact with her, about the car?' Peter replied 'No. No, she never came here for service'.

A notice alleged to have been found on a Morgan abandoned in a farmyard.
    'Born 1938 in Malvern, Worcestershire.
    Died 1961 in Surrey.
    Rust-in-Peace'.

Chris Lawrence, whilst discussing the Plus-4 Super Sports: 'In those days, it seems to me looking back on it, half the attraction of a tuned car was that it wouldn't idle, it wouldn't start, it made a ghastly noise, and it boiled as soon as it saw a traffic jam'.

Remark made by Mary Lindsay about Dave Saunter after finishing the all-comers' race at the Bentley Drivers' Club meeting at Silverstone in 1978: 'How can I have a dice with him if he won't stay on the circuit?'

One day in New Zealand John Rock Evens, his wife and 10-month-old son, were travelling at about 80 mph in a 50 mph limit. John looked in his mirror and to his horror saw a Police patrol car with lights flashing coming up fast behind him. He lifted his foot and hoped that the patrolman was answering an emergency call and had not been pacing him. No such luck. The car pulled level with him and the driver signalled him to stop. He did so, desperately trying to think of some excuse. The Police Officer got out of the patrol car and walked back to John. Before he could say anything the Police Officer said: 'Don't say anything. I have a Morgan myself!' So the Morgan Owners' Club of New Zealand was born.

MORGANS TAKING SHAPE

The photographs on the following three pages, all of them taken by the Central Photographic Unit, Fort Dunlop, are a graphic reminder of the traditional skills and crafts which are such an essential ingredient of the manufacture of these classic and so highly coveted sports cars.

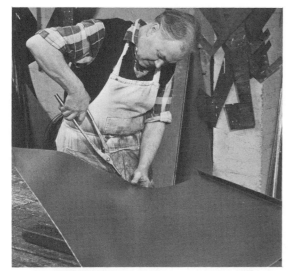

Left: Trimming a body panel. Below left: Attaching a wing panel to the ash frame. Below: Assembly of wood chassis frames.

Below: Final adjustments to a Plus-8 door frame. Right: Rover and Ford engines awaiting installation. Below right: Rolling chassis in the body assembly shop.

Left: Machinists preparing interior body trim panels. Below left: A four-seater's tonneau is checked for fit. Below: Front screen fitment as assembly nears completion.

Appendix

Major competition results 1954-1979

DATE	EVENT	ENTRANT	RESULT
Jan. '54	VSCC Measham Rally	A. L. Yarranton	1st overall
Feb. '54	TEAC Cat's Eyes Rally	B. Clark	1st overall
Mar. '54	RAC Rally	J. H. Ray	7th overall
		A. Newsham	8th overall
Mar. '54	BARC Goodwood race	B. de Mattos	1st overall
Mar. '54	Hereford MC Welsh Rally	A. L. Yarranton	Peter Wray Trophy
Apr. '54	Northampton DMC autocross	H. M. Denton	1st overall
Jun. '54	RSAC Scottish Rally	J. Ray	1st in class
Jul. '54	London MC driving tests	B. Clark	1st overall
Jul. '54	Brighton Rally	Dr. J. T. Spare	1st overall
Sep. '54	LMC London Rally	Mrs. N. Mitchell	Ladies award
Sep. '54	Shelsley Walsh autocross	A. L. Yarranton	1st overall
Nov. '54	MCC RedeX Rally	A. L. Yarranton	*2nd overall
		W. A. G. Goodall	*1st in class
		P. H. G. Morgan	*1st in class
		P. W. S. White	*2nd in class
			*Team award
Dec. '54	MGCC Gothland Rally	K. N. Lee	1st overall
Jan. '55	MCC Exeter Trial	H. H. Gould	*1st class award
		Dr. J. T. Spare	*1st class award
		I. D. L. Lewis	*1st class award
		W. A. G. Goodall	1st class award
			*Team award
Jan. '55	Stott Trophy Rally	K. H. James	1st overall
Feb. '55	Maggi Carlo Rally	Dr. J. T. Spare	1st overall
Feb. '55	MGCC Bronte Rally	D. Butterwick	1st overall
Feb. '55	Plymouth MC 200 Trophy	Dr. J. T. Spare	1st overall
Mar. '55	Sebring 12 Hours race	Rothschild/Kunz	3rd in class
		Dr. Weitz/Mackenzie	5th in class
Mar. '55	Amersham autocross	H. Denton	1st overall
Apr. '55	Hereford MC Welsh Rally	B. Phipps	Wray Trophy
		J. T. de Blaby	Lion Trophy
		Miss A. M. Jervis	Lynx Trophy
Apr. '55	Worcester MC Spring Rally	B. Phipps	1st overall

DATE	EVENT	ENTRANT	RESULT
Apr. '55	N. Staffs MC Oulton Park race	H. M. Denton	1st overall
May '55	London MC autocross	P. Norgard	1st overall
May '55	Morecambe Rally	A. L. Yarranton	1st in class
May '55	BARC Aintree race	J. Moore	1st overall
Jun. '55	RSAC Scottish Rally	R. K. N. Clarkson	1st in class
		Miss A. Neil	Ladies award
Jun. '55	Scarborough Rally	A. Walker	1st overall
Jul. '55	SCCA Beverly race, USA	G. Andre	1st overall
Jul. '55	Circuit of Ireland	S. Moore	Team award
		J. F. F. Howe	Team award
Sep. '55	LMC London Rally	A. L. Yarranton	Harradine Trophy
		Mrs. Y. B. Jackson	Ladies award
Sep. '55	Oulton Park race	P. Reece	1st overall
Oct. '55	Fairchild race, USA	G. Rubini	1st overall
Nov. '55	MCC National Rally	Miss A. Palfrey	Ladies award
Feb. '56	EAMC Winter Rally	E. Cleghorn	1st overall
Feb. '56	YSCC Yorkshire Rally	C. W. Whiteley	1st overall
		Mrs. Y. B. Jackson	Ladies award
Mar. '56	RAC Rally	Dr. J. T. Spare	3rd overall
			1st in class
Apr. '56	Morecambe driving tests	C. Hall	1st overall
Apr. '56	Birmingham Post Rally	P. H. G. Morgan	Team award
		W. A. G. Goodall	Team award
		A. L. Yarranton	Team award
Apr. '56	TEAC Day of Dicing	A. J. Blair	1st overall
May '56	Morecambe National Rally	A. L. Yarranton	*1st overall
		B. Phipps	*Team award
May '56	RSAC Scottish Rally	Miss A. Neil	Ladies award
Jun. '56	Scarborough Rally	D. A. Walker	1st overall
Jun. '56	AMOC Silverstone relay race	R. E. Meredith	Team award
		B. Phipps	Team award
		J. McKechnie	Team award
Sep. '56	SUNBAC Silverstone race	R. E. Meredith	1st overall

DATE	EVENT	ENTRANT	RESULT
Sep. '56	LMC London Rally	Mrs. Y. B. Jackson	Ladies award
		A. L. Yarranton	1st in tests
Sep. '56	Worcester AC autocross	W. A. G. Goodall	1st overall
Nov. '56	MCC National Rally	P. H. G. Morgan	*1st in class
		B. Phipps	1st in class
		W. A. G. Goodall	*Team award
		A. L. Yarranton	*Team award
Mar. '57	V. T. Fellowes Trial	M. B. Jarrett	Shenstone Trophy
Apr. '57	MCC Land's End Trial	P. H. G. Morgan	1st class award
		W. A. G. Goodall	1st class award
Apr. '57	MGCC Night Rally	A. Newsham	1st overall
May '57	Hereford MC driving tests	A. L. Yarranton	1st overall
Jul. '57	Harlow AC Rally	C. Johnson	1st overall
Sep. '57	LMC London Rally	Mrs. P. Mayman	Ladies award
Nov. '57	Boanerges Rally	Mrs. P. Mayman	Ladies award
Nov. '57	HMC Night Rally	Miss V. Domleo	1st overall
Mar. '58	RAC Rally	A. L. Yarranton	1st in class
		W. A. G. Goodall	2nd in class
Mar. '58	Colmore Trophy Trial	J. S. Parry	1st overall
Apr. '58	Midland AC National Rally	Mrs. P. Mayman	Ladies award
May '58	Worcester MC Spring Rally	W. A. G. Goodall	1st overall
May '58	Tulip Rally	Sims/Stokes	2nd in class
May '58	Taunton MC driving tests	P. H. G. Morgan	1st overall
		Mrs. P. Livingstone	Ladies award
May '58	Morecambe National Rally	Mrs. P. Mayman	Ladies award
Jun. '58	Rally of the Downs	H. A. Appleby	1st overall
Jul. '58	MAC Shelsley Walsh hill-climb	A. L. Yarranton	1st overall
		J. F. Livingstone	2nd overall
Jul. '58	Prescott hill-climb	P. H. G. Morgan	Team award
		J. F. Brown	Team award
		R. E. Meredith	Team award
Aug. '58	Taunton MC autocross	T. W. J. Bryant	1st overall
Sep. '58	Jeans Cup Rally	Mrs. P. Mayman	Ladies award
Sep. '58	LMC London Rally	Mrs. P. Mayman	Ladies award
		A. L. Yarranton	1st in tests
Oct. '58	Bournemouth Rally	Mrs. P. Mayman	Ladies award
Feb. '59	Rallye Militaire	B. Harper	1st overall
Mar. '59	BARC Goodwood races	C. J. Lawrence	1st overall
Mar. '59	S & DMC March Rally	C. Janes	1st overall
Apr. '59	Highland Rally	Mrs. P. Mayman	Ladies award
Apr. '59	Birmingham Post Rally	Mrs. P. Mayman	Ladies award
		W. A. G. Goodall	*1st in class
		P. H. G. Morgan	*Team award
		A. L. Yarranton	*Team award
Jul. '59	BARC Goodwood race	C. J. Lawrence	1st overall
Aug. '59	BARC Oulton Park race	C. J. Lawrence	1st overall
Aug. '59	BARC Crystal Palace race	C. J. Lawrence	1st overall
Aug. '59	Bolton-Le-Moors Rally	Mrs. P. Mayman	Ladies award
Sep. '59	Jeans Gold Cup Rally	Mrs. P. Mayman	Ladies award
Sep. '59	BARC Mallory Park race	C. J. Lawrence	1st overall
Sep. '59	LMC London Rally	B. Harper	1st overall
		Mrs. P. Mayman	Ladies award
Oct. '59	Bournemouth Rally	Mrs. P. Mayman	Ladies award
Nov. '59	RAC Rally	P. H. G. Morgan	1st overall
Jan. '60	Monte Carlo Rally	Sims/Jones	3rd in tests
Jan. '60	Welsh Rally	B. Harper	1st overall
Mar. '60	Express & Star Rally	Mrs. P. Mayman	2nd overall
		B. Harper	1st in class
Apr. '60	Birmingham Post Rally	Mrs. P. Mayman	Regent Trophy
		B. Harper	1st in class
May '60	Tulip Rally	Sims/Hercock	1st in class
Aug. '60	BARC Oulton Park race	C. J. Lawrence	1st overall
Sep. '60	BARC Goodwood race	C. J. Lawrence	1st overall
Oct. '60	Mini-Miglia Rally	B. Harper	2nd overall
Dec. '60	Warwick Farm race, Aus.	D. McKay	1st overall
Dec. '60	BRSCC Brands Hatch race	C. J. Lawrence	1st overall
Feb. '61	Express & Star Rally	B. Harper	1st overall
Jun. '61	Barbon Manor hill-climb	P. M. Bradley	1st overall
Jul. '61	London MC Snetterton race	H. Braithwaite	1st overall
Aug. '61	Guards Trophy race Goodwood	R. Shepherd-Barron	1st in class
Aug. '61	RAC TT Goodwood	C. J. Lawrence	3rd in class
Sep. '61	BARC Mallory Park race	P. W. Marten	1st overall
Sep. '61	Autosport 3-Hrs. Snetterton	H. Braithwaite	Class champion
Nov. '61	Press-on-Regardless, Canada	A. Sands	Team award
		E. Russell	Team award
		S. Broady	Team award
Mar. '62	Sebring 12-Hours	Rogers/Bailey	1st in class
Mar. '62	Wellesbourne speed trials	J. Terry	1st overall
May '62	Spa Grand Prix	R. Shepherd-Barron	2nd in class
May '62	Nurburgring 1000 Kms	Savoye/Savoye	3rd in class
Jun. '62	BARC Goodwood race	W. H. Jones	1st overall
Jun. '62	BARC Goodwood race	P. Arnold	1st overall
Jun. '62	Le Mans 24-Hours	Lawrence/Shepherd-Barron	1st in class
Aug. '62	Brands Hatch Int. race (Champ.)	C. J. Lawrence	1st in class

DATE	EVENT	ENTRANT	RESULT
Sep. '62	Autosport 3-Hrs.	C. J. Lawrence	3rd overall
		P. Arnold	1st in class
Mar. '63	BRSCC Brands Hatch race	P. Arnold	1st overall
Mar. '63	Sebring 12-Hours	McNeil/Clarens	4th in class
Apr. '63	MMKCC Silverstone races	A. Dence	1st overall
Apr. '63	BARC Oulton Park race	A. Dence	1st overall
May '63	Spa Grand Prix	C. J. Lawrence	1st in class
		P. Arnold	2nd in class
May '63	Nurburgring 1000 Kms	Slotemaker/Braithwaite	1st in class
		Arnold/Carnegie	2nd in class
May '63	100-mile race, Panama	P. Kennett	1st overall
May '63	Oulton Park race	J. Dangerfield	1st overall
May '63	BARC Goodwood race	J. Dangerfield	1st overall
Jun. '63	BARC Goodwood race	A. Dence	1st overall
Aug. '63	RAC TT Goodwood	A. Dence	17th overall
Sep. '63	Coppa Inter-Europa Monza	C. Smith	15th overall
Sep. '63	BARC Goodwood race	A. Dence	Brooklands Mem. Trophy
Sep. '63	BARC Aintree race	G. G. Spice	1st overall
Oct. '63	Derbyshire Trial	W. A. G. Goodall	1st class award
Jan. '64	BARC production car trial	A. Lefevre	1st overall
Mar. '64	Llandow race	R. Meredith	1st overall
Apr. '64	BARC Goodwood race	B. Kendall	1st overall
May '64	AMOC Silverstone relay race	Hon. B. Feilding	2nd team award
		R. Meredith	2nd team award
		J. K. McKechnie	2nd team award
Jun. '64	Curborough sprint	J. Harper	1st overall
Oct. '64	Oddicombe hill-climb	D. Van Horn	1st overall
Nov. '64	SCCA Am. Road Race Champs.	E. Jones	C. Prod. Champ.
Apr. '65	BRSCC Mallory Park race	A. T. House	1st overall
Apr. '65	SWAC Llandow races	B. M. Jenkins	1st overall
May '65	MMKMC Silverstone race	A. T. House	1st overall
May '65	Guards 1000 race Brands Hatch	Lawrence/Spender	1st in Part 2
May '65	Castle Combe race	R. Meredith	1st overall
Aug. '65	SWAC Llandow race	B. Jenkins	1st overall
Sep. '65	Autosport Champ. Snetterton	A. House	1st in class B
Nov. '65	Guy Fawkes Trial	A. F. Lefevre	Special award
Nov. '65	Track Mark Trial	A. F. Lefevre	1st overall
Jan. '66	MCC Exeter Trial	W. H. D. Lowe	1st in class
		W. A. G. Goodall	1st class award
		M. G. Bellamy	1st class award
		H. C. Roberts	1st class award
		A. F. Lefevre	1st class award
		G. M. Margetts	1st class award
Mar. '66	BARC Goodwood race	C. J. Lawrence	1st overall
May '66	BRSCC 6-Hrs. Brands Hatch	Pugh/Kendall	8th overall
		Tucker/Blyth	10th overall
May '66	BARC Goodwood race	C. J. Lawrence	1st overall
Jun. '66	BARC Goodwood race	J. Donnelly	1st overall
Jul. '66	Hemerdon hill-climb	R. W. Harper	1st overall
Aug. '66	SWAC Llandow race	B. V. M. Jenkins	1st overall
Sep. '66	BARC Mallory Park race	G. Miles	1st overall
Jan. '67	MCC Exeter Trial	P. H. G. Morgan	1st in class
May '68	BARC Santa Pod slalom	H. E. Postlethwaite	Team award
		G. Martin	Team award
		D. Massey	Team award
Jun. '68	Wiscombe Park hill-climb	D. Way	1st in class
		D. Van Horn	1st in class
Aug. '68	Great Auclum hill-climb	D. Way	1st in class
Sep. '68	Wiscombe Park hill-climb	D. Way	1st in class
Sep. '68	Pontypool Park hill-climb	D. Way	1st in class
Mar. '69	Prescott hill-climb	H. E. Postlethwaite	1st in class
Apr. '69	Harewood hill-climb	D. Way	1st overall
Apr. '69	MCC Land's End Trial	P. H. G. Morgan	1st in class
Jun. '69	Prescott hill-climb	D. Way	1st in class
Jul. '69	Harewood hill-climb	J. N. J. Upton	1st in class
Jul. '69	Sutton Valence hill-climb	J. C. Churchill	1st in class
Mar. '70	Castle Howard hill-climb	N. R. Hargreaves	1st in class
May '70	Gurston Down hill-climb	D. Way	1st in class
Jul. '70	Pontypool Park hill-climb	D. Parsons	1st in class
Jul. '70	Gurston Down hill-climb	A. Roberts	1st in class
May '71	Loton Park hill-climb	M. Wyatt	1st in class
May '71	Barbon Manor hill-climb	R. J. Smith	1st in class
May '71	Gurston Down hill-climb	B. Harrison	1st in class
Jun. '71	Pontypool Park hill-climb	B. Harrison	1st in class
Jul. '71	Shelsley Walsh hill-climb	B. Harrison	1st in class
Aug. '71	Prescott hill-climb	L. Harrison	1st in class
Aug. '71	Trengwainton hill-climb	E. Scoby	1st in class
		M. Wyatt	1st in class
Aug. '71	Tregrehan hill-climb	W. Holt	1st in class
Sep. '71	Ditcham hill-climb	J. Gillham	1st in class
Oct. '71	Gurston Down hill-climb	J. Harrison	1st in class
		J. Gillham	1st in class
Apr. '72	Prescott hill-climb	A. Robinson	1st in class
Apr. '72	MCC Land's End Trial	M. J. Croome	Field Trophy

DATE	EVENT	ENTRANT	RESULT
Jun. '72	Pontypool Park hill-climb	L. Ryan	1st in class
Jul. '72	Shelsley Walsh hill-climb	W. Holt	1st in class
Sep. '72	RECC Snetterton race	A. Bridgeland	1st overall
Sep. '72	Rothmans Brands Hatch race	R. Gray	1st overall
Sep. '72	Suffolk Stages Rally	Barbour/James	2nd overall
Oct. '72	Gower hill-climb	B. Harrison	1st in class
Jan. '73	MCC Exeter Trial	H. B. Woodall	1st in class
		M. G. Owen	1st class award
		W. A. G. Goodall	1st class award
		M. J. Croome	1st class award
Apr. '73	Loton Park hill-climb	W. Holt	1st in class
May '73	MCC Edinburgh Trial	M. J. Croome	1st in class
		H. B. Woodall	1st in class
Jun. '73	London CC Brands Hatch race	C. J. Lawrence	1st overall
Jun. '73	Gurston Down hill-climb	B. Harrison	1st in class
Jul. '73	Snetterton Morgan race	M. Hayward	1st overall
Jul. '73	Prescott hill-climb	W. Holt	1st in class
Aug. '73	MSCC driving tests	K. Hill	1st Morgan
Sep. '73	RECC Snetterton race	R. Gray	1st overall
Oct. '73	Silverstone Champ. race	R. Gray	1st overall
Oct. '73	Penrice Castle hill-climb	W. Holt	1st in class
Apr. '74	Castle Howard hill-climb	P. M. Fay	1st in class
Apr. '74	BARC Mallory Park race	R. Gray	1st overall
May '74	Prescott hill-climb	J. Berry	1st in class
May '74	Loton Park hill-climb	R. Meere	1st in class
Jun. '74	Barbon Manor hill-climb	D. Rutherford	1st in class
Jun. '74	London CC Brands Hatch race	R. Gray	1st overall
Jun. '74	Prescott hill-climb	P. Meredith	1st in class
Jun. '74	Penrice Castle hill-climb	M. Hall	1st in class
Jul. '74	RECC Snetterton race	R. Wells	1st overall
Aug. '74	Bentley DC Silverstone race	J. MacDonald	1st overall
Aug. '74	Cadwell Park hill-climb	P. Fay	1st in class
Aug. '74	SUNBAC Silverstone race	R. Gray	1st overall
Sep. '74	Loton Park hill-climb	D. Rutherford	1st in class
Sep. '74	Lydden Hill sprint	R. Wells	1st overall
Nov. '74	NSCC Croft 1st race	J. MacDonald	1st overall
Nov. '74	NSCC Croft 2nd races	J. MacDonald	1st overall
Mar. '75	Jaguar DC Silverstone race	R. Gray	1st overall
Mar. '75	Castle Howard hill-climb	P. Fay	1st in class
Mar. '75	BRSCC Croft race	J. Britten	1st overall
Mar. '75	Rufforth race	J. Britten	1st overall
Mar. '75	MCC Land's End Trial	M. G. Owen	1st in class
		G. M. Margetts	1st class award
		W. A. G. Goodall	1st class award
		H. B. Woodall	1st class award
Apr. '75	Prescott hill-climb	B. Holt	1st in class
Apr. '75	Curborough hill-climb	M. Hall	1st in class
May '75	Prescott hill-climb	R. Meredith	1st in class
May '75	Scammonden hill-climb	D. Birch	1st in class
May '75	Silverstone 6-Hr. relay	Libra Morgan	1st team
May '75	Tregrehan hill-climb	I. Dobie	1st in class
May '75	Harewood hill-climb	T. Donald	1st in class
Jun. '75	Snetterton race	R. Gray	1st overall
Jun. '75	BARC Snetterton race	R. Gray	1st in class
Jun. '75	Shelsley Walsh hill-climb	A. Duncan	1st in class
Jul. '75	BRSCC Oulton Park race	R. Gray	1st overall
Aug. '75	Lancs. AC Woodvale hill-climb	A. Smith	1st in class
		D. Rutherford	1st in class
Aug. '75	Gurston Down hill-climb	A. Kennedy	1st in class
Aug. '75	Bentley DC Silverstone race	Sir A. Brocklebank	1st overall
Aug. '75	Cadwell Park hill-climb	D. Styring	1st in class
Sep. '75	SUNBAC Silverstone race	R. Gray	1st overall
Sep. '75	NSCC Croft race	A. Palmer	1st overall
Sep. '75	Doune hill-climb	T. Donald	1st in class
Sep. '75	Brands Hatch race	R. Gray	1st overall
Jan. '76	MCC Exeter Trial	W. A. G. Goodall	1st class award
		M. G. Owen	1st class award
Mar. '76	MAC Silverstone race	R. Gray	1st overall
Mar. '76	BRSCC Mallory Park race	R. Gray	1st overall
Apr. '76	Harewood hill-climb	P. Fay	1st in class
		A. Smith	1st in class
May '76	8 Clubs Silverstone race	G. Dennis	1st overall
May '76	Baitings Dam hill-climb	N. Howell	1st in class
May '76	Barbon Manor hill-climb	D. Rutherford	1st in class
Jun. '76	Harewood hill-climb	A. Smith	1st in class
		M. Granville	1st in class
		M. Hall	1st in class
		M. Ridley	1st in class
Jun. '76	Curborough hill-climb	N. Howell	1st in class
		M. Hall	1st in class
Jun. '76	Loton Park hill-climb	D. Rutherford	1st in class
Jul. '76	RECC Snetterton race	D. Rutherford	1st overall
Jul. '76	Baitings Dam hill-climb	N. Howell	1st in class
		A. Smith	1st in class
Aug. '76	Baitings Dam hill-climb	P. Fay	1st in class
Aug. '76	Shelsley Walsh hill-climb	A. Duncan	1st in class
Aug. '76	Loton Park hill-climb	D. Rutherford	1st in class

DATE	EVENT	ENTRANT	RESULT
Aug. '76	Bentley DC Silverstone race	R. Gray	1st overall
Oct. '76	Castle Howard hill-climb	Mrs. M. Robson	1st in class
Mar. '77	8 Clubs Silverstone race	Mrs. M. Lindsay	1st overall
Apr. '77	Castle Howard hill-climb	M. Robson	1st in class
May '77	Harewood hill-climb	P. Garland	1st in class
May '77	Wiscombe Park hill-climb	M. Kennedy	1st in class
May '77	Barbon Manor hill-climb	D. Wright	1st in class
Jun. '77	Harewood hill-climb	M. Hall	1st in class
Jul. '77	BMRMC Donington race	P. Keen	1st overall
Jul. '77	Scammonden hill-climb	D. Wright	1st in class
		M. Robson	1st in class
Jul. '77	Baitings Dam hill-climb	M. Robson	1st in class
		N. Howell	1st in class
Jul. '77	Shelsley Walsh hill-climb	P. Garland	1st in class
Jul. '77	Donington evening race	P. Keen	1st overall
Jul. '77	Harewood hill-climb	P. Garland	1st in class
Aug. '77	Loton Park hill-climb	N. Garland	1st in class
Aug. '77	BRDC Silverstone race	R. Wells	1st overall
Aug. '77	Bentley DC Silverstone race	C. Cooke	1st overall
Sep. '77	Prescott hill-climb	B. Gilmore	1st in class
Sep. '77	BRSCC Snetterton race	B. Wykeham	1st overall
Mar. '78	Oddicombe hill-climb	I. Doble	1st in class
Apr. '78	BRSCC Donington race	C. Morgan	1st overall
May '78	BRDC Silverstone race	C. Morgan	1st overall
May '78	Prescott hill-climb	P. Garland	1st in class
May '78	Croft race	B. Wykeham	1st overall
May '78	AMOC Brands Hatch race	M. Lucassen	1st overall
Jun. '78	BRDC Silverstone race	B. Stapleton	1st overall
Jun. '78	Loton Park hill-climb	P. Garland	1st in class
Jun. '78	BRSCC Brands Hatch race	B. Wykeham	1st overall
Jul. '78	BRSCC Castle Combe race	B. Wykeham	1st overall
Jul. '78	BMRMC Donington race	P. Keen	1st overall
Jul. '78	Harewood hill-climb	T. Bridgen	1st in class
Jul. '78	Loton Park hill-climb	D. Rutherford	1st in class
Aug. '78	BRDC Mallory Park race	C. Morgan	1st overall
Aug. '78	Laguna Seca historic race USA	B. Howlett	1st overall
Aug. '78	BMRMC Silverstone race	C. Morgan	1st overall
Aug. '78	BRDC Silverstone race	C. Morgan	1st overall
Aug. '78	BRDC Donington race	C. Morgan	1st overall
Aug. '78	Bentley DC Silverstone race	C. Cooke	1st overall
Sep. '78	BARC Thruxton race	C. Morgan	1st overall
Sep. '78	BRDC Silverstone race	C. Morgan	1st overall
Sep. '78	BRSCC Cadwell Park race	C. Morgan	1st overall
Sep. '78	Doune hill-climb	P. Garland	1st in class
Oct. '78	Donington 6-Hr. relay race	Anglemog Vikings	1st team
		Anglemog Saxons	2nd team
Oct. '78	LDMC Oulton Park hill-climb	A. Smith	1st in class
Oct. '78	Romford MC Snetterton race	N. Stechman	1st overall
Dec. '78	BRSCC Brands Hatch race	T. Palmer	1st overall
Apr. '79	BARC Thruxton race	R. Wells	1st overall
Apr. '79	BRSCC Snetterton race	R. Wells	1st overall
May '79	AHC Snetterton sprint	N. Stechman	1st overall
May '79	BRSCC Brands Hatch race	R. Wells	1st overall
May '79	BRSCC Castle Combe race	C. Morgan	1st overall
May '79	750MC Mallory Park race	N. Stechman	1st overall
Jun. '79	BRSCC Oulton Park race	C. Morgan	1st overall
Jun. '79	DRC Donington race	R. Wells	1st overall
Jun. '79	Silverstone race	R. Wells	1st overall
Jun. '79	Brands Hatch race	C. Morgan	1st overall
Jun. '79	BARC Harewood hill-climb	N. Stechman	1st in class
		D. Wright	1st in class
		M. Robson	1st in class
		P. Fay	1st in class
Jul. '79	HSCC Donington race	M. Lucassen	1st overall
Jul. '79	BRSCC Cadwell Park race	C. Morgan	1st overall
Jul. '79	BRSCC Snetterton race	C. Morgan	1st overall
Jul. '79	BARC Harewood hill-climb	P. Garland	1st in class
Aug. '79	Int. 6-Hrs. Brands Hatch	Wykeham/Classic/ Spero	18th overall
Aug. '79	BRSCC Brands Hatch race	C. Morgan	1st overall
Aug. '79	BARC Loton Park hill-climb	P. Garland	1st in class
Aug. '79	Bentley DC Silverstone races	P. Askew	Stapleton Trophy
		J. MacDonald	1st overall
Sep. '79	Mallory Park race	R. Wells	1st overall
Sep. '79	BARC Harewood hill-climb	J. Ball	1st in class
Sep. '79	COMCC Goodwood sprint	P. Askew	Wimsett Trophy
Oct. '79	BRSCC Mallory Park race	C. Morgan	1st overall
Dec. '79	BARC Brands Hatch race	M. Paul	1st overall

Footnote: Pressure of space has meant that the foregoing list of Morgan competitions results has had to be an arbitrary choice from the vast number of successes achieved by drivers during the period covered. As far as possible I have attempted to select those performances which seemed the most significant at the time and in relation to the strength of the opposition, but if there are any inconsistencies I can only apologise to the drivers concerned, as I do to the many successful drivers whose exploits unfortunately I have been obliged to exclude from this table.